The
Guiding Light
of
*Lao Tzu*

Cover art by *Jane A. Evans*

The cover art is adapted from the painting of Ma Yüan of pines in "The Tao of Painting" by Mai-Mai Sze. "Pine trees are like people of high principles whose manner reveals an inner power."

# The Guiding Light of Lao Tzu

A New Translation and Commentary on the TAO TEH CHING

By

*Henry Wei*

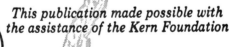

*This publication made possible with the assistance of the Kern Foundation*

The Theosophical Publishing House
Wheaton, Illinois U.S.A.
Madras, India / London, England

The Theosophical Publishing House
306 West Geneva Road
Wheaton, Illinois 60187
A publication of the Theosophical Publishing House
a department of the Theosophical Society in America.

Library of Congress Cataloging in Publication Data
Lao-tzu
    The guiding light of Lao Tzu.

    "A Quest book."
    Includes index.
    I. Wei, Henry, 1909-            II. Title.
BL1900.L26E5      1982b        299'.51482      81-53011
ISBN 0-8356-9562-0
ISBN 0-8356-0558-2 (pbk.)

Printed in the United States of America

Drawings are from Mai-Mai Sze's *The Tao of Painting:
A Study of the Ritual Disposition of Chinese Painting.*
Bollingen Series XLIX.
Copyright ©1956 and 1963 by Princeton University Press.

To the memory of my brother, Wei Tat (1901-1977), author of *An Exposition of the I-Ching* and translator of the entire *Ch'eng Wei Shih Lun (Doctrine of Mere-Consciousness)*, by Hsuan Tsang, a Buddhist luminary of the T'ang dynasty.

# Contents

# Preface

This work, which includes a new and faithful translation of the *Tao Teh Ching*, is an attempt to interpret that book in terms of mysticism and meditation. The purpose is to bring out such wisdom in the Taoist canon as is conducive to spiritual cultivation and self-improvement.

Mysticism has sometimes been confused with occultism. Some common ground, it is true, exists between the two fields, but they are essentially different. Broadly speaking, occultism aims at satisfying man's curiosity about the mysteries of the universe. In a sense it is akin to modern science, only it lays much more stress on the supersensible field. Mysticism, however, sets high value on rectification of the heart or purification of the emotions in order to attain identification with Tao, or union with the Divine, or the gaining of enlightenment.

Meditation, in one form or another, is a very old practice. It is much older than Lao Tzu and the Lord Buddha. It is, for instance, frequently referred to in the Psalms of the Old Testament. It is a spiritual process common to almost all faiths, but seems to be well developed and especially prized in Hinduism, Buddhism, and Taoism. In the long course of its history, it underwent development into various forms. In recent decades, it has become quite popular in Western countries where it is often employed as a kind of therapy for gaining personal poise, relieving stress and tension, or repairing a damaged psyche. Mystic meditation is not without such therapeutic virtues, but aims higher, much higher. Its goal is union with the holy and divine.

This writer has long been aware that scattered in various chapters of the *Tao Teh Ching* is a wealth of material that can be related to mystic meditation and yoga. As time went on, he became increasingly unable to resist the temptation to gather together such material and develop it into a consistent and coherent treatise on the subject. The upshot of that effort is the six chapters in Part I of this work.

Part II is a faithful and conscientious translation of the Taoist canon. It does not include anything like a comprehensive commentary. The reason is twofold. First, it is deemed desirable to avoid repetition, for a wide range of the important truths embodied in the *Tao Teh Ching* has already been presented in the Introduction as well as in the six chapters of Part I. Secondly, anything like a comprehensive commentary is bound to increase considerably the bulk of this work. However, efforts have been made to expose the general significance of each chapter and to explain the peculiar notions and controversial terms that exist here and there in the text. Last but not least, cross references are furnished to facilitate the location of those chapters that contain more or less similar ideas.

In sending forth this modest work, the author fervently hopes it will satisfy the need of that segment of the reading public that is interested in the ancient wisdom of China as well as in meditation. If it can in any way help the readers attain a better understanding of Taoist mysticism and cherish a deeper desire for spiritual cultivation, the labor that has gone into the preparation of this work will not be regarded as having been in vain.

As my views and ideas tend toward mysticism and yoga rather than toward speculative philosophy, I can well anticipate criticisms from certain quarters. However, I shall always welcome criticisms and try to learn from them with, as my fellow Chinese would say, "A hollow heart." To parody Lao Tzu:

By good criticism I shall benefit;
By bad criticism I shall also benefit.

Before concluding I should like to take this opportunity to tender my thanks to Mr. Clarence Pedersen, Publications Manager of the House, for his deep interest in my work. To Mrs. Rosemarie Stewart, former Senior Editor, and her associates, my thanks are due for their helpful suggestions for the improvement of the book by removing a number of repetitions and by using a better arrangement in Part Two. To Mrs. Shirley Nicholson, present Senior Editor, I owe gratitude for her many perceptive criticisms, cogent comments, and valuable suggestions. Needless to say, the author alone is responsible for any misinterpretations or misstatements that may be found.

Henry Wei

Still, I am conscious now that behind all this beauty, satisfying though it may be, there is some spirit hidden of which the painted forms and shapes are but modes of manifestation, and it is with this spirit that I desire to become in harmony. I have grown tired of the articulate utterances of men and things. The Mystical in Art, the Mystical in Life, the Mystical in Nature—this is what I am looking for. It is absolutely necessary for me to find it somewhere.

Oscar Wilde, *De Profundis*

# Introduction

Lao Tzu may rightly be regarded as an immortal inspirer whose teaching constitutes a bright beacon for the guidance of the human spirit to supreme fulfillment.

Born almost twenty-six centuries ago, Lao Tzu led a long, quiet and studious life and then mysteriously vanished from the human scene, leaving behind a compact parcel of sublime wisdom clothed in glorious poetry. This is perhaps what should be expected, considering the kind of man Lao Tzu was. He was not exactly a hermit or recluse, but a scholar who simply loved a contemplative life. Far from courting publicity or jostling for the limelight, he preferred to stay in obscurity in some solitary abode or in the silence of the library, devoting himself to inner culture and to the pursuit of truth and enjoying communion with the enlightened spirits of the past. He thus rendered his life an enigma perhaps even to his contemporaries, let alone posterity.

Paucity of reliable data concerning his life has given rise to some absurd speculations and fantastic legends. His parentage remains unknown. Like some other human prodigies, he was probably born out of wedlock. Legend says

1

that his mother dreamed of a falling star entering her bosom and later became pregnant—a pregnancy which lasted for over eighty years! Finally, from her left side, her baby came out—an old man with snow-white hair. Hence the name Lao Tzu, which in Chinese could mean *Old Son* as well as *Venerable Master.* As he had long ears, a sign of intelligence and wisdom, he was given the personal name Erh, meaning *ear* in Chinese. As his birth site was beside a plum tree, he was surnamed Li, Chinese sound for *plum.* This incident, whether fictitious or authentic, has had some great historical significance. It happened that the founder of the famous T'ang dynasty (A.D. 618-906) was also surnamed Li, and in order to show reverence for their great ancestor he and his descendants lent their royal influence to the promotion of Taoism.

Ssuma Ch'ien (145-86 B.C.), an historian noted for his on-site research and fidelity to the truth, has included a biographical treatise on Lao Tzu in his famous *Shih Chi* (Historical Records). According to this treatise, Lao Tzu was a southerner from the state of Ch'u (now Hunan and Hupei provinces), whose family name was Li, with Erh as his personal name, Po-yang as his courtesy name, and Tan as his posthumous title. Though a southerner, he went to the metropolis Loyang (in what is now Honan province) and served as Custodian of the Imperial Archives of the Chou House (1122-256 B.C.). While in that capacity, he granted an interview to Confucius, who was his junior by about fifty years and who wanted to consult him about some questions regarding rituals. In reply, he said to his young guest:

> Those people you talk about have long been dead and have become dried bones. Only their words survive. The superior man rides in a carriage when the time is auspicious; when it is not, he hides his face and limps away. I have heard that a clever merchant will conceal his wealth of goods from view so that his store appears empty, and that a superior man of eminent moral excellence will behave as if he were a simpleton. Better strip yourself of your proud airs and numerous desires, your complacent demeanor and excessive ambitions. They won't do you any good. This is all I have to say to you.

Having heard this reply, Confucius made his exit and later said to his disciples:

> I know that birds can fly, fish can swim, and beasts can run. Those that run can be snared, those that swim can be caught with a net, and those that fly can be shot down with arrows. As to the dragon, I don't know how it can ride upon the wind and clouds and soar to high heaven. I saw Lao Tzu today, He can truly be likened to a dragon.

After reporting this interview between the two sages, Ssuma Ch'ien points out in his treatise that Lao Tzu was a scholar of a retiring disposition and may have lived for more than two hundred years, possibly until 129 years after the death of Confucius, for he was fond of cultivating Tao (Way) and Teh (Virtue) as well as the art of nourishing life. The last paragraph of the treatise states that Lao Tzu lived a pure life and always conducted himself correctly with serene spontaneity and natural ease.

Lao Tzu aparently enjoyed his office as Custodian of the Imperial Archives, for he held it for a long time. It was not until the Chou House showed glaring signs of decay and decline that he finally took his departure and decided to exile himself. As he reached the pass leading westward, the warden of the pass, Yin Hsi, said to him: "Since you are retiring from the world, will you please write a book for my enlightenment?" Lao Tzu consented and wrote a book in two parts about the meaning of Tao and Teh, consisting of a little over 5,000 words. A book of this modest size is well within the writing capacity of a single person. So the suggestion that it may have been written by several persons does not have much merit. It is also credible that Lao Tzu was able to finish the writing on short notice and in a very short time; for he was a scholar, a librarian, and a contemplative to boot. The ideas in the book may well represent the fruits of his life-long meditation. So when the occasion arose, he had no difficulty in setting them forth beautifully and coherently. No wonder that his work soon afterwards became a strong intellectual stimulus and contributed considerably toward the development of various classical schools of Chinese philosophy.

At first, the work was simply called *Lao Tzu*. Later, during the Western Han dynasty (202 B.C.-A.D. 9), it was dignified with the title *Tao Teh Ching*, or Classic of the Way and its Virtue.

After completing the work, Lao Tzu left for the western region. What finally happened to him is unknown. There is a story that he travelled to India and reincarnated as Gautama Buddha. But this kind of story obviously cannot be verified.

As can be expected from the spiritual output of such a sublime sage, the *Tao Teh Ching* sparkles with bright gems of wisdom couched in provocative paradoxes. Before long, it attracted the attention and excited the interest of some very keen minds, notably Han Fei Tzu (d. 233 B.C.), a great leader of the Legalist school, and Chuang Tzu (369-286 B.C.), second only to Lao Tzu as a Taoist mystic and philosopher. In his works, Han Fei Tzu devoted two chapters to commenting on the *Lao Tzu*. Chuang Tzu, however, did not write any commentary but played with Lao Tzu's ideas, mixed them with his own, and produced a new work with great philosophic depth as well as literary beauty and persiflage, to the delight and admiration of all its readers.

The first detailed and comprehensive commentary on the *Lao Tzu* or *Tao Teh Ching* was written by a recluse called Ho Shang Kung (d. 159 B.C.). This is not his actual name but a sobriquet meaning "Old Man by the River." The name of the recluse was either unknown or purposely concealed. The nature of his commentary tends toward yoga and mysticism; in other words, it interprets Lao Tzu's ideas in terms of instruction for spiritual cultivation aiming at longevity or immortality as well as personal experience of Tao. Mystics always feel that what satisfies and nourishes the soul is not discursive knowledge but the inner tasting of the truth.

Incidentally, a story runs that Ho Shang Kung could practice levitation at will. It is said that Emperor Wen Ti once went to consult him about the meaning of certain passages in the *Tao Teh Ching*. During the meeting he noticed that Ho Shang Kung did not pay him the respect due to him; so he asserted his sovereign power and declared that all people on earth were his subjects. On hearing this, Ho Shang Kung rose into the air to an appreciable height, indicating he did not have to remain on earth. This extraordinary feat greatly impressed Wen Ti and made him adopt a humble and deferential attitude.

The commentary by Ho Shang Kung was preferred later by a sect called the religious Taoists. Probably it may have played a significant role in inspiring the genesis of religious Taoism (*Tao Chiao*).

The second detailed and comprehensive commentary was written by Wang Pi (A.D. 226-249). This commentary is predominantly philosophical in nature. It is noted for its exposition of metaphysical and transcendental ideas, and has exerted considerable influence in establishing the *Tao Teh Ching* as a canon of the Taoist school of philosophy (*Tao Chia*). In passing, it may be fitting to mention that Wang Pi was a rare genius, an intellectual prodigy. He wrote a detailed and learned commentary not only on the *Tao Teh Ching* but also on the *I Ching* or *Book of Changes*, and passed away at the young age of only twenty-four! Most people at that age have not even made the first attempt to understand the two abstruse classics.

In the course of the succeeding centuries, commentaries on the *Tao Teh Ching* came out in great profusion, attesting to the immense interest and importance attached to the work. About a thousand of those commentaries are known to have existed: some 700 in Chinese and over 250 in Japanese, plus a small number in Western languages.

There also have been numerous translations of the Taoist canon. The earliest was in Sanskrit and was done by Tripitaka-Master Hsuan Tsang, a Buddhist luminary of the T'ang dynasty. The next earliest translation was in Latin and appeared about 1750. It was apparently done by a Jesuit missionary who had been in China. In 1828, the first Russian version came out. Forty years later, the first English version was published. Since then there have been many other translations into Western languages, especially into English. To date, there are upwards of forty English translations in the field, vying with one another for superior merit. Thus the influence of the *Tao Teh Ching* has become virtually worldwide. No other Chinese work, not even any of the Confucian classics, can approach it in popularity and prestige. Its influence has been circumscribed, however, by the fact that even the best translation would fail to do it justice. For in the original version there are subtle rhythms, pictorial images, and tonal values that are simply untranslatable and yet are the very qualities that would produce a strange effect on the mind and tend to awaken its intuition.

The numerous commentaries and translations constitute eloquent evidence that the *Tao Teh Ching* has a wide appeal. But why? There are various reasons. First, Lao Tzu was a revolutionary thinker, and some of his radical ideas might have found a sympathetic chord in the heart of many people who are not satisfied with the *status quo*. Second, while the *Tao Teh Ching* was intended for the edification of the prince or the ruler, it in fact has the welfare of the people in view. It is against war, against violence, against official corruption, against exorbitant taxation, against all undue interference with the life of the people. It is all in favor of human rights. Third, Lao Tzu strongly hints that man is potentially immortal and suggests ways to fulfill this popular human aspiration. Fourth, it has a high degree of literary beauty and poetic charm. Many of its passages can be easily memorized and quoted on various occasions. Fifth, it is quite similar to Christianity in some of its moral viewpoints. There are Christians all over the world who may be curious about the similarity of the visions of truth.

Following are some parallels in the teachings of two eminent spiritual leaders—Lao Tzu (L), and Christ (C):

L: "It (space) is hollow, yet it never fails to supply. The more it is worked, the more it gives forth." (Ch. 5)

C: "Ask, and it shall be given you; seek, and ye shall find; knock, and it shall be opened unto you."
(Matthew 7:7)

L: "The Sage putting himself behind, finds himself in front." (Ch. 7)

C: "If any man desire to be first, the same shall be last of all, and servant of all." (Mark 9:35)

6

L: "A hall filled with gold and jade can hardly be safe-guarded." (Ch. 9)

C: "Lay not up for yourselves treasures upon earth, where moth and rust doth corrupt, and where thieves break through and steal." (Matthew 6:19)

L: "To show pride in one's wealth and high rank is to pave the way for one's own doom." (Ch. 9)

C: "How hardly shall they that have riches enter into the kingdom of God! (Luke 18:24)

L: "In attuning your breath to induce tenderness, can you become like a new-born babe?" (Ch. 10)

C: Except ye be converted, and become as little children, ye shall not enter into the kingdom of heaven. (Matthew 18:3)

L: "As he does not justify himself, he is prominent." (Ch. 22)

C: "Ye are they which justify yourselves before men; but God knoweth your hearts." (Luke 16:15)

L: "The strong and violent will die an unnatural death." (Ch. 42)

C: "All they that take the sword shall perish with the sword." (Matthew 26:52)

L: "Which is more dear: fame or health? Which is more valuable: health or wealth?" (Ch. 44)

C: "For what is a man profited if he shall gain the whole world and lose his own soul?" (Matthew 16:26)

L: "No misfortune greater than not knowing contentment; no fault greater than hankering after wealth." (Ch. 46)

C: "Take heed and beware of covetousness: for a man's life consisteth not in the abundance of things he possesseth." (Luke 12:15)

L: "To the good, I show goodness; to the not good, I also show goodness." (Ch. 49)

C: "Love your enemies, bless them that curse you, do good to them that hate you, and pray for them which despitefully use you and persecute you." (Matthew 5:44)

L: "When Heaven wants to deliver a person from harm, it grants him compassion as a protective charm." (Ch. 67)

C: "Blessed are the merciful; for they shall obtain mercy." (Matthew 5:7)

L: "My teaching is very easy to understand, and very easy to carry out." (Ch. 70)

C: "My yoke is easy and my burden is light." (Matthew 11:30)

L: "The big and strong will be laid low; the soft and tender will be lifted up." (Ch. 76)

C: "Every one that exalteth himself shall be abased; and he that humbleth himself shall be exalted." (Luke 18:14)

In general, it may be said that both Christ and Lao Tzu were radical revolutionaries aiming at transformation of the human heart as a basis for the transformation of human society. While Christ wants to establish the kingdom of Heaven on earth, Lao Tzu wants to have the Eternal Tao prevail in the world.

The *Tao Teh Ching*, while similar to Christianity in many essential teachings, is a far shorter work than the Bible, even shorter than any of the four Gospels. If "brevity is the soul of wit," as Shakespeare has said, the *Tao Teh Ching* is the wittiest work in the world. In English literature, Francis Bacon is reputed to have the most condensed style, especially in his essays. Compared with Lao Tzu, Bacon appears long-winded and verbose. In hardly 5,350 words, divided into eighty-one chapters and in essentially poetic form, Lao Tzu's spiritual legacy covers a vast variety of subjects ranging from personal culture to political ideals, and expounds both the immanent and the transcendent aspect of Tao. Apart from being brief and pithy, it is peppered with paradoxes. Oscar Wilde, often called the prince of paradox, would have loved its witty sayings, perhaps also its general teaching. Anyway, he did show great admiration for Chuang Tzu in his review of Herbert Gile's translation of Chuang Tzu's works. There is, however, a great difference between the paradoxes of Wilde and those of the ancient Chinese philosopher. Wilde's paradoxes are brilliant and often would provoke a flashing smile or a ripple of laughter. They are good for enlivening a social party. Lao Tzu's paradoxes are profound, provocative, and challenging. They might give you a jolt at first and then move you to deep thought. They are good as subjects for meditation.

Only a true sage with sublime wisdom and superior spirituality could produce such a work as the *Tao Teh Ching*. Lao Tzu's ideas are, beyond doubt, not all original; some of them can be found in the *I Ching* and the *Shu Ching (Book of History)*, traditionally considered the oldest books in China. In fact, in several chapters of the *Tao Teh Ching* there are clear indications that some lines are quotations, although the sources are not revealed. However, whatever ideas Lao Tzu may have derived from the ancient cultural heritage must have been spiritually digested by him before expression in his unique and inimitable style. At this statement some sinologists may raise their eyebrows. For there has been considerable controversy among them as to whether Lao Tzu was really a historical figure, or whether he was really the author of the *Tao Teh Ching*, or whether this Taoist canon could have been a literary product of the sixth century B.C. The controversy has lasted many decades, since the 1920s. But no convincing, much less conclusive, evidence has been found, and so no verdict has been reached that commands general acceptance. The present writer is not at all interested in expressing an opinion on the matter which seems to him as dry as gunpowder. He is, however, inclined to follow the view of the late Dr. Hu Shih, who is well known inside and outside China for his critical acumen and for his scholarly research in Chinese history and culture. In his *Outline History of Chinese Philosophy* (in Chinese) he agreed with Ssuma Ch'ien that Lao Tzu was an elder contemporary of Confucius and was indeed the author of the *Tao Teh Ching*.

The influence directly or indirectly exerted by this extraordinary work on Chinese life and culture is profound and far-reaching—amazingly out of all proportion to its small size. Side by side with Confucianism, Taoist philosophy forms one main current of Chinese thought and molds a different popular way of life. While Confucianism may be said to constitute the Yang or positive aspect of life and culture, Taoism constitutes the Yin or passive aspect, the two balancing and complementing each other. While Confucianism manifests its influence mainly in the ethical and the political sphere, Taoism manifests its influence in the literary, the artistic, and the spiritual. Throughout the ages, it has been a fertile fount of inspiration for Chinese poetry, painting, and calligraphy, and has fostered a spirit of contentment, a deep love of nature, and a strong sense of simplicity and innocence in the psyche of the Chinese people. For this reason, it facilitated the introduction of Buddhism into China and later greatly enriched that alien faith. Taoism played a great role especially in the development of Ch'an (Zen) Buddhism. It also strengthened the metaphysical aspect of Confucianism and contributed to the emergence of Neo-Confucianism in the Sung dynasty (A.D. 960-1279).

Furthermore, it inspired the founding of the only indigenous religion of China: the Taoist religion or religious Taoism. Founded by Chang Tao-ling toward the end of the second century A.D., religious Taoism in its own right has exerted great influence on the Chinese people. It has shaped many of the popular beliefs, customs, and festivals. It has played a signal part in the development of medicine, acupuncture, and the practical arts and crafts as well as alchemy, astrology, divination, and martial art (kung fu). In the third volume of his excellent work, Science and Civilization in China, Joseph Needham pointed out that Taoists have made significant contributions to the development of such sciences as chemistry, mineralogy, and geography. Through secret societies, Taoism has also furnished leadership in quite a number of rebellions in the history of China, and therefore has been responsible for many a change of dynasties.

The Tao Teh Ching embodies the spiritual insights of Lao Tzu and provides wholesome pabulum for the spiritual growth of man. It conceives Tao as all-embracing, as both immanent and transcendent, and as eternal and infinite, preceding the Creator of Heaven and Earth and continuing to sustain Heaven and Earth. It characterizes Tao as a pro-

10

found mystery, immutable, subtle, elusive and ineffable, yet vital, creative, pervasive and powerful. Such views of Tao have important effects on the human mind. They tend to initiate man into the realm of fancies and mysteries, widen the horizon of his contemplation, inspire in him a profound sense of awe, and heighten his power of imagination and creativity. Furthermore, it leads man to realize that, willy-nilly, he has to depend and obey Tao for his life and happiness. Even Heaven and Earth cannot be free from such dependence and obedience. How much less so is man! Dictators and despots may for some time have the power to oppress the people under their rule, but before Tao they are impotent and helpless and have to bend their stiff neck or else suffer the consequences. When the oppressed people feel that Tao is on their side, they will rise to overthrow their oppressors.

There is a strong strain of mysticism weaving through the *Tao Teh Ching*. Lao Tzu was truly a mystic, who apparently had experience in spiritual union with Tao through meditation or other practices. In reading the Taoist canon, one can hardly escape the feeling that the ideas and ideals expressed in that work are based on the spiritual insights derived from Lao Tzu's mystic experience. Lao Tzu was by no means secretive about the possibility of such experience. In the very first chapter of the Taoist canon, he clearly points out that Tao cannot be expressed in words, but this does not mean that Tao cannot be encountered and experienced by the human spirit. In fact, in the same chapter he sets forth two methods of meditation—one without desire and one with some desire—for the purpose of attaining the mystic goal. In some later chapters, especially in Chapter 10, he becomes quite explicit in his instructions on meditation and yoga for the same sublime purpose.

In the light of Taoist mysticism, the supreme goal of life is union or identification with Tao. Lao Tzu makes this point amply clear in Chapter 20 of the *Tao Teh Ching*, wherein he contrasts himself with the worldlings. While the latter love fun, sex, good food, and other worldly matters, he himself prefers to taste and enjoy Tao. This personal choice definitely shows that he considers Tao as man's supreme goal. He does not criticize, much less rebuke, the worldlings for their love of worldly pursuits. But there is no doubt that he wants to guide them along toward Tao so that they may share his mystic experience and attain liberation or even immortality. This was perhaps his purpose in composing the *Tao Teh Ching*, which may rightly be regarded as a body of doctrines for the understanding of Tao and the cultivation of virtue. The aim is to create a quiet and peaceful environment as well as a pure, serene, and undisturbed state of mind for spiritual cultivation. This sublime aim is made especially manifest in Chapter 80, where Lao Tzu presents the general contour of his ideal state, which is typified by a social atmosphere of peace and harmony, ideal for preparing and conditioning oneself for the attainment of the mystic goal.

The most important doctrine in regard to spiritual cultivation is *Wu Wei* or non-action in the sense of non-interference, that is to say, non-interference with the trend of nature or the flow of Tao. So much emphasis does Lao Tzu lay on this doctrine that Chinese scholars generally regard *Wu Wei* as synonymous with Tao (*Wu Wei Shih Tao*). Throughout the *Tao Teh Ching* the theme of Wu Wei recurs like a refrain in music. Whether in ruling a country or even in conducting a war, Wu Wei is considered a wise course to follow. Says Lao Tzu: "Practise non-interference and there will never be any misrule." He also says: "March as if without motion. Brandish arms as if having none. Attack as if without enmity. Seize as if without weapons."

On the other hand, interference is considered an evil. As war represents maximum interference with the flow of Tao, and political corruption involves interference with the life of the people, they are both seriously condemned.

The essence of Wu Wei is docile conformation to Tao or to one's original true nature. One of Lao Tzu's pet symbols for Tao is *P'u*. Literally *P'u* means wood in its virginal state, uncarved and unvarnished, thus aptly representing the simplicity and innocence of man's original true nature. As Lao Tzu sees it, there is some subtle but potent influence inherent in P'u. He says: "Though P'u may appear puny, yet the world dare not dominate it. If kings and nobles can preserve it intact, the ten thousand things will gladly pay them homage."

What specifically is meant by docilely conforming oneself to P'u or Tao? To this question Chapter 34 gives a good answer. In that chapter, Lao Tzu declares that Tao creates and sustains all things but does not claim ownership of any of them; and that while all things acknowledge Tao as their lord, Tao does not care for the honor. Furthermore, Tao is eternally devoid of desire. All this constitutes Tao's greatness. To follow or imitate Tao, therefore, means to be generous in giving and serving, at the same time humble, self-effacing and free from desires. This teaching is supplemented and reinforced in Chapter 40, where it is said that "cyclic reversion is Tao's movement. Weakness is Tao's function." Cyclic reversion means that Tao, after reaching the climax in its movement, will revert from one pole to the opposite pole. The lesson one should learn from this is moderation or contentment. In other words, one should not push any activity to the extreme limit, so as to avoid the reaction or setback which will inevitably occur when the limit is reached.

That weakness is the function of Tao may be difficult to understand, inasmuch as Tao is supposed to be omnipotent. But Lao Tzu makes the matter abundantly plain in one or two sentences. He likens Tao to water and says: "Water benefits the ten thousand things but does not contend, and stays in places detested by the multitude; in this respect, it comes very close to Tao." Tao functions just as water does. Thus in following Tao, one should not contend and should prefer to be lowly. In other words, one should be humble and meek and gentle and unpretentious. This is why in the *Tao Teh Ching* there are frequent warnings against pride, haughtiness, self-display, and avarice. On the other hand, a high premium is placed on such virtues as humility, simplicity, innocence, and contentment.

Lao Tzu sees greatness in humility, strength in weakness, and advantage in lowliness. The Sage is humble and places himself behind or below other people, yet eventually he finds himself on top of them or in front of them. He is humble and does not take credit for his achievements, yet credit will come to him in the end. He is humble and does not try to be great, yet for that very reason he becomes truly great.

As regards strength in weakness, Lao Tzu again uses water as an illustration. He says: "Nothing in the world surpasses water in softness and weakness; yet, among things that attack the hard and strong, nothing can do a better job than water."

And last, to show advantage in lowliness, he refers to the power of the female. He says: "The female always employs quiescence to subdue the male, and takes a low position." Further, in a different context, he says: "That rivers and seas can be kings of valleys is because they are good in staying low." These observations are at once cogent and convincing because they correspond to actual fact. It is true that women often exercise a strange power over men and assert their supremacy in the guise of submission. It is true too that the weakness of water and the lowliness of the sea bottom combine to form the seas and oceans, whose vast expanse and immense power have provoked Lord Byron's poetic outburst in "Childe Harold's Pilgrimage":

> Roll on, thou deep and dark blue ocean, roll!
> Ten thousand fleets sweep over thee in vain.

Lao Tzu undoubtedly wants people to conform their will to P'u, that is, to follow their original true nature. In Chapter 19, for instance, he urges people to "display plainness, embrace simplicity, reduce selfishness, and decrease desires." This remark shows deep wisdom, for underlying every action or interference there is a desire. Decrease desires, and there will be decrease of interference. In fact, it is desire that vitiates or obscures one's original true nature and makes it appear as if non-existent.

Scholars are generally agreed that the *Tao Teh Ching* was written for the edification of the prince or the ruler. It was patently intended to make him inwardly a saint and outwardly a king (*nei-sheng wai-wang*). Accordingly, two programs were prescribed for him to follow—one for handling governmental and other external affairs, and one for the cultivation of the inner life. The two programs are by no means mutually exclusive, much less in conflict. On the contrary, they are in harmony and promote or reinforce each other. The outer program, stressing Wu Wei or non-interference, aims to preserve a peaceful state of mind necessary for meditation. The inner program, stressing spiritual cultivation, aims to attain or retain the immanent Tao so as to render possible spontaneous action or non-interference. All this points to the conclusion that the *Tao Teh Ching* is an ideal guide for the ruler and for any serious-minded person seeking supreme life-fulfillment. No wonder it can endure more than two and a half millennia in Chinese history and survives various social and political vicissitudes, including two big book-burnings and some sharp rivalries between Taoism and Buddhism, especially during the T'ang and the Yuan dynasty.

In the modern period, far from heading toward oblivion as an anachronism, the *Tao Teh Ching* continues to attract attention and the circle of its influence and popularity seems to expand wider and wider with the progress of time. It thus proves itself to be a perennial charmer. Very possibly it will continue to exert a benign and uplifting influence for the welfare of mankind, at least by helping to slow down the feverish Utilitarian struggle and competition in the sorely troubled modern world.

道德經

Part One

# Chapter I

## Tao and Its Attainment

Possibly because of the spreading popularity of the *Tao Teh Ching*, the word *Tao* has now gained currency in Western countries and is being listed in some well-known English dictionaries.[1] It is, therefore, almost unnecessary to point out that the Chinese word literally means *way* or *path*. By the extension of ideas, it also means *method* or *principle*. To Lao Tzu, however, the way is not merely an ordinary way, nor merely a method or principle. It is something elusive, intangible, and mysterious. It is transcendental, infinite, and eternal, preceding even the birth of the universe. Lao Tzu was essentially a mystic, apparently fond of contemplating not only human society and human destiny but also the starry heavens and other natural phenomena. He may have wondered what gives rise to the stars, what makes the sun and moon shine, what activates the human mind, and so on. He probably guessed and realized that there is some mysterious force underlying as well as transcending the visible universe and governing all natural developments. He was curious about this mysterious force and, for convenience sake, called it Tao.

To the Taoists, therefore, attainment of Tao does not mean merely finding a way to do things. On the highest level, it means contact and harmony with that mysterious force. It may be taken as the counterpart of what the Christian mystics believe to be union with the Divine, or what the Buddhists claim to be the gaining of enlightenment.

The first chapter of the *Tao Teh Ching* is generally considered to be the most important and significant, for it sounds the keynote of the entire ancient but immortal classic. It sets forth Lao Tzu's main conceptions of Eternal Tao and his ways to attain the Tao. It may be translated as follows:

> The Tao that can be stated is not the Eternal Tao.
> The name that can be named is not the Eternal Name.
> The Unnameable is originator of Heaven and Earth.
> The Nameable is mother of the ten thousand things.
> Therefore,
> Always be desireless, so as to discern Tao's wonderful essence;
> Always have some desire, so as to discern its manifestations.
> These two come out from the same source,
> But are different in name.
> Their identical nature is a mystery.
> Mystery of mysteries—
> That is the gate of all the wonderful essence.

These dozen lines constitute a great enigma, shrouding some pregnant truth. Throughout the centuries, a vast number of great minds have attempted to draw out the real meaning, but so far no concordance of views has been reached. Their attempts, in fact, have caused some controversy. This is but natural and to be expected. Each scholar, no doubt, interpreted those lines according to his own peculiar background of experience and intellectual training. As their backgrounds differ, their interpretations also differ and give rise to controversy.

To this writer, the dozen lines embody three main ideas: (1) the basic nature of Tao; (2) the ways to attain Tao; and (3) the profound mystery of Tao.

The first idea is set forth in the first four lines. The saying that Eternal Tao cannot be stated or expressed in words clearly indicates that Eternal Tao is utterly transcendent, transcending time and space and consequently beyond human comprehension. Man cannot hope to perceive it with his senses or grasp it with his intellect. So fundamentally he knows nothing about it. How, then, can he say anything sensible about it? Even if his spirit or soul can contact it through meditation, as will be shown in due course, he cannot understand it, much less verify it by objective experiments in order to obtain some demonstrative evidence. As a result, he cannot express the Tao in any language, certainly not in a way intelligible to his fellow men who do not share his experience. Besides, language as a medium of expression has its limitations. It may be very effective in expressing things known and experienced in common by men. In dealing with highly abstract ideas it is often found to be deficient. Voltaire has well said: "Four thousand volumes of metaphysics will not teach us what the soul is."[2] In fact, even some truths in physics are inexpressible in words. Some laws of physics, for instance, can only be expressed in highly abstract mathematical equations. In this regard, note the following remark by Bertrand Russell:

> Ordinary language is totally unsuited for expressing what physics really asserts, since the words of everyday life are not sufficiently abstract. Only mathematics and mathematical logic can say as little as the physicist means to say.[3]

On the above considerations, it would seem that Lao Tzu is absolutely right when he says: "The Tao that can be stated is not the Eternal Tao."

The second line may be taken as the corollary of the first. Lao Tzu believes that Eternal Tao has an Eternal Name, but again he holds that this Name cannot correspond to any created word or sound. This shows logic and consistency in his thinking. Since Eternal Tao is beyond human comprehension and its attributes remain unknown, it naturally follows that no real name can be given to it. True, men can arbitrarily give it a name, but such a name is only in the nature of a label for the sake of convenience. It does not at all symbolize or reveal any essence of Eternal Tao.

So much for the first two lines. In the third and fourth lines, there appear the words "Unnameable" and "Nameable." "Unnameable" refers to Eternal Tao, and is considered the origin of Heaven and Earth. This means that Eternal Tao exists eternally and embodies the essence in which Heaven and Earth have had their origin. Clearly, then, Eternal Tao transcends Heaven and Earth. The meaning of the third line is given more adequate expression in the first part of Chapter 25, which may be translated as follows:

> There is something formless and perfect,
> Existing before the birth of Heaven and Earth.
> How still it is! How quiet!
> Abiding alone and unchanging,
> It pervades everywhere without fail.
> Well may it be called mother of the world.
> I do not know its name,
> But label it Tao.

"Something formless and perfect" is the Eternal Tao, as Lao Tzu subtly intimates. This verse is patently another way of saying that "The Unnameable is originator of Heaven and Earth."

The "Nameable" in the fourth line refers to the manifest aspect of Eternal Tao. It is this aspect that is believed to have mothered the ten thousand things. It is called the Nameable because the attributes of the manifestations can be known and therefore can be named. To make clearer the meaning of the third and fourth lines, it may be pertinent to cite some doctrines taught in the *I-Ching* or *Book of Changes*, which is older than the *Tao Teh Ching* by more than a thousand years, and upon which the Taoist classic is broadly based.

The *I-Ching* postulates the existence of an Absolute Reality called the *T'ai Chi* (Supreme Ultimate), as the First Cause.[4] The *T'ai Chi* corresponds to what Lao Tzu called Eternal Tao, i.e., the Unnameable. It is understood to have contained the two basic cosmic principles, Yin and Yang, in their potential or undifferentiated form. When T'ai Chi mysteriously underwent some quickening motion, it *produced* Yin and Yang (*T'ai Chi sheng liang yi*), Yin, being the passive principle, corresponds to Earth or Matter, Yang, being the active principle, corresponds to Heaven or Spirit. So the T'ai Chi or Eternal Tao or the Unnameable is called originator of Heaven and Earth. Yin and Yang correspond to what Lao Tzu called the Nameable, for after they have come into being their attributes can be known and named. It is the interplay of the two cosmic principles that produces the ten thousand things. So the Nameable is called mother of the ten thousand things.

It should be noted that the T'ai Chi did not become Yin and Yang, but *produced* them. If it became Yin and Yang, it would have disappeared, just as water disappears after decomposing into hydrogen and oxygen. But in producing Yin and Yang, Tai Chi continues to exist after the production, just as the mother continues to exist after giving birth to a baby or babies.

In the two lines after the word "Therefore" pertaining to desirelessness and desire, Lao Tzu says something exceedingly important and practical for spiritual cultivation. He declares that both the essence and the manifestations of Tao can be perceived and realized by the human soul or spirit. He points out the ways for the attainment of Tao. He virtually says: "Always get rid of desires in order to see the wonderful essence of Tao. Always concentrate on something desirable in order to see the manifestations of Tao." He does not use the word *meditate* at all, but he is actually setting forth the basic principles of the meditational process. He may even be revealing some of his personal experiences in meditation, and says by implication: "Therefore, I often practice meditation, sometimes by stripping myself of desires so as to see the wonderful essence of Tao, and sometimes by retaining some desire so as to see its manifestations."

As this interpretation or thesis seems somewhat unorthodox, the author considers it necessary to substantiate and justify it by answering some challenging questions that may be anticipated: Is there any historical evidence that Lao Tzu practiced meditation? Is there any convincing evidence that meditation will lead to attainment of Tao, or to the perception of the essence or the manifestations of Tao? Could the two meditational methods suggested by Lao

Tzu be in any way corroborated by methods later developed by experts in the art of meditation?

In reply to the first question, it can be said that there is at least some circumstantial evidence that Lao Tzu practiced meditation. Chuang Tzu, generally recognized to be the best exponent of Lao Tzu's teaching, tells the following story in his works:

> One day, Confucius went to see Lao Tzu and found him coming out from a bath to spread his hair to dry but appearing so motionless as to be like a corpse. Confucius had to wait for some time before finding a suitable moment to ask any question. Finally he said, "Did my vision deceive me, or could it really be true? A moment ago, Sir, your body looked like a piece of dry wood, and you stood there utterly alone and aloof as if your spirit had left this world and mankind." Lao Tzu replied, "Yes, I was in deep meditation on the birth of Heaven and Earth."[5]

This story may lack historical authenticity, but it does show that Chuang Tzu believed that Lao Tzu practiced meditation. In his biographical sketch of Lao Tzu, Ssuma Ch'ien, the great historian, also says that the old philosopher was an adept in the art of nourishing life.[6] This remark adds some evidence to the belief that Lao Tzu was a meditative mystic. Furthermore, it should be noted that the original Chinese title of the chapter under consideration is *T'i Tao*, meaning "realization of Tao." To achieve the realization of Tao, there must be a way. The only way that can be deduced from the content of the chapter is meditation.

As regards the second challenging question, whether meditation can lead to attaining the Tao, it may be fitting to point out that seers of almost all faiths are virtually agreed that man can come in contact with the Divine or the Godhead or Ultimate Reality through various spiritual practices. Among these practices meditation ranks very high, probably the highest. The outstanding and best known case to substantiate this view is furnished by the Lord Buddha, Gautama Sakyamuni (560-480 B.C.). How did he attain Tao, or Enlightenment as he called it? It was not by reading books, or attending lectures, or participating in debates and discussions. It was solely through meditation under the Bodhi tree.

In fact, it is only in reference to meditation that the two lines in question have any real significance. As a mere philosophical concept, their meaning seems rather vague. In his *The Way and Its Power*, Arthur Waley translates the two lines as follows:

> Only he that rids himself forever of desire can see the Secret Essences.
> He that has never rid himself of desire can see only the Outcomes.[7]

According to Chinese grammatical syntax, the two lines are either in the nature of instructions to some second person, or in the nature of first-person revelations or confessions. Yet Waley's translation is in the form of general statements relating to some third person. Also, this translation includes some extraneous words. In the original Chinese lines, there are no words corresponding to "Only he" and "He." Even more important is the meaning conveyed by Waley's translation. If the translation is considered in terms of meditation, it makes some sense. It may be taken as meaning that a sustained desireless mental state, as possibly happens during meditation, will lead to the perception of Tao's "Secret Essences"; and that a sustained mental state, possessed of some desire, will lead to the perception of Tao's "Outcomes." From a merely philosophical viewpoint apart from meditation the translation does not seem to have much merit. Regarding the first sentence, one wonders whether, in the long course of human history, there has ever been any person who could claim to have "rid himself forever of desire." Consider the case of Confucius, for instance, who has been traditionally respected by the Chinese as the "saint of all time." The prodigy, Wang Pi, generally recognized as a brilliant commentator on the *Tao Teh Ching* and the *I Ching*, even contended that Confucius attained a higher vision of Tao than Lao Tzu.[8] Yet, in the *Confucian Analects*, there is this confession by Confucius: "At seventy, I can follow the desires of my heart without transgressing the norm."[9] Thus even a great saint like Confucius, and at the age of seventy, still harbored some heart's desires, though not to an excessive degree. It seems that a man, without "forever" divesting himself of desires, could still see the essences of Tao, at least as Confucius did.

Waley's second sentence is also open to criticism. Does it not mean that any man who has desires can see the "Outcomes" of Tao? In the world, practically every man has desires most of the time. Does he see the "Outcomes" of Tao? Hardly.

In this connection, it may be of interest to point out that by a little change in punctuation in the Chinese original—by placing the comma before instead of after the word *yu* (desire), the meaning of the two lines becomes quite different. In favoring this way of punctuation, Professor Wing-tsit Chan has rendered the two lines as follows:

> Therefore let there always be non-being so we may see their subtlety,
> And let there always be being so we may see their outcome.[10]

What do these sentences mean? It is not the intent of this writer to be overly critical; but in all sincerity he must confess that he can hardly make any sense out of them. It should be noted that the two sentences clearly convey the impression that someone turns on "non-being" and "being" like an electric light, while other people—"we"—may see "their subtlety" or "their outcome." This appears rather odd even as a metaphysical surmise. Incidentally, there is no word in the Chinese original to correspond to the word "let," which appears in the translation.

On the above considerations, it would seem justifiable to say that the two lines in question have little worth from the viewpoint of speculative philosophy but are highly significant when viewed in terms of meditation.

Let us now attend to the third challenging question, namely, whether the two ways of meditation suggested by Lao Tzu could be corroborated by later theories of meditation. In doing so, it may be helpful, first of all, to try to get at the import of the two ways of meditating. Meditation without desires undoubtedly means meditation with a blank mind. Chuang Tzu, the apt disciple of Lao Tzu, has called this kind of meditation *Tso-wang* (lit., "sit-forget"), that is to say, sit with a blank mind. It is believed that the mind must be purified or emptied of all desires and impediments before it can be a suitable place for the manifestation of Tao, or before it can discern the wonderful essence of Tao. In fact, the wonderful essence of Tao may not necessarily be outside the mind; it could be the mind itself in its pristine purity. Water offers an apt illustration. When water is pure and perfectly quiescent, it attains a reflective clarity like that of a bright mirror. This is the wonderful essence of Tao or its reflection, so far as water is concerned. Similarly, when the human mind is pure and tranquil, it attains perfect clarity of perception and reflects the essence of Tao so perfectly as to be at one with it. Chuang Tzu has well said:

> Water becomes clear and transparent when in a quiescent state. How much the more wonderful will be the mind of a sage when poised in quiescence! It is the mirror of heaven and earth, reflecting the ten thousand things.[11]

As regards meditation with desire, it means meditation with the mind concentrating on something desirable—a word, an idea, or an object. The purpose is to set the mind in focus. Something desirable is patently better for the purpose than something unpleasant. It is better to meditate on beauty than on ugliness, on peace than on war, on a rose or lily or lotus than on a rat or spider or snake. It is believed that only a mind in focus is able to discern the manifestations of Tao.

Their nature being such as described above, the two kinds of meditation have definitely found echoes in the later theories of meditation in other countries, testifying to the soundness of Lao Tzu's instructions. For instance, Hinayana Buddhism prescribes two general types of meditation: one with form or *rupa-jhana*, and one without form or *arupa-jhana*. The former aims at gradual reduction of mental activities and proclivities, while the latter aims at recovery of original nature. The ultimate goal in both cases is the same, but the approach is different. These two types of meditation may not be identical with the two ways suggested by Lao Tzu. In basic principle, however, they may be regarded as similar to them.

Patanjali, the Hindu master of yoga and meditation, also taught two ways of meditation, namely, seedless meditation and meditation with seed. Seedless meditation is not based on any object. Meditation with seed involves sustained concentration on a single thought or object in a receptive attitude.[12] Seedless meditation will lead to the highest level *samadhi*, called *nirvikalpa samadhi* in the Vedas, the ancient scriptures of the Hindus. Meditation with seed, however, will lead only to the lower grades of *samadhi*. *Nirvikalpa samadhi* is said to be utterly inconceivable to the human intellect, for it is consciousness in its purest state.[13] In general, one may say that meditation without seed corresponds to meditation without desire, while meditation with seed corresponds to meditation with desire.

It should be noted in passing that in quite a number of the later chapters of the *Tao Teh Ching*, especially in Chapter 10, Lao Tzu also gives instructions on meditation and even yoga, thereby indicating his interest in the two subjects. Those instructions will be brought out and discussed in the following chapters of this work.

In the last five lines of the chapter under consideration, Lao Tzu stresses the mystery of Tao. "These two" refers to "wonderful essence" and "manifestations." These came out from the same source, i.e., from Eternal Tao, but they assume different aspects and therefore bear different names, though identical in nature. "Their identical nature is a mystery." For it must be their identical nature that causes their cyclic alternation from essence to manifestations and from manifestations back to essence, or from unity to multiplicity and from multiplicity back to unity. This cyclic alternate movement is spontaneous and continues in all eternity. Why? How? Nobody knows or can know. Hence the mystery. It is interesting to note that Plotinus, principal expounder of Neo-Platonism, has expressed some views which fully corroborate the above perception on the part of Lao Tzu. He says:

> The perfect and unchangeable life of the Divine Spirit overflows in an incessant stream of creative activity,

which ceases only when it has reached the lowest confines of being, so that every possible manifestation of Divine energy, every hue of the Divine radiance, every variety in degree as well as kind, is reached, somewhere and somehow. And by the side of this outward flow of creative energy there is another current which carries all the creatures back towards the source of their being. It is this centripetal movement that directs the active life of all creatures endowed with soul.[14]

Lao Tzu should be credited with true wisdom in having called attention early to both the essence and the manifestations of Tao, for one-sided concern about either the essence or the manifestations is unbalanced and hence undesirable. Speaking of Brahma, which corresponds to what Lao Tzu has called Tao, the modern Hindu poet Rabindranath Tagore deeply deplored the fact that Western people often attend mainly to the manifestations, while his fellow countrymen attend mainly to the essence. Note his own words:

In the great western continent we see that the soul of man is mainly concerned with extending itself outwards; . . . Its partiality is entirely for the world of extension, and it would leave aside—nay, hardly believe in—that field of inner consciousness which is the field of fulfillment. . . . In our country the danger comes from the opposite side. Our partiality is for the internal world. . . . We would realize Brahma in meditation only in his aspect of completeness, we have determined not to see him in the commerce of the universe. . . . That is why in our seekers we so often find the intoxication of the spirit and its consequent degradation. . . . But true spirituality, as taught in our sacred lore, is calmly balanced in strength, in the correlation of the within and the without.[15]

This lengthy statement seems too general and sweeping to be an accurate and correct comment on the Western peoples or even on the Hindus. But it does serve to dramatize the undesirability of leaning exclusively either to the essence or to the manifestations of Tao or Brahma.

The mysterious cyclic movement from essence to manifestations and from manifestations to essence is perhaps what makes some Taoists say that an enlightened person can see unity in multiplicity, quiescence in motion, and stability in change, and *vice versa*. Buddhism seems to support this view. It says that insight into manifestations is dharma;[16] that insight into the essence is wisdom; and that fusion of dharma and wisdom brings about enlightenment.[17] This idea may sound strange, but seems to be simply another way of saying that when the knower and the known have become one, or when the illusory polarity between subject and object has disappeared, then there will emerge enlightenment or realization of Tao.

All this is very mysterious, profoundly mysterious. It is mystery within mystery in a series of increasingly deeper mysteries. It is the "gate of all the wonderful essence" of Tao. In other words, the wonderful essence is deeply shrouded in layer after layer of mystery. It is hardly visible or conceivable. It may be likened to the reflected image of a star in the water at the bottom of a well. Because of this apparently infinite mystery, Eternal Tao can neither be verbally stated nor intellectually grasped. However, as Lao Tzu teaches, it is existential. Through meditation it can be realized by the human soul or spirit. The deeper the meditation, the deeper will the soul penetrate the mystery and the greater will be its perception of Tao's essence or manifestations.

That the soul can realize what is inaccessible to the intellect is by no means a peculiar idea. An erudite American theologian, the Rev. James Marsh, has aptly expressed the idea as follows:

> A man may be truly religious, and essentially a believer at heart, while his understanding is sadly bewildered with the attempt to comprehend and express philosophically, what yet he feels and knows spiritually.[18]

Thus, the first and most important chapter of the *Tao Teh Ching* ends on a high note of profound mystery. This is significant. It shows logical consistency and coherence as well as spiritual insight. Apparently speaking of the Godhead, some philosophers in medieval Europe once said: *"Omnia exeunt in mysterium;"* that is, There is nothing, the absolute ground of which is not a Mystery.[19] Now, Eternal Tao is Ultimate Reality. It is the absolute ground of everything. It, therefore, remains a mystery which cannot be explained or put into words. To say that it is not a mystery and can be explained is a contradiction in terms or confusion in thought. For how can that which is to explain all things be susceptible of an explanation? If unexplainable, it must forever remain a mystery.

# References

1. See, for instance, *Webster's New Collegiate Dictionary, Random House Dictionary,* and *Concise Oxford Dictionary.*

2. Quoted in W. Macneile Dixon, *The Human Situation.* New York: Longmans, Green & Co., n.d., p. 24.

3. Bertrand Russell, *The Scientific Outlook.* London: Allen & Unwin, 1931, p. 85.

4. Wei Tat, *An Exposition of the I-Ching.* Hong Kong, 1978, p. 12.

5. *Chuang Tzu,* Chapter 21.

6. Cf. Introduction.

7. Arthur Waley, *The Way and Its Power.* London: Allen & Unwin, 1934, P. 141.

8. Fung Yu-Lan, *The Spirit of Chinese Philosophy,* tr. E. R. Hughes. Boston: Beacon Press, 1962, p. 135.

9. *Lun Yu (Confucian Analects),* Vol. I, Chapter 2.

10. Wing-Tsit Chan, *A Source Book In Chinese Philosophy.* Princeton: Princeton University Press, 1963, p. 139.

11. *Chuang Tzu,* Chapter 13.

12. Clara Codd, *Introduction to Patanjali's Yoga.* Madras, 1966, pp. 12-13, 147-152.

13. Swami Prabhavananda, *The Spiritual Heritage of India.* New York: Doubleday & Company, 1963, pp. 262-264.

14. Quoted in Kenneth Walker, *The Mystic Mind.* New York: Emerson Books Inc., 1965, p. 99.

15. Rabindranath Tagore, *Sadhana.* New York: The Macmillan Company, 1916, pp. 125-127.

16. The word *dharma* has several meanings.

17. Chang Chung-yuan, *Tao: A New Way of Thinking.* New York: Harper & Row, Publishers, 1975, p. 5.

18. James Marsh, "Preliminary Essay" serving as Introduction to *Aids To Reflection,* by Samuel Taylor Coleridge. London: G. Bell and Sons, 1913, pp. xliii-xliv.

19. Ibid., p. 91.

# Chapter II

# The Mysterious Void

In the *Tao Teh Ching,* there are certain chapters which border on the esoteric. What they were intended to say appears mysterious and profound and is difficult to decipher, much less fathom. Prominent among them is Chapter 6. It is a very short chapter, consisting of only six lines; yet it seems to be replete with significance. In it Lao Tzu very ingeniously resorts to the use of similes and symbols to suggest the mystery of Tao and to show how Heaven and Earth came into existence and continue to exist.

Following is a faithful translation of the chapter:

> The Spirit of the Valley never dies.
> Hence comes the name Mysterious Female.
> The gateway of the Mysterious Female
> Is the root of Heaven and Earth.
> Continuous like a thread it seems to exist.
> Its utility is inexhaustible.

These few lines have puzzled not only many general readers but also a number of commentators. Some commentators explain them without much regard to the coherent meaning of the whole chapter. For instance, Huang Yuan-chi interprets *hsuan p'ien* (here translated Mysterious Female) as meaning Heaven and Earth.[1] If this interpretation were correct, then the third and fourth lines would seem to constitute a glaring case of tautology, which weakens rather than strengthens the sense of the whole chapter.

The translation of the first two lines also poses some problem. They are usually rendered by other translators as follows:

> The Spirit of the Valley never dies;
> It is called the Mysterious Female.

In the light of the wording of the original text, this translation seems almost compelling. However, it fails to capture the sense. The point is that Spirit is something active and dynamic and strong. It alone cannot be called the Mysterious Female; for female is passive, static, and weak. For this reason, it seems more appropriate to translate the second line thus: "Hence comes the name Mysterious Female." This would indicate that the Spirit and the Valley are two entities and they together form the Mysterious Female which, as will be made clear in due course, should be interpreted as a pregnant female embodying in its womb the male essence, just as the Valley embodies the Spirit.

The whole chapter may be regarded as representing Lao Tzu's theory of cosmogony; and this theory, as will be shown in a later section, has much to do with mystic meditation and with spiritual cultivation in general.

From the standpoint of philosophy, the chapter has hardly any significance. It does not show any reasoning process. It contains simply a number of dogmatic assertions, apparently intended to reveal visions of the truth as seen by Lao Tzu. No reason for them is given. One can only accept them or reject them.

In order to draw out its peculiar significance, the chapter should best be regarded as a symbolic aphorism or a poetic metaphor. This, anyway, is the general basis of the interpretation set forth in the following paragraphs. There is no claim here that this interpretation is necessarily the right one and has solved the mystery. It is set forth merely as a possible contribution toward understanding an important aspect of Taoist mysticism.

*Valley* is a symbol for emptiness or the Void. However, emptiness or the Void does not mean "nothing" in the usual sense. "The Spirit of the Valley never dies" means that there is spiritual essence in the Void always; and that wherever there is a Void, spiritual essence will be found there also. The Void and Spirit inseparably coexist. They presuppose each other, like heat and fire. So the Void is very mysterious. It may be discerned by the intuition, but cannot be grasped and controlled by the intellect. It definitely cannot be experimented upon, analyzed, and measured. In this respect, it is very similar to the Buddhist conception of *Sunyata* and the Confucian conception of *T'ai Chi* or Supreme Ultimate. This point will be explained presently.

The Valley or Void together with its undying or inherent Spirit is called by Lao Tzu *hsuan p'ien* or Mysterious Female. Why is it considered to be female? The reason is given in the next two lines:

> The gateway of the Mysterious Female
> Is the root of Heaven and Earth.

In other words, it is considered female because from its gateway Heaven and Earth come forth, as a baby comes forth directly from the womb of a woman.

Can the Female alone give birth to Heaven and Earth? This is impossible, just as it is impossible for a woman alone to give birth to a baby. The female must have had union with the male so as to be impregnated with the male principle or essence, for only when Yin (passive principle) and Yang (active principle) are in loving union can life be created. Neither the female alone, nor the male alone, can produce any living thing. This probably explains why Lao Tzu uses the term *hsuan* or *mysterious* to qualify the Female. For the Female that gives birth to Heaven and Earth is decidedly not an ordinary female but a female that has been subject to some mysterious influence. And this influence cannot be other than the male influence, i.e., the influence of Yang or Spirit. If the influence were female, there would be no mystery, no possibility of mystic union, and consequently no creation. Therefore, just as some art critic has suggested pregnancy to interpret the enigmatic or mysterious smile of Leonardo da Vinci's *Mona Lisa,* one considers it appropriate to interpret Lao Tzu's Mysterious Female as a pregnant female, i.e., a female that has been and is being impregnated with the male or Yang essence and who has a fertile womb whence Heaven and Earth and the ten thousand things are given birth.

The above interpretation corresponds more or less with that advanced by the great Confucian sage Chu Hsi (1130-1200). In his treatise on Lao Tzu, he says: *"Hsuan p'ien* is nature that has been spiritualized. *Hsuan* means 'wonderful' *(miao),* and *p'ien* is a female that has been impregnated and can produce things."

The two lines (3rd and 4th) not only indicate that Heaven and Earth come forth from the Mysterious Female, but also suggest that they continue to be attached to her through her gateway, which is called their root.

It is worthwhile to note in the last two lines that the gateway only "seems to exist." The use of the word "seems" *(jo)* is by no means casual but indicates some deep meaning. The gateway does not exist in the human world of sense but in the realm of ideas or noumena. It is, therefore, invisible and even inconceivable to men; to men it only seems to exist. Lao Tzu probably had this in mind. Or, he might have wanted to show that he advanced the view only inferentially. Since Heaven and Earth come forth through the gateway and are rooted in it, and since Heaven and Earth continue to exist, it is reasonable to infer that the gateway also continues to exist.

As the gateway is called the root of Heaven and Earth, it may be further inferred that the gateway continues to convey nourishment to Heaven and Earth from the Mysterious Female or the Valley with its undying Spirit. In other words, Heaven and Earth continue to draw nourishment from the Valley, just as trees draw nourishment from the soil through their roots. As the fertility or utility of the Valley is inexhaustible, Heaven and Earth will never lack nourishment, and so will continue to exist. It may be said that they are being reborn and revitalized eternally.

The Valley with its undying Spirit, which may aptly be called the mysterious Void, also serves as a symbol for Tao. What is the nature of Tao? In Chapter 21 of the *Tao Teh Ching*, Lao Tzu has this to say:

> Tao is something dreamily winking and waning.[2]
> Waning, winking, it embodies forms;
> Winking, waning, it embodies things.
> Failing and dimming, it becomes gloomy,
> Yet within it there is an essence.
> The essence is very real;
> Inside is something invariably vital.

These lines show that Tao, far from being without any content whatsoever, embosoms something spiritual and mysterious and very vital—just like the Void or Valley embosoming Spirit. The following lines from Chapter 4 are also relevant to the discussion here:

> Tao is hollow, yet its utility
> Seems unlikely to reach the limit.
> Profound indeed it is;
> It seems to be the fount of all things.
> . . . . . . . . . . . . . . . . . . .
> I do not know whose son it is.
> It apparently antecedes the Creator.

The first two lines support the view that Tao, though hollow like a Valley, yet is also inexhaustible in its resources and utility. The other lines indicate that Tao, like the Valley again, is the originator of Heaven and Earth and the ten thousand things; it may even be the precursor of the Creator.

It can thus be seen that the Valley with its undying Spirit is replete with precious potentialities and is the inexhaustible source of all things. While Lao Tzu poetically likens it to a Mysterious Female, in another place he also identifies it with a highly metaphysical concept, namely, Non-Being. In Chapter 40, he says:

> All things in the universe are derived from Being.
> Being is derived from Non-Being.

37

Non-Being as a metaphysical concept can hardly be made intelligible to people in general by means of ordinary language. So Lao Tzu resorts to the use of images and likens it to a hollow Valley or the mysterious Void. Nevertheless it is still often misinterpreted as meaning "nothing." This interpretation is quite correct from the standpoint of common sense; for from this standpoint whatever is beyond sensation and ideation is simply nothing. Spiritual seers, however, maintain that beyond sensation and ideation there can be some spiritual essence and that the Void is not just emptiness. To make this view appear in a clearer light, it may be of interest to point out that Lao Tzu's conception of the Void is quite similar to the Buddhist conception of *Sunyata* and the Confucian conception of *T'ai Chi.* The Sanskrit term *Sunyata* is often understood and translated as "nothing" or "empty." Mahayanist scholars, however, seriously contend that such translation or explanation is a gross error. They maintain that the term should be regarded as synonymous with *tathata,* meaning "suchness" or "thusness," and indicating things as they essentially are. In the famous Buddhist classic, *The Awakening of Faith,* "suchness" or void is said to have two aspects: the unconditioned or unchangeable, and the conditioned or changeable.[3] The latter refers to things that have birth and death, that are changing from moment to moment, that are in a state of becoming all the time. In other words, objects are devoid of so-called self-nature. So they are considered unreal, devoid of reality. Their existence is never independent but always depends upon, or is conditioned by, something else. They are not absolute but always relative.

The *unchangeable* void, however, is unborn and undying. It has always been and ever shall be. It embosoms all virtues and prototypes. In it is inherent the light of Prajna or intuitive wisdom which shines forever. Such being its attributes, *Sunyata* in its unconditioned aspect may be said to correspond quite fully with the mysterious Void or the Valley with its undying Spirit as conceived by Lao Tzu. Both may be empty in the material sense; but both have within them some mysterious, spiritual reality which somehow affects the phenomena of the world of sense.

The mysterious Void is also similar to the *T'ai Chi* or Supreme Ultimate as expounded in the famous Confucian classic, the *I Ching* or *Book of Changes*. The *T'ai Chi*, as postulated in the *I Ching*, contains within itself both the Yin and Yang principles in their potentiality, i.e., before their differentiation. Now, in the case of Lao Tzu's conception, the Valley itself may be said to represent the Yin principle, while its inherent Spirit represents the Yang principle. Both the *T'ai Chi* and the Valley with its Spirit, therefore, may be called the Mysterious Female, because they both resemble a pregnant woman embodying the Yang essence. Similarly, just as the Valley or the mysterious Void gives birth to Heaven and Earth, so the *T'ai Chi* underwent some mysterious quickening motion and differentiated into Yin and Yang, thereby causing the emergence of the universe.

In a sense, Lao Tzu's theory of cosmogony, though stated in only a few lines, is more profound than that set forth in the *I Ching* or some other works on metaphysics. According to his theory, the birth or creation of Heaven and Earth is not a once-for-all affair, as some humorist has said: "God created the universe, and then left for a vacation." That theory asserts that Heaven and Earth continue to be connected with the Void or Mysterious Female by means of the latter's gateway which constitutes their root and continues to nourish them.

Thus Taoism, Confucianism, and Buddhism, traditionally regarded as the three "religions" of China, are essentially similar in their basic conception of Ultimate Reality. The similarity between Taoism and Confucianism could be expected, for it is highly probable that Lao Tzu may have derived some of his ideas from the *I Ching*, which is one of the five Confucian canons. The similarity between the Buddhist and the Taoist conception is significant, indicating that seers are apt to have similar visions of the sublime truth.

Now, how does Lao Tzu's conception of the mysterious Void relate to meditation or spiritual cultivation in general? The relation is very significant. In fact, it provides a theoretic basis for meditation. According to some great Confucian scholars, influenced by both Taoism and Buddhism, every man is a little *T'ai Chi*, or mini-void. To use

Lao Tzu's symbols and images, man is also like a Valley with its undying Spirit or a Mysterious Female in miniature. In other words, man is also composed partly of the passive Yin principle or matter and partly of the active Yang principle or spirit. In Chapter 42, Lao Tzu expressly states that "the ten thousand creatures carry Yin and embrace Yang" in their being. At the time of its birth, the mini-void is perfectly pure and clear, and the Yang Spirit in it is, therefore, in full manifestation. If the mini-void continues to be pure and clear, the Yang Spirit will also continue to function at the maximum rate and everything will be in its ideal state. Man will enjoy inner unity, peace and harmony. Like the Mysterious Female, he will be highly creative, creating a wealth of love and beauty. He will experience a continuous flow of creative rhythm and delight. In such an ideal mental state, he has no need to practice spiritual cultivation or meditation. His life is already an Eden of happiness, to which meditation is supposed to lead.

Unfortunately, more often than not, man's whole being is subject to the influence of the senses and sensual desires which arise upon its encounter with external phenomena and circumstances. As these desires increase and keep on increasing, the mini-void becomes more and more impure with defilements and impediments, and the Yang Spirit becomes less and less effective in its manifestation, as if it were partially buried in a tomb or imprisoned in a dungeon. As the Buddhists would say, it is hidden beneath layers and layers of ignorance. It should be the sovereign ruler of man's whole being; but as life proceeds, its power is gradually usurped by the senses. A stage may be reached when it seems entirely lost to the human soul, and man in giving himself over to greed and sensual pleasures seems to have lost his spiritual treasure. This tendency is indeed very strong. Sages of both the East and the West have deplored the situation and taught that man's main purpose in life should be the exercise of his highest faculties in order to fulfill his true nature which is spiritual. The Arab prophet, Kahlil Gibran, is quite near the truth when he says: "Remember that Divinity is the true self of Man. It cannot be sold for gold; neither can it be heaped up as are the riches of the world today. The rich man has cast off his Divinity, and has clung to his gold. And the young today have forsaken their Divinity and pursue self-indulgence and pleasure."[4] A more vivid treatment of the subject is presented by the Confucian sage, Mencius, in the following parable:

> The Bull Mountain was once beautiful with its forest of trees. As it is located in the vicinity of a metropolis, however, its trees were cut down with axes and hatchets. How can it retain its beauty? In the course of its diurnal rest and its nourishment by dew and rain, it indeed would send up fresh sprouts from its soil. But then the sheep and cattle came to feed on them. As a result, the mountain became bare and bald. And when people see its bald appearance, they think it never produced any timber. Is this the true nature of the mountain?
>
> In what is inherent in man, is there no sense of love and righteousness? That which makes man disregard his good nature is similar to what the axes and hatchets have done to the trees. Battered incessantly day in day out, how can man's good nature retain its beauty? His diurnal rest and the balmy air of the dawn may indeed restore to his good nature a semblance of human aspiration and aversion. But then his daily activities tend to destroy it. As this destructive process recurs again and again, he fails to preserve his nocturnal breath with its recuperative potency, and this failure reduces him to a state little different from that of the birds and beasts. And when people see him in this beastly state, they think he never had any human attributes. Is this the normal nature of man? Forsooth, with proper nourishment and care, every creature flourishes; without proper nourishment and care, every creature decays.[5]

When the Yang Spirit in the mini-void is blacked out, that is, when man's true nature is completely eclipsed by passions and desires, man may well become little different from a beast; but this is an extreme case which may be beyond salvation. In most cases, the Yang Spirit only grows dim, which means that man's true nature is only partially eclipsed. There is hope in such cases. With proper care and nourishment, the soul would recover its bright Yang Spirit and flourish. In other words, spiritual cultivation will then be a desirable course, in fact an urgent necessity.

41

How to restore the purity of man's original nature so that it will become a pure mini-void again for the proper function of the Yang Spirit? This is indeed the main problem of spiritual cultivation.

As a solution for the purpose of mental or spiritual purification, Lao Tzu attached great importance to the avoidance or elimination of desires. In Chapter 16 of the *Tao Teh Ching,* he exhorts people to empty their mind to the utmost extent. In Chapter 19, he teaches people to live plainly, embrace simplicity, preserve their pristine purity, reduce selfishness, and lessen desires. Then in Chapter 48, he declares:

> To learn, one increases day by day;
> To cultivate Tao, one reduces day by day.
> Reduce and reduce and keep on reducing,
> Till the state of non-interference is reached.

Chuang Tzu, well-known for his lyrical and humorous exposition of Lao Tzu's teaching, has coined another name for purification of the Void. He called it "fasting of the mind," and explained it in an imaginary anecdote in which Confucius is made to teach his favorite disciple Yen Hui a lesson. Says Confucius: "Concentrate your mind on some goal. Do not hear with your ears but with your mind. Do not hear with your mind but with your primordial breath. Let hearing stop with your ears. Keep sensible images off your mind. Empty and purify your breath and quietly wait for the approach of Tao. Tao gathers only in the Void. The Void is the fasting mind." In response, Yen Hui says: "The reason why I could not use this method is my awareness of my individuality. Before I can make use of this method, that awareness should first be got rid of. Is this what you call the Void?" "Precisely," replies Confucius. After some digression, Confucius continues: "Be attentive to the state of emptiness. The empty chamber manifests a bright glow *(hsu-shih sheng pai).* Good fortune will stay there forever."[6]

The remark "The empty chamber manifests a bright glow" does not say explicitly that the bright glow never dims, but the implication is obvious. As long as the chamber remains empty and the Void exists, the glow will be there. Thus the remark may be taken as synonymous with the saying: "The Spirit of the Valley never dies."

Similar emphasis on purification of the heart or mind can be found in Confucianism. In the classic *Tah Hsueh (Great Learning)*, it is said: "When subject to passion and resentment, the heart won't be normal; when subject to fear and horror, the heart won't be normal; when subject to pleasure-loving notions, the heart won't be normal; when subject to sorrow and anxiety, the heart won't be normal." In other words, the heart must be cleared of all disturbing emotions before it can function correctly and normally. Mencius, the greatest sage after Confucius, has expressed a similar view. He said: "In nourishing the heart, there is nothing better than the lessening of desires." Another Confucian sage, Chu Hsi, a principal pillar of Neo-Confucianism, was fond of dwelling on the theme of what he called *Hsu Ling Pu Mei*, or "empty intelligence never dims." This is almost the same in meaning as the remark "The Spirit of the Valley never dies." Just as Spirit and Valley are two entities in constant association, so are emptiness and intelligence. Thus Chu Hsi in his works frequently exhorts people to purify their mind so as to restore its "empty intelligence."

In Christianity, purity of heart together with its reward is well set forth in the sixth of the eight Beatitudes enunciated by Jesus Christ, which reads: "Blessed are the pure in heart; for they shall see God."[7] St. Paul also has expressed some cogent views on the subject. He said: "Know ye not that ye are the temple of God, and that the Spirit of God dwelleth in you? If any man defile the temple of God, him shall God destroy; for the temple of God is holy, which temple ye are."[8]

The Lord Buddha also laid stress on the necessity of purifying one's heart or mind. In the *Surangama Sutra*, he gives the following instructions to his favorite disciple Ananda: "If you wish to tranquilize your mind and restore its original purity, you must proceed as if you were purifying a jar of muddy water. You first let it stand until the sediment settles to the bottom when the water will become pure, which corresponds with the state of mind before the defilements of the evil passions had troubled it. Then you carefully strain off the pure water which is the state of the mind after the five defilements of ignorance, form, desire, grasping, decrepitude, have been wholly removed. When the mind becomes tranquilized and concentrated into perfect unity, then all things will be seen, not in their separateness, but in their unity wherein there is no place for the evil passions to enter, and which is in full conformity with the mysterious and indescribable purity of Nirvana."[9]

It is clear, then, that noted Chinese sages and some world teachers and saviors have prized the sterling value of important doctrines of the *Tao Teh Ching*. A pure heart is generally regarded as an indispensable condition for spiritual advancement and well-being. On the other hand, desires and passions are considered deleterious and distractive elements that cloud the vision and obstruct the manifestation of Tao.

There is a wide variety of ways to get rid of desires and to purify the heart. However, from the standpoint of Taoism and Buddhism, there is no doubt that the best way is meditation. As has been noted in the preceding chapter, Lao Tzu envisages two kinds of meditation, and maintains that meditation will lead to the attainment of Tao. The various features of mystic meditation as suggested by Lao Tzu will be discussed in detail in the following chapter. In passing, it may be pertinent to point out here that Buddhism lays even stronger stress on meditation as the way to salvation—to attainment of Nirvana. Meditation is seen by the Buddhists not only as effective in getting rid of desires and purifying the heart, but even as instrumental in purging away one's past bad karma which usually retards one's spiritual progress and is extremely difficult to dissipate and eliminate. It is believed that at certain stages in the course of meditation some intense heat or burning sensations will arise from the base of the spinal cord and will serve as a powerful purgative agent to burn up one's bad karma, thereby accelerating one's spiritual advance to Nirvana:

> As a beginning the now one-pointed attention may be turned to other body parts or processes than the breathing, until, by the tingling, burning sensations that follow upon such focused attention, the meditator increasingly knows-feels that his body is indeed only a composite of physical factors, transient in nature . . . . This burning is

also seen as a process of purification, in which past bad karma is "burned up"—the only way to escape its effects—and the forces of purity, good karma, within one are further strengthened.[10]

# References

1. Huang Yuan-chi, *Tao Teh Ching Ching Yi* (Essential Meaning of the *Tao Teh Ching*). Taipei: Tzu-Yu Ch'u-Pan She, 1960, I, p. 9.

2. The two Chinese words *huang* and *hu* are usually regarded as meaning "elusive and evasive." This is substantially correct, for things in the process of change, especially from light to darkness or vice versa, always appear elusive and evasive. Here the two words are translated "winking and waning" just to make the meaning a little more vivid.

3. Beatrice Lane Suzuki, *Mahayana Buddhism*. New York: Collier Books, 1963, pp. 41, 44-45. Cf. also Alan W. Watts, *The Way of Zen*. New York: The New American Library, 1964, p. 71.

4. Kahlil Gibran, *The Voice of the Master*, tr. Anthony R. Ferris. New York: Bantam Books, 1967, p. 65.

5. *Mencius*, Book VI, Section 1, Chapter 8.

6. *Chuang Tzu*, Chapter 4.

7. Matthew, 5:8

8. I Corinthians, 3:16-17.

9. Dwight Goddard, ed., *A Buddhist Bible*. Thetford, Vermont, 1938, p. 201.

10. Winston L. King, *Buddhism and Christianity*. London: George Allen and Unwin, 1963, p. 161.

# Chapter III

# Features of Mystic Meditation

To many people in the West meditation may seem to be of recent origin because they have only recently heard of it. Actually meditation in one form or another is a very ancient practice. Reference to the subject appears frequently in the Bible, especially in the Psalms. Following are some instances:

"My mouth shall speak of wisdom; and the meditation of my heart shall be of understanding."[1]

"I call to remembrance my song in the night: I commune with mine own heart: and my spirit made diligent search."[2]

"My meditation of him shall be sweet: I will be glad in the lord."[3]

"O how love I thy law! it is my meditation all the day."[4]

Recent and current literature on the subject shows that meditation is often employed as a therapeutic device for the relief of tension and strain, for the development of poise, and for the rehabilitation of a damaged psyche or a perverted personality. This is a very valuable device, but it is not mystic meditation.

Mystic meditation aims higher, much higher. It may be of help in developing a balanced and poised personality, but only as a side effect or a by-product. It aims essentially at attaining union or identification with Tao, or with God, or with Brahma, or with the Divine Spirit. While these names are different in sound and appearance, they may be said to denote the same reality—Ultimate Reality. Tao or God or Brahma or the Divine Spirit is ineffable and cannot be grasped, much less controlled, by the human intellect. But Lao Tzu and other mystic teachers say that it could be personally experienced or realized through meditation. Hence mystic meditation.

In Chapter 1 of the *Tao Teh Ching*, Lao Tzu implies that the human mind can, through meditation, attain a state of supreme enlightenment and have a taste of the wonderful essence and manifestations of Tao. In Chapter 10 of his inspiring work, he lays down a number of principles and procedures for the purpose. From the standpoint of common sense, the general meaning of this chapter is quite plain but does not seem to have much significance. It is simply a kind of moral lesson, exhorting people to be attentive, poised and collected, to relax, to purify their heart and mind, to practice non-action or non-interference, to be humble and meek, and to eschew pride and self-assertion. From the standpoint of mystic meditation, however, the significance of the chapter cannot be overestimated, for therein Lao Tzu not only lays down some principles and techniques of mystic meditation but also sets forth some norms for measuring success at certain stages of the meditation.

The chapter can be divided into two parts. The first part brings out the six features of mystic meditation and their respective targets, each of which is expressed in the form of a question. The second part urges the meditator to imitate Tao so as to practice humility and charity and avoid contention.

The first feature of mystic meditation concerns concentration. Lao Tzu says:

> In harmonizing your *hun* and *p'o* to embrace the One,
> Can you concentrate without deviating?

*Hun* and *p'o* constitute the soul as the Chinese conceive it, *hun* being the Yang or male aspect, and *p'o* being the Yin or female aspect. The two aspects must be in harmony in order to embrace the One. Otherwise, the soul will suffer a sharp conflict—a state of civil war, as Shakespeare says in *Hamlet*:

> The genius and the mortal instruments
> Are then in council; and the state of man,
> Like to a little kingdom, suffers then
> The nature of an insurrection.

Such a troubled soul cannot embrace the One, in fact, is unfit for any kind of spiritual cultivation. From the standpoint of common sense, to embrace the One may mean to dwell on one single object or one single idea so as to become one-pointed in one's attention or vision. This is an important and highly cherished aim of meditation, for one-pointed or concentrated attention will raise the power of the psyche, just as concentration of the sun's rays through a prism will increase the heat of the sunlight. Another commonsense meaning of embracing the One is to stay in unity; in other words, to let the two aspects of the soul to stay in unity. This method is a little different from the preceding one, but will lead to the same goal.

Other meanings of embracing the One depend on the metaphysical concept of the One. In metaphysics, the One is a highly abstruse concept which is rather difficult to grasp. In China the metaphysical concept of the One was formed at a very early date, much earlier than Lao Tzu's time. In the *Shu Ching (Book of History)*, one of the two oldest Chinese classics, it is recorded that when Emperor Shun was about to abdicate his throne, he gave the following advice to his successor, Yu the Great:

> The heart of man is precarious;
> The heart of Tao is tenuous.
> Concentrate on the Essence;
> Concentrate on the One;
> Hold fast to the Center.[5]

To the Confucians as well as the Taoists, the above advice contains the arcanum of Tao, which was transmitted from

48

sage to sage only orally. Hence the meaning of "the One" was never formally explained in writing and remains vague or is left to anybody's guess.

In Western countries, Plotinus, the principal propounder of Neo-Platonism, is prominent among philosophers in setting forth his conception of the One. According to him, the One is supreme and ineffable, transcending the totality of all things. From the One comes "Intelligence or the Intelligible World." From Intelligence there emerges the "Soul" which is on the border of the Intelligible World, and whose attributes are dissipated and scattered into the world of sense.[6] This conception of the One is almost identical with Lao Tzu's conception of Tao, which regards Tao not only as ineffable and mysterious but as something absolute and undifferentiated, existing before the birth of Heaven and Earth.[7] It is, however, different from Lao Tzu's conception of the One. According to Lao Tzu, the One is not supreme but is derived from Tao. He says:

Tao gave birth to One;
One gave birth to Two;
Two gave birth to Three;
Three gave birth to the ten thousand things.[8]

This view, apart from maintaining that the One comes from Tao, has another important implication, namely, that while Tao produces all things, it produces them through the One, which was produced before everything else. This interpretation is supported and supplemented by what is said in Chapter 39 of the *Tao Teh Ching,* which, in part, may be translated as follows:

Heaven, obtaining the One, has become clear;
Earth, obtaining the One, has become steady;
Spirits, obtaining the One, have become divine;
Valleys, obtaining the One, have become full;
Creatures, obtaining the One, have become alive.

This passage clearly shows that the One came into existence earlier than Heaven and Earth and the other things, for it must be there first before Heaven and Earth and the others can obtain it.

According to Lao Tzu, therefore, the One, though not supreme, is exceedingly creative and may be called the creative principle of Tao. As such, it corresponds to the Yang or active principle expounded in the *I Ching*. Furthermore, as Heaven and Earth and other created things owe their respective individual natures to the One, the One may be considered the essential or true nature of all individual things, including man. In other words, the One represents man's true nature. To embrace the One, then, means to embrace or contemplate man's true nature. Incidentally, this view anticipated to a great extent the basic guideline of Bodhidharma, founder of Ch'an (Zen) Buddhism in China in the fifth or sixth century, A.D. That guideline is:

> Direct pointing at the mind of man;
> Seeing into one's own true nature.

Whatever its meaning, to embrace the One is difficult to sustain for any length of time, especially for beginners. The point is that the mind is very difficult to control. People are sensitive to all sorts of stimuli and distractions, external and internal. Consequently the mind is agitated by desires and aversions, by worries and anxieties, by joys and sorrows. Some people are apt to lose their mind without knowing it. As the great Confucian sage Mencius has said: "When people lose a dog or a chicken, they realize that they should get it back. But when they lose their mind or heart, they do not realize that they should recover it."[9] A Hindu poet-saint, Thayumanavar, has expressed a similar idea in a different way. He said: "You can control a mad elephant. You can shut the mouth of the bear and the tiger. You can ride a lion .... But to enjoy peace by controlling the mind is rare and difficult."[10] Undoubtedly aware of the volatile condition and centrifugal tendency of the mind, Lao Tzu therefore asks: "Can you concentrate without deviating?" The question implies a challenge. Lao Tzu practically says: "It is necessary but very difficult to concentrate for some reasonably long period of time without deviating. Can you do it?"

Undeviating concentration for some length of time, then, constitutes the target for the first feature of mystic meditation. At the same time it also serves as a criterion for measuring the progress of the meditator. If the period of concentration becomes longer and longer, it means the meditator is making progress.

The second feature of mystic meditation is breath control. It is a matter of common knowledge and experience among meditators and yogis that there is a close relation between the breathing process and the physico-mental state, and that breath control is an important technique for improving general health and prolonging life. Hindu yoga prescribes quite a number of breathing methods, including breathing only with the left or the right nostril. This method is rather inconvenient and should be practiced with caution. The Chinese Taoists lay great stress on counting the breaths, especially in the initial stage of breath control. Lao Tzu, however, does not specify any method of controlling the breath, but seems to be in favor of the natural breathing process. He says:

> In attuning your breath to induce tenderness,
> Can you become like a new-born babe?

Here he also points out the aim of breath control, namely, to induce tenderness. He seems to think that any breathing method that will achieve this aim would be satisfactory. As to why it is desirable to induce tenderness, the reason is not far to seek. He believes that tenderness or softness is the essential characteristic of life, while rigidity or hardness is the essential characteristic of death.[11] In other words, the more tender the body, the more life it will have, and consequently the mind will be raised to a higher state of awareness necessary for the direct perception of truth. William Penn may not have read the *Tao Teh Ching*, but he has made a statement which is worth quoting here. He says:

> Men may tire themselves in a labyrinth of search, and talk of God. But if we would know Him indeed, it must be from the impressions we receive of Him; and the softer our hearts are, the *deeper* and *livelier* those impressions will be upon us.[12]

Furthermore, Lao Tzu considers tenderness a potent factor capable of overcoming the hard and the strong.[13]

Lastly, to induce tenderness is only another way of saying "to relax." The importance of relaxation to our health,

51

mental and physical, is a matter of common sense and needs no elaboration here.

In asking the question, "Can you become like a new-born babe?" Lao Tzu undoubtedly implies that the state of the infant is the ideal norm for ascertaining the success of breath control. The infant with its "soft sinews and tender bones" is the perfect symbol of tenderness. In fact, in the eyes of Lao Tzu, the infant with its pristine purity and innocence is the perfect symbol of Tao itself. In this respect, Lao Tzu sees eye to eye with Jesus Christ who considers reversion to the state of a child as necessary for salvation, for entrance into the kingdom of heaven.[14] Wordsworth, the mystic poet, might have been inspired by Lao Tzu or by Christ when he wrote the following lines:

> Not in entire forgetfulness,
> And not in utter nakedness,
> But trailing clouds of glory do we come
> From God, who is our home:
> Heaven lies about us in our infancy![15]

All this leads to the conclusion that Lao Tzu considers it highly important and desirable for one to breathe as naturally, rhythmically, and placidly as an infant does, so as to induce a state of tenderness like that of an infant. This step is essential to mystic meditation which aims at identification with Tao.

Later Taoists went farther than Lao Tzu and maintain that perfect breathing is "foetus breathing" *(t'ai hsi)*. In other words, one should breathe like the foetus in the womb of the mother. The Taoists maintain that foetus-breathing is so faint and soft as to seem all but extinguished, and that a fine feather would remain motionless if held beneath the nostrils. (This poetic expression came long before the scientific knowledge that a foetus cannot breathe air.) They also say that foetus-breathing is the precursor or accompaniment of a thrilling sense of joy, usually referred to as ecstasy or *samadhi.*

The third feature of mystic meditation is purification of the heart and mind. Lao Tzu says:

> In cleansing and purifying the Mystic Mirror,
> Can you make it free from all stain?

This is tantamount to saying that one should, during meditation or in preparation for meditation, wipe one's heart and mind clean, perfectly clean. The heart or mind with some stain in it is not good enough, not perfect. In a very real sense this teaching is closely related to that contained in Chapter 6 of the *Tao Teh Ching* which deals with the Mysterious Void (discussed in the preceding chapter). In Chapter 6 Tao or Ultimate Reality is symbolized by the Mysterious Void or the Valley with its undying Spirit, which must not be defiled by desires emanating from an impure heart or unclean mind.

The heart or mind of man is often bombarded by a thousand and one distractions and temptations. For this reason man is daily wandering away from Tao or Ultimate Reality, and his original pure nature is apt to be obscured or buried, as it were, under a thick layer of dust. This deplorable condition has been vividly pointed out by Shelley in the following lines:

The One remains, the many change and pass;
Heaven's light for ever shines, Earth's shadows fly;
Life, like a dome of many-colored glass,
Stains the white radiance of Eternity,
Until Death tramples it to fragments.[16]

In pursuing spiritual cultivation, one should lead a pure and clean life and avoid or remove the "many-colored glass" so as to preserve or restore the "white radiance of Eternity." Symbolism apart, one should purge one's heart and mind of all inordinate affections and sensible images in order to regain one's ingenuous innocence and receive the inflow of Divine Spirit or restore its manifestation.

The fourth feature of mystic meditation is Wu Wei or the serene and effortless performance of one's daily duties. Wu Wei literally means no action. More correctly it means no interference or no willful action. It denotes the stage where man's will ceases to operate, while his Tao begins its natural and spontaneous flow and manifests its innate freedom. Lao Tzu says:

In loving the people and ruling the state,
Can you practice non-interference?

53

This saying may have surprised and puzzled quite a number of people. They may have asked: Why suddenly raise the question of government and politics? It is not difficult to find the answer.

In writing the *Tao Teh Ching,* Lao Tzu primarily had the ruler or king or emperor in mind. He wanted to capture the ear of the ruler, through whose sovereign power he expected to have his teaching realized throughout the land. Whenever the word *sage* appears in that wonderful classic, it refers to the supreme ruler. The ruler's duty is, of course, to rule the state and love the people. In so doing, however, he is apt to meet with difficulties and troubles and consequently have plenty of cares and worries and anxieties that are highly disturbing to his mind. Such a mind is not conducive to successful meditation. So Lao Tzu advises him to cultivate Tao and practice Wu Wei, in other words, to deal with his daily duties calmly and serenely with his intelligence and not with his temper. He should be able "to rule a big country like frying a little fish."[17] Furthermore, he should not "push people around" or "cut the people to his own shape."[18] Only when he succeeds in thus practicing Wu Wei will he be able to maintain his peace of mind and even tenor of life so necessary for fruitful meditation.

Wu Wei is to be a perdurable or abiding way of life. At all times life has to proceed at a serene and placid tempo. Even in waging war or going into battle, the ruler or the general is expected to practice Wu Wei so as to preserve his presence of mind instead of letting outside circumstances distract or distort it. In Chapter 68 of the *Tao Teh Ching,* Lao Tzu says:

A good warrior is not warlike;
A good fighter does not lose his temper;
A good conqueror is not pugnacious.
A good leader of men is humble.

If Lao Tzu addressed himself to the common people, he would undoubtedly give the same advice, for there is no difference between ruler and people so far as meditation is concerned. He would exhort them to avoid being too eager for success, too worried about possible failure, too prone to interfere in other people's affairs, or too strenuous in their efforts to win wealth or fame or power. On the other hand, they should take things easy and maintain their poise and composure always, so as to constantly condition themselves for fruitful meditation and for the realization of Tao. In the *Tao Teh Ching*, Lao Tzu harps upon the theme of Wu Wei again and again, no doubt considering it salutary and necessary for spiritual cultivation.

In Chinese history, Emperor Shun was noted for following the principle of Wu Wei. Confucius once spoke of him thus: "Was it not Shun who ruled the country through Wu Wei? He simply assumed a respectful position and set his face toward the south. What else did he do?"[19]

Chuang Tzu, with his lively wit, has dramatized the effects of Wu Wei in a charming parable, which appears in Chapter 12 of his works and may be translated as follows: "Huang Ti (Yellow Emperor) was once enjoying his vacation on the north side of the Red River and found himself deep in the Kun Lun mountains. As he looked southward to the place whence he had come and whither he would return, he realized he had lost his mystic pearl. He at once directed Wisdom to search for it. Wisdom did, but failed. Huang Ti then directed Keen Sight to conduct the search, but the search was again in vain. He next dispatched Philosophy to do the job, but still without success. Finally he approached Nothing or Wu Wei, and Wu Wei found the wonderful pearl. Thereupon, Huang Ti said: 'How wonderful that Wu Wei could succeed in finding the treasure.' "

In ordinary life, the view of Wu Wei as expounded by Lao Tzu and Chuang Tzu is positively sound in at least one sense. For instance, a student may have a problem in physics or mathematics to solve. He may revolve and revolve it in his mind but fail to find the solution. He may try again and again, racking his brain, but still in vain. At last, he gives up trying and goes to bed to enjoy his sleep. When he awakes—lo and behold!—the very solution which he tried so hard to find swims serenely into his ken without any effort on his part.

The fifth feature of mystic meditation is the willingness or capacity to play the female role during mystic union. Lao Tzu says:

When the Heavenly Gate opens and closes,
Can you play the part of the Female?

This saying symbolizes the mystic union of the two principles Yin and Yang, or the passive and the active principle, or the female and the male. Since Heaven is Yang, the opening of the Heavenly Gate suggests the outflow of Yang. The opening and closing of the Heavenly Gate indicates that Yang manifests itself in a rhythmic fashion. Yang or the Heavenly active principle is ready and eager to unite with Yin, the passive principle. Anything female or anything charged with the passive principle will be attracted by, and consequently unite with, the Heavenly active principle. If man can condition himself to play the female role, he will be drawn to the Heavenly principle like iron filings to a magnet and thus enjoy mystic union.

Men in general are probably too proud of their masculine status to play the female role. Lao Tzu apparently knew this, and that's why he asks: "Can you play the part of the Female?" There is always a challenge lurking in such a question. To meet the challenge, men should know that every human being, in fact, every creature, is composed of both Yin and Yang. This is one of the eternal and immutable truths taught in that wonderful classic, the *I Ching* or *Book of Changes*. In Chapter 42 of the *Tao Teh Ching*, Lao Tzu says: "The ten thousand things carry Yin and embrace Yang." A man is predominantly Yang but not all Yang, while a woman is predominantly Yin but not all Yin. Furthermore, the Yin or Yang status of a man is relative. In relation to his wife, he is Yang; in relation to the king or emperor or any ruler, he is Yin. The ruler is Yang in relation to all his subjects; but in relation to Heaven or Tao or God, he is Yin. In prerepublican China, for instance, all people had to kowtow when in the presence of the emperor; but the emperor himself had to kowtow to Heaven when he offered his annual sacrifices.

What is meant by playing the female role? The following confession by Pierre Teilhard de Chardin may perhaps shed some light on the subject:

I made myself limitlessly humble, as docile and tractable as a child, so as not to run counter in any way to the least desires of my heavenly guest but to make myself indistinguishable from him and through my submission to him, to become one with the members of the physical organism which his soul so completely directed. I went on and on without respite trying to purify my heart so as to make my inmost being ever more transparent to the light which I was sheltering within me.[20]

Teilhard was not speaking of any female role. He was describing his humble and submissive attitude toward what he called his "heavenly guest" or Christ. But probably this attitude is very similar to the female role.

Lao Tzu did not so much as drop a hint about the nature of mystic union, much less about its effects. According to the revelations of later mystics in various countries, he was undoubtedly wise in his silence, for the mystic experience is said to be entirely personal and could not be communicated from one person to another. In other words, the mystic union is something extremely mysterious. It may be called the mystery of mysteries. It is perhaps the most mysterious feature of mystic meditation, possibly of mysticism in general, whether Eastern or Western, whether Taoist or Christian. Mystic union represents the unique experience stemming from "the flight of the alone to the Alone," as the famous mystic Plotinus has so well expressed it. Unfortunately it cannot be easily attained, much less isolated and measured and experimented upon in the laboratory. Its actuality is entirely based on the experience and confession of the mystics themselves who were completely convinced of its authenticity. By all reports, the mystic or divine union is an exceedingly exhilarating experience, superior in joy and sweetness to all other human experiences, but its nature is ineffable. After the experience, people usually become less subject to the influence of external events and circumstances and more detached from the conventional values of the world. For their scale of values has radically changed. Consequently their attitude toward life in general has also changed. They would, moreover, become better in health, sharper and deeper in understanding, and clearer in spiritual vision. Meister Eckhart, the celebrated German mystic of the fourteenth century, has expressed the following view on the matter:

> Mystic union brings to the soul power, wisdom, knowledge and indescribable happiness. Man becomes steadfast in all his activities, strong in virtue, never overwhelmed by either joy or sorrow. The soul knows itself and knows God in his essential being.[21]

Those who have experienced mystic union feel that they are blessed with the ecstatic consciousness of Ultimate Reality and consequently consider all else as secondary and unessential, even vain and empty. Note, for instance, the reaction of St. Teresa, the famous Spanish mystic:

> Oh what a mockery is everything in this world that does not lead and help us to attain to this state [union with God], even though all the earthly pleasures, riches and happiness that can be imagined could last for eternity.[22]

Some skeptics have maintained that the mystics are victims of hallucination or self-hypnosis. But the mystics replied that far from being in a state of hallucination or self-hypnosis, their awareness was at its highest during the mystic experience.

In Christianity, the mystic union experienced by St. John of the Cross (1542-1591) is perhaps the best known. Volumes have been written on the subject as well as on his life. His *Spiritual Cantos* has been carefully edited and subjected to detailed expositions. Stanzas 22 and 27 of that work respectively read as follows:

> The Bride has entered
> Into the pleasant garden of her desire,
> And at her pleasure rests,
> Her neck reclining on the gentle arms of the beloved.
>
> There he gave me his breast;
> There he taught me a science most delectable;
> And I gave myself to him indeed, reserving nothing;
> There I promised him to be his bride.[23]

The above poems are self-explanatory and one does not have to read between the lines to get the general import. They support Lao Tzu's view that mystic union can take place between man and a heavenly or divine principle.

The experience of Saint Teresa of Avila furnished another well-known case of mystic union. As indicated in her work *The Interior Castle*, she practiced meditation intensely and frequently; and in her autobiography she confessed that she frequently had mystic experiences of various kinds, such as visions and ecstasies. Following is one of her confessions:

> It pleased the Lord that I should sometimes see the following vision. I would see beside me, on my left hand, an angel in bodily form . . . . In his hands I saw a long golden spear and at the end of the iron tip I seemed to see a point of fire. With this he seemed to pierce my heart several times so that it penetrated to my entrails. When he drew it out, I thought he was drawing them out with it and he left me completely afire with a great love for God. The pain was so sharp that it made me utter several moans; and so excessive was the sweetness caused me by this intense pain that one can never wish to lose it, nor will one's soul be content with anything less than God.[24]

In her works, St. Teresa often referred to her divine lover as the "heavenly bridegroom." Her later visions, however, became more and more predominantly religious and less erotic in character.

Experience of mystic union has also been recorded by mystics of other faiths but its expression as well as its nature varies, indicating that the union may have been felt differently. However, the Hindu poet, Rabindranath Tagore, referred to the subject, as revealed in the Upanishads, in the following passages:

> Therefore the Upanishads say: "He who knows Brahman, the true, the all-conscious, and the infinite as hidden in the depths of the soul, which is the supreme sky (the inner sky of consciousness), enjoys all objects of desire in union with the all-knowing Brahman."
>
> The union is already accomplished. The *paramatman*, the supreme soul, has himself chosen this soul of ours as his bride and the marriage has been completed. The solemn *mantram* has been uttered: "Let thy heart be even as my heart is."[25]

Here, as in Christian mysticism, such images as "bride" and "marriage" are used to suggest the mystic union.

Tantrism, one of the many forms of Hinduism, also deals with the subject of mystic union, but in a different manner. It objectifies the matter. Instead of considering it a union between man and Cosmic Spirit or Tao, Tantrism regards mystic union as some peculiar intercourse between a man and a woman and has prescribed some strange ritual for the purpose. It tends to be erotic in its doctrines. It holds that "Buddhahood abides in the female organ," that "lust is to be crushed by lust," and "everything is pure to a pure man."[26]

Lama Anagarika Govinda, the learned German scholar of Tibetan mysticism (including Tantrism), has expressed a rather skeptical and critical attitude toward the above Tantrist practice of mystic union. He seems to consider it a corrupt form of "authentic Tantrism." In his opinion, the union should not be actual intercourse between a man and a woman, but the union between man's "male and female nature." Note his own words:

> In other words, instead of seeking union with a woman outside ourselves, we have to seek it *within ourselves* ('in our own family') by the union of our male and female nature in the process of meditation. This is clearly stated in Naropa's famous 'Six Doctrines' upon which the most important yoga-method of the *Kargyutpa* School is based, a method which was practiced by Milarepa, the most saintly and austere of all the great masters of meditation, whom certainly nobody could accuse of sexual practices![27]

If we compare the various descriptions of mystic union as set forth above, we may find that the union as conceived by Lao Tzu is quite similar to that as experienced by the Christian mystics or as revealed in the Upanishads. In all these three cases, man is understood as being capable of attaining union with some mysterious Cosmic influence, or Cosmic Spirit, or Divine Being.

The sixth and last feature of mystic meditation is perfect equanimity. Lao Tzu says:

> When your light shines forth in all directions,
> Can you ignore it with perfect equanimity?

The word "light" here may mean one's spiritual light, or the light of one's learning or influence. Light arising to illumine one's vision during meditation is a familiar experience among mystics. Chuang Tzu referred to "the glow in the empty chamber."[28] Jesus Christ also noted this phenomenon, for he says: "The light of the body is the eye: if therefore thine eye be single, thy whole body shall be full of light."[29] Theologians may have some erudite interpretation of this saying, but to a lay person the saying simply means that when a man has brought his faculties to a focus, he will feel himself bathed in a mysterious light.

There have been some attempts to explain this strange phenomenon. According to one theory, the light is produced when the pituitary gland at the base of the brain sends its pulsations upward to the pineal gland inside the brain. "The arc of the pulsation of the Pituitary Body mounts upward, more and more, until, just as an electric current strikes some solid object, the current finally strikes the Pineal Gland, and the dormant organ is awakened and set all glowing with the pure Akashic Fire."[30] In passing, it may be of interest to note that the pineal gland was believed to be the vestige of an ancestral eye and was regarded by the French philosopher Descartes as the seat of the soul or the *sensus communis*.[31]

Whatever may be the cause of the visionary light or glow, there is no doubt that man can experience it at an advanced stage of meditation, a stage perhaps higher than that of mystic union. The light, however, is extremely evanescent. A little thought, a slight exercise of the intellect, will cause it to vanish; just as a little puff of wind will ruffle the placid surface and spoil the reflective clarity of pure still water. This is why Lao Tzu asks: "Can you regard it with perfect equanimity?" The question undoubtedly has to be answered in the affirmative. One must be able to face the light with nonchalance, as if unaware of it. In other words, one's mind must be in a state of perfect equanimity in order to sustain the vision of the light.

This mysterious light is probably akin to what in Buddhism is called *prajna*, or intuitive wisdom, which is said to be the source of all knowledge but itself is not an object of knowledge. It is also extremely evanescent. Hence the following warnings frequently appear in the Mahayana Sutras: "Do not think of exercising *Prajna*, nor think of not exercising *Prajna*, nor think of doing anything with *Prajna* in any possible way you can think about it; for then you will not be exercising *Prajna*."[32] In other words, the mind must be in a state of perfect equanimity, must suspend the operation of the intellect, and must be utterly passive, if it wants to retain the awareness of *prajna*.

It is worthy of note that the pinnacle of spiritual cultivation, or spiritual transfiguration, has always been associated with the manifestation of intense effulgent light. The spiritual transfiguration of the Buddha, for instance, is described in the *Surangama Sutra* as follows:

> The whole audience having heard Ananda's sincere plea to the Lord, rose from their seats and made obeisance to the Lord and then waited attentively to hear the Lord's sacred Dharani. As they waited in solemn silence there appeared a most wonderful sight. From the crown of the Blessed One's head there streamed forth a glorious splendor in the likeness of a wonderful lotus blossom, and in the midst of the abundant foliage and seated in the cup of the blossom was the Lord Tathagata's Nirmanakaya (appearance body). From the crown of the Lord's head there radiated outward uncounted beams of light that shot outward in all the ten directions, and in each of the bright beams of light were figures of transcendently mysterious Vajra-gods permeating everywhere in the open spaces of the Universes and suggesting the lightning-like potencies of all the transcendental powers.[33]

With less exuberant imagery, the Bible presents the following account about the spiritual transfiguration of Jesus Christ:

> And after six days Jesus taketh Peter, James, and John his brother, and bringeth them up into an high mountain apart.
> And was transfigured before them: and his face did shine as the sun, and his raiment was white as the light.[34]

It is not by chance, then, that Lao Tzu's system of mystic meditation winds up with the prospect of "light shining forth in all directions."

As has been noted, the word *light* may be used metaphorically to mean the light of one's splendid achievements and social influence. Even if light is considered in this sense, the person concerned should regard it with equanimity, as if unaware of it. The reason is simple. To Lao Tzu humility is a sublime virtue, while pride or vanity is a deadly sin which precludes true spiritual glory and draws one's attention and vitality outward toward multiplicity.

The remaining portion of the chapter under consideration amplifies this view. It deals with what Lao Tzu calls mystic virtue and therefore accords well with the first portion. In the first portion, Lao Tzu sets forth the various techniques and objectives of mystic meditation. In the second portion, he counsels people to practice mystic virtue in daily life so as to constantly prepare and condition themselves for mystic meditation. To practice mystic virtue means "to produce (things) but not to claim ownership, to act but not to presume on the result, and to lead (people) but not to manipulate (them)." In essence, mystic virtue presupposes such qualities as humility, detachment, noncontention, and Wu Wei or noninterference, all stressed throughout the *Tao Teh Ching*. It must be cultivated and practiced by people who want to succeed in mystic meditation and to taste its fruits.

Ordinarily, people are apt to be gripped by their selfish desires and struggles, distracted and disturbed by the ups and downs of mundane fortune. Those who have cultivated mystic virtue, however, are of a different type. They are meek and gentle and charitable to their fellow men and always at peace with the world. They appear as if conscious of a higher calling and guided by a higher vision of truth. They are indifferent to power and material possessions and their minds are free from cares and worries. They are really extraordinary personages though by no means uncommon. Authentic history records quite a large number of mystics, saints and sages who could look upon worldly glories as empty bubbles and could transcend them as naturally as adults outgrow their childhood toys.

# References

1. Psalms, 49.3.

2. Ibid., 77.6.

3. Ibid., 104.34.

4. Ibid., 119.97.

5. *Shu Ching (Book of History)*, "Ta Yu Mu" *(Plan of Yu the Great)*.

6. Emile Brehier, *The Philosophy of Plotinus*, tr. Joseph Thomas. The University of Chicago Press, 1958, pp. 45-46, 56.

7. *Tao Teh Ching*, Chapters 1 and 25.

8. Ibid., Chapter 42.

9. *Mencius*, Book 6, Part I, Chapter 11.

10. Swami Sivananda, *Concentration and Meditation.* Hong Kong, 1959, p. 32.

11. *Tao Teh Ching*, Chapter 76.

12. Richard Mudie-Smith, *Thoughts for the Day.* London: Methuen & Co., 1906, p. 80.

13. *Tao Teh Ching*, Chapters 43 and 78.

14. Matt., 18.3-6.

15. From the poem "Ode on Intimations of Immortality."

16. From the poem "Adonais."

17. *Tao Teh Ching*, Chapter 60.

18. Ibid., Chapter 58.

19. *The Analects*, Part XV, Chapter 4.

20. Pierre Teilhard de Chardin, *Hymn of the Universe.* New York: Harper & Row, 1961, p. 52.

21. James M. Clark, *Meister Eckhart.* New York: Thomas Nelson and Sons, 1957, pp. 90-91.

22. St. Teresa of Avila, *The Interior Castle.* London, 1906, p. 147.

23. St. John of the Cross, *Spiritual Canticle,* tr. and ed., E. Allison Peers. Garden City: Doubleday & Company, 1961, Image Books edition, pp. 371, 407.

24. E. Allison Peers, tr. and ed., *The Complete Works of Saint Teresa of Jesus.* New York: Sheed & Ward, 1950, I, pp. 192-193.

25. Rabindranath Tagore, *Sadhana.* New York: The Macmillan Company, 1916, p. 160.

26. Quoted in Charles W. Morris, *Paths of Life.* The University of Chicago Press, 1973, p. 49.

27. Lama Anagarika Govinda, *Foundations of Tibetan Mysticism.* New York: Dutton & Co., 1960, p. 103.

28. Chuang Tzu, Chapter 4.

29. Matt., 6.22

30. Clara M. Codd, *The Technique of the Spiritual Life.* Madras, 1958, pp. 75-76.

31. Norman Kemp Smith, *Descartes: Philosophical Writings.* New York: The Modern Library, 1958, pp. 150-151.

32. Beatrice Lane Suzuki, *Mahayana Buddhism.* New York: Collier Books, 1963, p. 45.

33. Dwight Goddard, *A Buddhist Bible.* Thetford, Vermont: 1938, p. 271.

34. Matt., 17.1-2.

# Chapter IV

## Mystic Meditation and Immortality

Mystic meditation, as conceived and taught by Lao Tzu in the *Tao Teh Ching,* is closely related to the subject of immortality. In fact, it is supposed to play an important role in achieving that favorite aspiration of mankind.

Chapter 16 is one of four or five chapters in the Taoist canon that embody the main notions of Lao Tzu on immortality. In that chapter, Lao Tzu dwells on quiescence and emptiness as essential prerequisites for mystic meditation and a meaningful life. He says at the very outset of the chapter:

> Empty your mind to the utmost extent.
> Maintain quiescence with your whole being.

What will happen if one follows these directions? As if answering this expected question, Lao Tzu then proceeds to explain the outcome of quiescence by his observation of what happens in nature. He adds:

The ten thousand things are growing with one impulse,
Yet I can discern their cyclic return.
Luxuriant indeed are the growing things;
Yet each again will return to the root.

He implies that the luxuriant trees and plants will reach their prime in summer; then they will begin to decline. When winter comes their foliage and flowers and fruits will be gone and they will wither and return to their roots. What happens when they return? According to Lao Tzu:

Returning to the root means quiescence;
Quiescence means renewal of life.

In other words, when things return to their roots a state of quiescence will ensue. During this state of apparent death the roots in the underground darkness will mysteriously generate vitality to be preserved in readiness for another cycle of life in spring—for the renewal of life.

Now let us consider the significance of the above remarks in connection with meditation and with human health, life, and destiny. According to the Taoists, the two directives ("Empty your mind to the utmost extent" and "Maintain quiescence with your whole being") imply that the state of quiescence works wonders not only with plant life but also with human life. During meditation the state of quiescence will sometimes lead to a sudden ecstasy of joy highly beneficial to physical and mental health. Sometimes it will lead to a higher consciousness or a higher degree of awareness which affords a penetrating insight into reality. In the *Tao Teh Ching* itself, there are other chapters where the wonderful and salutary effect of quiescence is set forth in more than one way. Following are some instances chosen from various chapters:

Quiescence is the master of rashness.[1]

When desirelessness leads to quiescence,
The world will set itself on the right course.[2]

Quiescence subdues heat.
Purity and quiescence are the norms of the universe.[3]

The female always employs quiescence to subdue the male.[4]

Chuang Tzu, the greatest Taoist philosopher after Lao Tzu, describes the effect of spiritual quiescence thus: "Water becomes clear and transparent when in a quiescent state. How much the more wonderful will be the mind of a sage poised in quiescence! It is the mirror of Heaven and Earth, reflecting the ten thousand things."[5]

More interesting evidence concerning the striking effect of quiescence is furnished in the experiences of mystics. The following poem by William Wordsworth is especially charming:

> Nor less, I trust,
> To them I may have owed another gift
> Of aspect more sublime; that blessed mood,
> In which the burthen of the mystery,
> In which the heavy and the weary weight
> Of all this unintelligible world,
> Is lightened: that serene and blessed mood,
> In which the affections gently lead us on,
> Until, the breath of this corporeal frame
> And even the motion of our human blood
> Almost suspended, we are laid asleep
> In body, and become a living soul.[6]

In another well-known poem, Wordsworth provides no less eloquent evidence. It is as follows:

> Earth has not anything to show more fair:
> Dull would he be of soul who could pass by
> A sight so touching in its majesty:
> . . . . . . . . . . . . . . . . . .
> Never did sun more beautifully steep
> In his first splendour valley, rock, or hill;
> Ne'er saw I, never felt, a calm so deep!
> The river glideth at his own sweet will:
> Dear God! the very houses seem asleep;
> And all that mighty heart is lying still![7]

The quiescence of Wordsworth's mind, interfused with the quiescence of the glorious sight, produced what may be called a rendezvous with Reality.

Wang Wei, one of the great poets of the illustrious T'ang dynasty, also felt the mystic effect of quiescence and expressed his inner experience in a poem, part of which may be freely translated as follows:

Of late I realized the meaning of quiescence,
And kept aloof from the crowd's presence.
Suddenly the truth dawned on my mind—
Quiescence is indeed full of joy divine.

The value of quiescence has, of course, been realized by some of those who practiced meditation. Note, for instance, the confession of Ch'en Hsien-chang (A.D. 1428-1500), an outstanding Neo-Confucian well-known and highly respected especially in southern China:

> Because (I felt) my ability did not equal that of others, I ardently began to study in my twenty-seventh year under Mr. Wu .... However, I failed to experience any final result. Hence on returning to Pai-sha, I kept in seclusion and exclusively devoted myself to the search for the right method of employing one's efforts .... Thereupon I cast aside the complexities of his (Wu's method), and sought for a simple one of my own, entirely through 'quiet sitting.' After a long time I finally came to perceive the very structure of my mind, which mysteriously became visible to me, even as if it were a concrete object. Throughout the varied reactions involved in my daily activities, I could follow whatever I desired, just like a horse that is guided by the bit and bridle .... Thereupon I came clearly to have trust in myself and said: 'Does not the effort of being a sage consist in this?' And to those who came to study with me, I exclusively taught quiet sitting.[8]

Western monks have also found quiet meditation highly relaxing and rewarding. In his famous *Decline and Fall of the Roman Empire*, Edward Gibbon referred to the subject in the following passage:

> The opinion and practice of the monasteries of mount Athos will be best represented in the words of an abbot who flourished in the eleventh century. 'When thou art alone in thy cell,' says the ascetic teacher, 'shut thy door, and seat thyself in a corner, raise thy mind above all things vain and transitory; recline thy beard and chin on thy breast; turn thy eyes and thy thoughts towards the middle of thy belly, the region of the navel; and search the place of the heart, the seat of the soul. At first, all will be dark and comfortless, but, if you persevere day and night, you will feel an ineffable joy; and no sooner has the soul

discovered the place of the heart than it is involved in a mystic and ethereal light.'[9]

Speaking of Western meditation and mystics, one cannot but recall the experiences of St. Teresa of Avila. In her work *The Interior Castle* as well as in her autobiography, she set forth in detail her inner experiences and frankly made known the fact that during meditation or what she called "prayer of quiet" and "prayer of union" she often fell into a trance, which she believed to be a divine blessing.

The above instances can be multiplied, but they are perhaps sufficient to show that quiescence is not merely a state of restfulness and an end in itself, but an intermediate stage leading to deeper and deeper spiritual understanding and insight.

In a very real sense, quiescence is a precursor of emptiness or the Void. Just as muddy water will become clear and transparent after the mud has sunk to the bottom, a quiescent mind will become empty and lucid after the distracting thoughts and emotions have subsided. An empty or blank mind will be better able to encounter spiritual realities. Furthermore, a sound body and a sound mind are interdependent. In other words, a sound mind will lead to a sound body and will be conducive to the restoration of vigor and vitality. It is no mystery, therefore, that Lao Tzu considers quiescence essential to the "renewal of life."

But a pure empty mind does more than contribute to the renewal of life; a pure empty mind is veritably the Mysterious Void or the Valley with its undying Spirit. It is where Tao or the Divine Spirit is said to manifest in full. In other words, it will lead life to the highest goal which is none other than Tao, and Tao is eternal and immortal. This is perhaps why Lao Tzu does not stop on the point of life-renewal, but proceeds to point out that the renewal will bring about a series of significant results culminating in immortality. He maintains that renewal of life accords with "the Immutable," and that "not knowing the Immutable will end up in disaster." In other words, he who does not renew his life by cultivating quiescence and emptiness of mind and, instead, wastes his life force in idle and frivolous activities, will meet with misfortune such as ill health or even death. On the other hand—

> Knowing the Immutable, one will be broad-minded;
> Being broad-minded, one will be impartial;
> Being impartial, one will be kingly;
> Being kingly, one will attain the Divine;
> Attaining the Divine, one will merge with Tao,
> And become immortal and imperishable,
> Even after the disappearance of the body.

Thus quiescence and emptiness of mind yield one advantage after another and eventually lead to immortality—spiritual immortality.

In another chapter (the 52nd), Lao Tzu sets forth a similar concept but a different road to immortality. The relevant passage is highly cryptic and puzzling. It may be translated as follows:

> The world has a beginning as its mother.
> Having got hold of the mother,
> Know her children;
> And having known the children,
> Further hold on to the mother,
> And you will survive the disappearance of the body.

To draw out the meaning of this apparently nonsensical passage, it seems necessary to treat it as a symbolic metaphor. "Mother" symbolizes the life force. "Having got hold of the mother, know her children" means that the life force can be directed for the purpose of procreation, i.e., for the production of children. "Having known the children, further hold on to the mother" means reversing the process of procreation, i.e., instead of using the life force for the production of children, one turns it back to the source. This will lead to life immortal, after the disappearance of the body.

It may seem absurd or fantastic to interpret the above puzzling passage in this way. But the interpretation in itself is by no means innovative or original. It is in consonance with the basic theory of Taoist yoga. According to that theory, the human male on reaching the age of sixteen has his spiritual intelligence *(shen shih)* fully developed, and his Yang or masculine force or vital essence is in the plenitude of its potency. This is the pivotal and most important stage in his life. For then his Yang force has two significant alternatives. If it is allowed to follow the downward course, it will become the ordinary semen for the production of babies, and the father will eventually die. However, if allowed to follow the contrary or upward course, it can be sublimated into the prenatal *(hsien t'ien)* vital force for the development of an immortal spiritual being.[10]

After indicating that reversal of the natural process will lead to immortal life, Lao Tzu makes some other enigmatic statements in the same chapter as follows:

> Stop up the aperture of the vessel,
> And shut the doors (of the senses),
> And you will not be devitalized all your life.
> Open the aperture of the vessel,
> And fulfill your carnal affairs,
> And your whole life will be beyond salvation.

These statements seem to convey a warning against resuming the downward course of the vital essence, as man is apt to do if he is unable to resist temptations and once more indulges in sensual pleasures. Lao Tzu is telling people to remain pure and chaste and avoid sensual temptations so as to continue the reversal of the natural process. If this can be done, people will never "become devitalized" and will succeed in their attempt at sublimation of the Yang force.

In the remaining portion of the same chapter, Lao Tzu says:

> Make use of the light,
> Withdraw its brilliance inward.

This directive is also important for spiritual cultivation. It means that people should not squander their inward light or mental energy in outward activity, but should preserve it for mystic meditation, aiming at union or identification with Tao.

In yet another chapter (the 28th) of the *Tao Teh Ching,* Lao Tzu amplifies his conception of immortality, and says that through cultivating Eternal Virtue one can return to the spiritual state of an infant, or to the Infinite, or to Tao. Here are the interesting lines:

He, who knows the Male
And yet holds on to the Female,
Becomes the ravine of the world.
Being the ravine of the world,
He is always in union with Eternal Virtue,
And returns to the state of the new-born babe.
He, who knows the white (Yang)
And yet holds on to the black (Yin),
Becomes a model for the world.
Being a model for the world,
His Eternal Virtue becomes unerring,
And he returns to the Infinite.
He, who is aware of glory
And yet holds on to ignominy,
Becomes the valley of the world.
Being the valley of the world,
His Eternal Virtue then becomes sufficient,
And he returns to the state of virgin wood.

There is a threefold presentation here, but all the three versions seem to amount to the same thing. All three metaphors, the newborn babe, the Infinite, and the virgin wood, symbolize Tao. The way to the first objective is by sticking to the female, to the second is by sticking to Yin, and to the third is by sticking to ignominy or humility. All these ways are passive in nature, in full accord with the basic teaching of Lao Tzu, and all lead to Tao, i.e., to immortality, for Tao is immortal. While these passive ways are favorable to mystic meditation, mystic meditation in turn fosters them, develops them, and strengthens them, for mystic meditation requires such techniques as breathing like an infant, assuming the female role, and practicing non-action and humility.

The various teachings of Lao Tzu concerning immortality, as discussed in the above sections, all point to the conclusion that Lao Tzu's conception of immortality is spiritual—not physical. It involves disappearance of the physical body. It is tantamount to the return to the Infinite or to the state of the new-born babe or virgin wood. It essentially means identification with Tao—existence in some spiritual realm. In this respect, Lao Tzu was in perfect agreement with Socrates and Plato who envisaged the immortality of the soul but not the body, as has been charmingly set forth in Plato's famous work, the *Phaedo*.

Jesus Christ, too, would approve of Lao Tzu's conception of immortality. According to a story in the Bible, Jesus believed in resurrection, but the Sadducees of his time did not. Some of them wanted to embarrass Jesus by asking him a puzzling question. Jesus gave them an enlightening answer. The story is as follows:

> The same day came to him the Sadducees, which say that there is no resurrection, and asked him,
> Saying, Master, Moses said, If a man die, having no children, his brother shall marry his wife, and raise up seed unto his brother.
> Now there were with us seven brethren: and the first, when he had married a wife, deceased, and, having no issue, left his wife unto his brother:
> Likewise the second also, and the third, unto the seventh.
> And last of all the woman died also.
> Therefore in the resurrection whose wife shall she be of the seven? for they all had her.
> Jesus answered and said unto them, Ye do err, not knowing the scriptures, nor the power of God.
> For in the resurrection they neither marry, nor are given in marriage, but are as the angels of God in heaven.[11]

This story indicates that Jesus realized, as Lao Tzu did, that immortality is spiritual (for angels are spiritual beings), not physical. This notion about immortality is also in line with that set forth in the Old Testament: "Then shall the dust return to the earth as it was: and the spirit shall return unto God who gave it."[12]

It is true that in at least two chapters of the *Tao Teh Ching* (the 50th and the 55th), Lao Tzu expressed some views which may be construed to mean that he also believed in the possibility of physical immortality.[13] But these views are equivocal. Lao Tzu is by no means explicit, much less definite, on the subject. His main emphasis is on spiritual immortality.

Chuang Tzu is also equivocal in his views on physical immortality. While believing that man should and could attain a transcendent state of joy and freedom, he told stories about immortals on earth and their wonderful powers and practices. These stories will be presented in a later chapter where immortality is treated from another angle. [14]

The views of Lao Tzu and Chuang Tzu on immortality influenced to a very great extent the thinking and practice of the later Taoists. Some Taoists who loved the world so much as to want to stay in it forever interpreted the equivocal views on physical immortality to suit their purpose. Others who were spiritual in their outlook were inspired by the teachings on spiritual cultivation and inner development. The remaining portion of this chapter will trace the evolution of certain Taoist practices so as to show how the views on physical immortality gradually died out after causing some disillusionment, and how those on spiritual immortality underwent various modifications and amplifications and persist down to the present day.

In Chuang Tzu's time, in the troubled period of the Warring States, there were already many people interested in physical immortality seeking the elixir of eternal life. Some princes of the various states actually fitted out expeditions to search for the elixir in islands where immortals were supposed to dwell and might hand out the elixir. As those expeditions turned out to be failures one after another, some were determined to concoct the elixir themselves. Hence the rise of alchemy. The most famous alchemist was Tsou Yen, a contemporary of Chuang Tzu. He was said to have written numerous works on his favorite subject, but most of them were lost soon afterwards. He had, however, many followers who claimed to be experts on the speculative science. Tsou Yen enjoyed great popularity and was respected by the rulers of the various states, indicating the wide interest in alchemy at that time. In his famous work *Shih Chi (Historical Records)*, the great historian Ssuma Ch'ien included a biographical treatise coupling Tsou Yen with the Confucian sage Mencius. Ssuma Ch'ien said, among other things, that while Mencius was usually shown a cold shoulder by the princes, Tsou Yen was accorded red-carpet welcome wherever he went.

In the same period, there were also people who sought to attain physical immortality by internal alchemy, that is, by breath-control, by imbibing the essence of the sun and the glory of the moon, and by doing some peculiar system of calisthenics, similar perhaps to the *asanas* of Hindu yoga.

In the century following the death of Chuang Tzu, interest in physical immortality became intensified and alchemy developed into a special study. Specialists in the field were called *Fang Shih* or scholars with recipes (for immortality). Some of them enjoyed great prestige and were apparently highly honored. They succeeded in winning the confidence and trust of the powerful and astute Ch'in Shih Huang Ti, or First Emperor of the Ch'in dynasty (221-207 B.C.), who followed their advice and dispatched overseas expeditions to seek the elixir of immortality. One of the expeditions, under the command of Hsu Fu and consisting of 3,000 young boys and girls, never returned to China but possibly reached Japan, where to this day the grave of Hsu Fu still exists.[15]

Hardly a century after Ch'in Shih Huang Ti passed away, another great and powerful empire-builder, Emperor Wu, or Wu Ti, of the Earlier Han dynasty (207 B.C.-A.D. 9) was won over to the belief in physical immortality. He was even more serious than Ch'in Shih Huang Ti. He offered periodic sacrifices to the spirits, and built grand terraces where he would wait for the descent of some spiritual or supernatural beings to help him attain his ambition. But he also failed and went the way of all flesh. His cousin Liu An, better known as the philosopher Huai Nan Tzu, however, was reported to have succeeded. According to a traditional story, he positively discovered the elixir of immortality and, after taking it, ascended to heaven in broad daylight. The story further stated that in the course of his ascent he accidentally dropped the vessel containing the elixir into his courtyard; and his dogs and chickens, after lapping up the elixir, also ascended to heaven![16] If this story were true, there were earthly animals in heaven long before Mohammed ascended thereto with his horse.

Meanwhile, interest was shown in internal alchemy, a form of spiritual cultivation, and this gave rise to a number of studies on the subject. One of these studies is the *San T'ung Ch'i* (Three In Accord). This interesting but highly cryptic work, later eulogized as "King among Elixir Clas-

76

sics," was composed by Wei Po-yang, a recluse who lived in the latter part of the Later Han dynasty (A.D. 25-220). In that work, Wei explained alchemy in terms of the principles as propounded in the *Tao Teh Ching,* the *I Ching,* and some earlier works on alchemy. He believed that man could attain immortality by reforming his personality and sublimating his vital force. The method he set forth involves repose in quiescence and desirelessness, withdrawal of the light inward, stopping up the openings of the senses, and preservation of the vital force—all for the purpose of developing an "inner pearl," symbol for some spiritual entity which is said to be invisible. If this method is diligently followed for three years, accompanied by the practice of breath-control, the inner pearl will emerge. Being fully established in Tao, it can travel far, through fire and water unharmed, either materialize itself or dissolve itself at will, and can enjoy perpetual happiness undiluted by any sorrow. Eventually it (the spiritual entity) will ascend to heaven and take its place among the divine beings.[17]

The method in its general features is similar to that set forth in the *Tao Teh Ching,* though not entirely so. The result is also somewhat different. Lao Tzu spoke of "return to the state of the new-born babe," "return to the Infinite," and "return to Tao" as the fruits of spiritual cultivation. He did not mention anything like the inner pearl or any spiritual entity within the body. It is true that Wei Po-yang also spoke of "return to the Infinite," as indicated by the phrase "ascend to heaven," but he mentioned the development of an inner pearl as a medium for the purpose. The difference is perhaps insignificant, for there must be some entity that returns to the Infinite or to Tao, although Lao Tzu does not refer to it.

Quite possibly, Wei's notions were not original but were derived from some previous Taoist works or from the lives of the ancient saints and sages. This possibility became apparent in another passage in the *San T'ung Ch'i,* where he set forth the method by which the ancient saints and sages attained the status of *hsien* (immortals or spiritual beings), and which was in general the same as the method he pointed out. The passage may be translated as follows:

The ancient saints and sages embosomed mystic virtue and embraced their true essence and practiced breath-control so as to sublimate their vital force till it became pure Yang. In order to do this, they withdrew from society and concealed themselves so that they can preserve their vital force and nourish their spirituality, harmonize their virtue with the sun and moon and stars, improve their health and strength, get rid of all evil influences, and maintain always their pristine spirit *(cheng ch'i)*. Having thus accumulated their merits over a long course of time, they were transformed into *hsien*.[18]

In a later passage in the *San T'ung Ch'i*, the interplay of Yin and Yang and the union between K'an and Li (supposed to be dynamic agents of Yin and Yang) are set forth as essential for one's spiritual cultivation. The two major symbols employed in the passage are "frivolous girl over the river" *(ho-shang ch'a-nu)* and "yellow shoots from the roots" *(huang-ya wei-ken)*. The frivolous girl, it is said, is intelligent and active and often goes off on a tangent. In order to restrain her, yellow shoots from the roots must be employed. According to Liu I-ming, editor and commentator of the *San T'ung Ch'i*, the frivolous girl denotes the mind of man as represented by the middle Yin line of the Li trigram ☲ of the *I Ching*, while the yellow shoots from the roots denote the mind of Tao as represented by the middle Yang line of the K'an trigram ☵. When the mind of man is restrained by the mind of Tao, it will not only cease to be frivolous, but even nourish the mind of Tao, and the constant harmony between the two minds or between K'an and Li will be highly creative.[19]

This is a strong hint of the mystic union suggested in Chapter 10 of the *Tao Teh Ching*. Later it was generally called the doctrine of *Ch'u K'an T'ien Li* (Taking from K'an to fill Li).[20] The theories of the *San T'ung Ch'i* reinforce to a great extent the doctrines of the *Tao Teh Ching*, and help promote the teaching of Lao Tzu in the succeeding centuries.

Wei did not show any interest in external alchemy, the speculative science aiming at turning base metals into gold or manufacturing an external pill of immortality. He did not refer to it in his work, although some of his contemporaries were studying the subject or even wrote treatises about it.

78

These treatises aroused the interest and stimulated the research of Ko Hung, who lived in the first part of the Tsin dynasty (265-420). Ko was a great scholar and poet and gathered a large number of works on alchemy and occult matters. He himself was a prolific writer and was best known for his *Pao P'u Tzu* (Embracer of Simplicity).

Ko placed great emphasis on moral cultivation, even considering it an indispensable basis for attaining immortality. But his moral cultivation is not quite the same as the cultivation and accumulation of virtue taught by Lao Tzu; rather it savors of Buddhism and Confucianism. It requires a proper fulfillment of the family and social relationships as envisaged by Confucius, and an expansion of one's love to embrace all living things as taught by the Buddha.[21]

His method of breath-control is also different from that suggested by Lao Tzu. It will be recalled that according to Lao Tzu, one should breathe like an infant. Ko, however, went much further and said that one should breathe like the foetus in the womb in order to secure the ideal effects. He also taught that in learning to circulate the breath, one should first try to hold it as long as possible. When one was able to hold it for the duration of one thousand heart beats, one would daily become younger and younger. [22]

Ko was especially interested in external alchemy. He positively believed that by taking various medicines made of gold, jade, or silver one can ascend to heaven in broad daylight, become an earth genie and enjoy immortality, make use of the power of ghosts and gods, become visible or invisible at will, turn grey hair into black, regenerate lost teeth, and recover one's eyesight.[23]

Ko had the making of the scientist in him, and many of his views appear quite modern and objective. And he did conduct experiments to develop the pill of immortality, hoping thereby to confirm his conviction. In his time, external alchemy may be said to have reached its high-water mark of development, but seemed to be rapidly dying out not long afterwards.

Interest in internal alchemy or spiritual cultivation aiming at forming the interior pill *(nei tan)* or spiritual foetus *(shen t'ai)*, however, continued and underwent further development. The Taoist master who contributed substantially to such development was Lu Tungpin, commonly venerated and worshipped as Lu Tzu or Grandmaster Lu. Historically he belonged to the T'ang dynasty (618-906). He was born in 755; but as to when he became a *hsien* or immortal, there is no record. He is one of the well-known Eight Immortals of China. He is to the religious Taoists what a Bodhisattva is to the Buddhists. The Taoists believe that his spirit will respond to their prayers and will guide them to good fortune and away from disaster. He was originally a Confucian scholar and aspired to become a high government official. Lack of success in the scholarly examinations, however, diverted his interest to inner culture. Consequently he practised yoga and meditation in a cave in the famous sacred mountain Hua Shan in Shensi province in northern China. Eventually he was ferried over by his guru, Chung-li Ch'uan, to the transcendental sphere. His teachings were recorded in a book called *T'ai-i Chin-hua Tsung-chih,* an essential portion of which was translated into German by the perceptive and learned sinologue Richard Wilhelm, with a lengthy commentary by the famous psychologist C. G. Jung who considered the work "a pearl of great insight." The work was later translated from German into English by Cary F. Baynes under the title *The Secret of the Golden Flower.* Many of the ideas embodied in the work are not different from those in Wei Po-yang's *San T'ung Ch'i* but are clothed in a new garb.

The golden flower is a symbol for Light or the primordial Yang principle. This Light is said to dwell in the "Spiritual Heart" between the two eyes, where it rules as the master. It is considered important to make the Light circulate. What starts the circulation is the two eyes which can direct it inward or outward. The inward or "backward-flowing method" is necessary for developing the golden flower. It is believed that the Light will thus protect the animus (creative part of the soul) and subdue the anima (receptive part of the soul). In other words, it will be effective in "burning out completely the slag of darkness" in the soul so that the soul can return "to the purely creative."[24] The back-flowing method is carried out through meditation. One is instructed during meditation to breathe rhythmically and noiselessly, turn seeing and hearing inward, keep the heart quiet, avoid distractions, and lower the lids of the two eyes.

> Then one illumines the house of the abysmal (water, *K'an*) with both eyes. Wherever the Golden Flower appears, the true Light of polarity goes out to meet it . . . . It is not only the Light in the abyss, but it is creative Light meeting creative Light. As soon as these two substances meet each other, they unite inseparably, and unceasing life begins; it comes and goes, rises and falls of itself, in the house of the primordial power. One is aware of effulgence and infinity. The whole body feels lighter and would like to fly.[25]

Another Taoist master of note is Ch'en T'uan, whose life spanned a major portion of the tenth century. He was the author of more than six hundred poems in addition to a number of prose works, including the *Chih Hsuan P'ien (Treatise on Mystic Insights)* with eighty-one chapters.[26] Ch'en T'uan is especially noted for his *Wu Chi T'u* (Diagram of the Ultimateless). According to a Taoist source, he received this diagram from Lu Tung-pin.[27] This diagram has tremendous philosophical and metaphysical significance. According to the two learned scholars Huang Tsung-yen (1616-1686) and Chu Yi-tsun (1629-1709), when Ch'en was pursuing inner culture in Hua Shan, he had the diagram carved on the surface of a nearby cliff.[28] Dr. Fung Yu-lan, in his well-known work *The History of Chinese Philosophy,* reports that Huang and Chu described the *Wu Chi T'u* thus:

> This diagram "consisted of several successive tiers arranged as follows: (1) At the bottom a circle labeled 'Doorway of Mysterious Female.' (2) Above this another circle, inscribed: 'Transmuting the Essence so as to Transform It into the Vital Force; Transmuting the Vital Force so as to Transform It into the Spirit.' (3) The next and central portion represented the elements wood and fire on the left side, metal and water on the right, and earth in the center, all interconnected by lines. It bore the title: 'The Five Forces Assembled at the Source.' (4) Above this was a circle (or probably several concentric circles), made up of interlocking black and white bands, and entitled: 'Taking from *K'an* to Supplement *Li*.' (5) A topmost circle with the

inscription: 'Transmuting the Spirit so that It May Revert to Vacuity; Reversion and Return to the Ultimateless.' "[29]

Such being its description, the diagram should be considered as an authentic design of Taoist origin, for it graphically demonstrates the ascending or back-flowing Taoist method of sublimating the vital essence into spiritual essence.

The most significant of the circles in the Diagram is the one immediately above the central group of circles. Yet its significance has escaped the perception of the two scholars Huang and Chu as well as Dr. Fung and his learned translator. They thought that the circle included some "concentric circles" and was "made up of interlocking black and white bands." Such observations entirely miss the point. This is rather surprising in view of the fact that the inscription clearly says "Taking from *K'an* to Supplement *Li.*"

The truth to be pointed out is that that circle embodies the two trigrams *K'an* ☵ and *Li* ☲. The *Li* trigram is on the left, and *K'an* is on the right. They are different from their usual forms in that (1) the lines are curved instead of being straight; and (2) Yang is represented by a white curved line instead of a straight unbroken one, and Yin is represented by a black line instead of a broken one. Why such deviations from the usual forms of the two trigrams? Because the symbol was designed to show the two trigrams embracing each other so as to dramatize their marriage or loving union. During the union something is taking place. Like attracts like. The major Yin force of *K'an* draws out the Yin force of *Li,* while the major Yang force of *Li* draws out the Yang force of *K'an.* Thus after the union *K'an* becomes the all-Yin *K'un* trigram ☷, while *Li* becomes the all-Yang *Ch'ien* trigram ☰.

*K'an* symbolizes the lower *tan t'ien* (elixir field) located about two inches and a half below the navel, while *Li* symbolizes the upper *tan t'ien* between and behind the eyebrows. To take the Yang of *K'an* to fill the Yin of *Li* means to draw the vital essence from the navel area upwards to nourish and strengthen the brain so as to form the spiritual essence or "foetus" symbolized by the *Ch'ien* trigram.

# Diagram Of The Ultimateless
## Wu Chi T'u

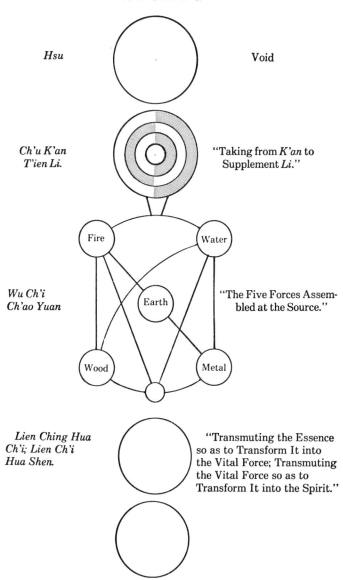

*Hsu*       Void

*Ch'u K'an T'ien Li.*      "Taking from *K'an* to Supplement *Li*."

Fire    Water

*Wu Ch'i Ch'ao Yuan*      Earth      "The Five Forces Assembled at the Source."

Wood    Metal

*Lien Ching Hua Ch'i; Lien Ch'i Hua Shen.*      "Transmuting the Essence so as to Transform It into the Vital Force; Transmuting the Vital Force so as to Transform It into the Spirit."

## "Doorway of the Mysterious Female"
### Hsuan P'in Chih Men

The topmost circle represents the Void or the "Ultimate-less." To it the spiritual essence will return, and this represents the goal of inner culture—the ultimate destiny of man as envisioned by the Taoists.

The whole process of *Ch'u K'an T'ien Li* is an elaboration and integration of three concepts suggested by Lao Tzu: (1) reversal of the natural trend of the vital essence (Chapter 52); (2) mystic union (Chapter 10); and (3) return to the Infinite or Tao (Chapter 28). However, there is a great difference between the mystic union as suggested by Lao Tzu and that conceived by the later Taoists. The former means union of man with Tao or some mysterious cosmic spirit and may be called an interpenetration of the divine nature with the human. The latter means union between the Yin and Yang principles within the human body and seems to be a psycho-physiological phenomenon which occurs when a number of physical and mental conditions are brought into harmonious coexistence; it is very similar to the mystic union as taught in Tibetan mysticism.[30]

In passing, it is interesting to note that when the *Wu Chi T'u* came into the hands of Chou Tun-yi (1017-1073), father of Neo-Confucianism, it underwent a change of name as well as interpretation.[31] Chou called it the *T'ai Chi T'u* (Diagram of the Supreme Ultimate), and his interpretation starts from the top downward instead of from the bottom upward as intended by the Taoists. To him the topmost circle represents the *T'ai Chi* which gave rise to the two modes Yin and Yang as represented by the *K'an* and *Li* trigrams in union. From the two modes evolved the so-called Five Elements which, after various interactions, engendered the two sexes: *Ch'ien* determining the male sex and *K'un* the female sex. The circle at the bottom was interpreted to mean the creation of the ten thousand things. Note this Diagram with its various inscriptions.

Chou's interpretation is supposed to be based on the philosophy of the *I-Ching* or *Book of Changes*. It should be noted, however, that there is no mention in the *I-Ching* about the Five Elements, which seems to be a Taoist conception.

# Diagram Of The Supreme Ultimate
## T'ai Chi T'u

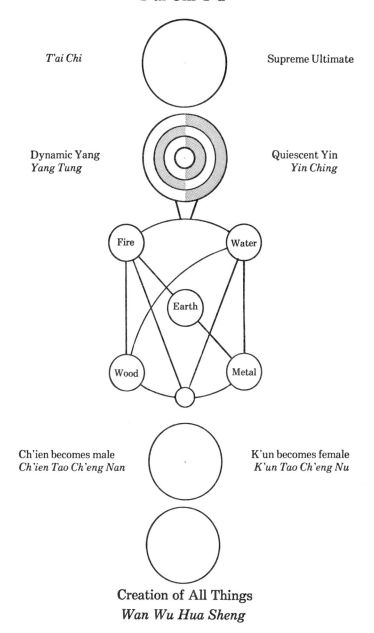

*T'ai Chi*                    Supreme Ultimate

Dynamic Yang                  Quiescent Yin
*Yang Tung*                    *Yin Ching*

Fire          Water

Earth

Wood          Metal

Ch'ien becomes male           K'un becomes female
*Ch'ien Tao Ch'eng Nan*       *K'un Tao Ch'eng Nu*

## Creation of All Things
*Wan Wu Hua Sheng*

In general the Chinese have been in favor of Chou's inter-pretation. Usually a Chinese would first choose to be a Con-fucianist and to get married or to be involved in public af-fairs. Only when disappointed in this would he turn Taoist. The Chinese follow, consciously or unconsciously, the well-known advice of the sage Mencius: "When you have oppor-tunities to express your talents and abilities, let your benefi-cence embrace the whole world; when denied such opportu-nities, just attend to your own well-being."

The next and last noteworthy Taoist master is Chang Tzu-yang, who lived in the latter part of the eleventh cen-tury. In his *Wu Chen P'ien (Treatise on Awakening to Truth)*, a work consisting of ninety-eight poems, he devel-oped further the theory of *Ch'u K'an T'ien Li*. He showed no knowledge of the works by Lu Tung-pin and Ch'en T'uan. His ideas are rather akin to those in Wei Po-yang's *San T'ung Ch'i*. He, however, employed some new symbolism and more sexual imagery than they. For example, in the third verse of Section I of the above treatise, he says: "Through the good offices of the go-between, husband and wife have a wonderful time."[32] This idea is virtually re-peated in verse 19 of Section II: "The Yellow Dame volun-teered as the go-between, so husband and wife united as one heart."[33] In the 16th verse of Section II, the trigrams *K'an* and *Li* are used instead of husband and wife. It reads: "Take the hard nucleus of *K'an* to transform the Yin in the bosom of *Li*, and a strong Yang entity will be formed which will hide itself or fly into the sky as the heart desires."[34] This Yang entity is also referred to as a "mystical pearl." It is called "interior pill" or "spiritual foetus" by other Taoists.

Chang also initiated the process of breath circulation, in-volving the counting of the breaths. However, he only men-tions the process without elaboration. He merely says: "Let the breath circulate thoroughly during the various phases denoting the two-hour periods. Having counted fully the Yin and Yang breaths, one will automatically commune with the Divine.[35]

Later Taoist masters that are relatively well known were Wu Ch'ung-hsu who lived toward the end of the Ming dynasty (1379-1644), Liu Hua-yang, a contemporary of

Emperor Ch'ien Lung (who reigned 1736-1796), and Chao Pi-ch'en who lived in the latter part of the nineteenth century. The various works by Wu and Liu have been included in a collection titled *Wu-Liu Hsien-tsung Ch'uan-chi* (Complete Works of Masters Wu and Liu). The work left by Chao is called *Hsing-ming Fa-chueh Ming-chih* (Clear Pointers into the Secrets of Cultivating Nature and Life). The method of spiritual cultivation taught in these works is still based on the theory of *Ch'u K'an T'ien Li*, but its main feature is the special technique of breath circulation and control.

This cycling process requires constant attention and wilful efforts. Sometimes it has to be speeded up, sometimes to be slowed down, and sometimes to be given a rest or "bath." It therefore is quite different from Lao Tzu's way of breathing like an infant. Some Taoists, however, claimed that it was based on the following remark by Chuang Tzu in one of his essays: "Follow the *tu* channel as a general principle *(yuan tu i wei ching),* and you can protect your body, preserve your life intact, support your parents, and live your span of life to the full."[36]

The process is not only intricate and delicate but also has to be carried out for several years. Moreover, it needs smooth and correct operation from beginning to end. A little mistake, even at an advanced stage, can prove disastrous. No mortal, therefore, could reasonably be expected to achieve success in it entirely by his own efforts. So, just as Christians recognize there is a limit to human effort and rely on holy grace for their ultimate salvation, the Taoists rely on some spiritual being or *hsien* to ferry them over to the other shore. Every Taoist master acknowledged that he had been guided and helped by a *hsien;* and after he had become a *hsien* himself, he in turn offered help and guidance to the qualified aspirants.

The above survey and review show that the path to immortality suggested by Lao Tzu more than two thousand years ago in various chapters of the *Tao Teh Ching,* after undergoing certain modifications and amplifications through the centuries, has persisted down to the present day.

It may be worthwhile to point out that the works by Wei Po-yang, Ko Hung, Chang Tzu-yang, Chao Pi-ch'en, and Lu

Tung-pin have all been translated into English and some other Western languages.

# References

1. *Tao Teh Ching*, Chapter 26.

2. Ibid., Chapter 37.

3. Ibid., Chapter 45.

4. Ibid., Chapter 61.

5. *Chuang Tzu*, Chapter 13.

6. From the poem "Lines Composed above Tintern Abbey."

7. From the poem "Upon Westminster Bridge."

8. Fung Yu-lan, *History of Chinese Philosophy*, tr. Derk Bodde. Princeton University Press, 1953, II, p. 594.

9. Edward Gibbon, *Decline and Fall of the Roman Empire*, ed. J. B. Bury. London: Methuen & Co., VI, pp. 506-507. Mount Athos is on the coast of Macedonia.

10. Wu Ch'ung-hsu, *Ch'ien Shuo* (Plain Talk), pp. 5ab. This work is included in *Wu Liu Hsien-Tsung Ch'uan-Chi* (Complete Works of Masters Wu and Liu). Taipei: Chen Shan Mei Publishing Co., 1962.
Wu is by no means the author of the theory. He probably learned it from much earlier Taoist works such as the *Su Wen* (Plain Questions) attributed to Huang Ti, and *T'ai-i Chin-hua Tsung-chih* (Secret of the Golden Flower) attributed to Lu Tung-pin.

11. Matt., 22.23-30.

12. Eccl., 12.7.

13. Infra, p. 94-97.

14. Infra, p. 98-100.

15. Capt. F. Brinkley and Baron Kikushi, *A History of the Japanese People*. New York: The Encyclopaedia Britannica Co., 1915, p. 144.

16. Herbert A. Giles, *A Chinese Biographical Dictionary*. Taipei: Ch'eng Wen Publishing Company, 1968, pp. 488-489.

17. Wei Po-yang, *San T'ung Ch'i* (Three In Accord), ed. Liu I-ming. Taipei: Chen Shan Mei Publishing Co., 1966, pp. 47-48.

18. Ibid., p. 49.

19. Ibid., p. 52.

20. Supra, p. 80-84.

21. Ko Hung, *Pao P'u Tzu Nei P'ien*, tr. James R. Ware, Cambridge: The M.I.T. Press, 1966, pp. 43-44.

22. Ibid., pp. 138-139.

23. Ibid., pp. 183-189.

24. Cary F. Baynes, tr., *The Secret of the Golden Flower*. London: Kegan Paul, Trench, Trubner & Co., 1947, pp. 28-31.

25. Ibid., pp. 60-61

26. *Sung Shih* (History of the Sung Dynasty), Chapter 457, Biographies No. 216.

27. Shao T'ien-shih, ed., *Ko Hsien-weng Chih-tao Hsin-ch'uan* (Venerable Immortal Ko's Spiritual Transmittence of the Supreme Tao). Taipei: Tzu Yu Ch'u Pan She, 1968, pp. 3-4.

28. Fung Yu-lan, op. cit., p. 441.

29. Ibid.

30. Supra, p. 60.

31. Fung Yu-lan, *op. cit.*, p. 442.

32. Chang Tzu-yang, *Wu Chen P'ien* (Awakening to the Truth), ed. Tung Te-ning. Taipei: Tzu Yu Ch'u Pan She, 1965, p. 8.

33. Ibid., p. 26.

34. Ibid., p. 24.

35. Ibid., p. 51.

36. *Chuang Tzu*, Chapter 3.

# Chapter V

# The Fruits of Mystic Meditation

There are many kinds of meditation. They all appear to bear good fruits of some sort or another. Books on the subject never fail to claim that meditation produces appreciable beneficent effects on both the inner character and the outward conduct of the meditator. The general picture of an experienced meditator may be presented as follows: He usually displays a calm and serene attitude toward life. He is poised and relaxed, as if free from stress and inner conflicts. He seems to have perfect control over himself, as if his Higher Self were exercising its sovereignty over his whole being. He handles his daily affairs smoothly and soberly, and is gentle and generous in his interpersonal relations. His eyes are bright and serene. His voice is clear and sonorous, yet he seldom speaks. He usually has a healthy and radiant complexion, and his youthful appearance in general is apt to belie his age.

In China, meditation has maintained a long and rich tradition since Lao Tzu's time, and its salutary effects were early recognized. In later ages it seemed to have been popular among scholars as well as recluses. For instance, in the Sung and the Ming dynasty, such noted scholars as Chu Hsi, Ch'eng Yi, Ch'eng Hao, Wang Yang-ming, and Ch'en Hsien-chang all studied and practiced meditation. Su Tung-po, famous poet, painter, and calligrapher of the Sung dynasty, did the same and found it good not only for maintaining physical health and developing mental poise but also for healing various diseases.[1]

Meditation may well be called exploration of "inner space." For a common feature of the various forms of meditation is the withdrawal of the attention inward into the innermost recess of the soul. In our daily life, our attention usually turns outward toward multiplicity. We seldom enjoy peace and calmness of soul. Such being the case, we are highly liable to suffer from strain and stress, and cannot contact the emanations from Tao or from any divine source. As Meister Eckhart has well said:

> When the flesh wars against the spirit, where distraction is opposed to unity, where time opposes eternity, God does not work. He who would praise God must be holy and be collected and be spiritual and not at all scattered.[2]

Meditation is an effective means to remedy the situation and to counter the centrifugal tendency of our attention. For meditation aims to reverse this usual tendency. It turns our attention inward into itself by gathering together our scattered attention and mental energy from various attachments. In so doing, it gradually leads to detachment from the external world, to reduction of outward activities, and to the restraint and subordination of the senses. On the other hand, it promotes our inner unity and harmony. We will feel an ineffable sense of supreme peace, and our personality will become more and more integrated.

Meditation is also credited with the efficacy of deepening our self-awareness and expanding our mental capacity. For it directs our attention to penetrate deeper and deeper into the consciousness and, in so doing, may awaken dormant centers, causing a sudden release of unsuspected psychic potentialities. It is perhaps this sudden development that sometimes engenders a feeling of mystery unfolding in the heart in the course of meditation.

Mystics have intimated that in meditation a new aspiration is sometimes born in the soul and will shine forth with a new joy and a new peace. This is said to be an inspiring experience that satisfies and harmonizes all our faculties, integrates the whole personality, and lifts the spirit to a transcendental atmosphere—to a new dimension of life and reality.

The most fantastic fruits or powers are claimed by yoga meditation. According to some Hindu treatises on the subject, yoga meditation can lead to various supra-human powers: to become as small as an atom, to become visible or invisible at will, to have no weight and to move like wind, to be transported to any place at will, to see things of vast dimensions, to know one's past life, to prophesy, and many others.

Mystic meditation does not aim at acquiring any of those extraordinary powers. However, it has its own peculiar fruits. Some of them are moral attributes or virtues, but some are quite unusual, almost incredible, though not so fantastic as the fruits claimed for yoga meditation. In order to understand them, it is necessary to have some clear notion of the concept of Teh or virtue.

As its name implies, the *Tao Teh Ching* embodies Lao Tzu's doctrines on both Tao and Teh. The work was originally divided into two sections, one dealing with Tao and ending with Chapter 37 and the other dealing with Teh and beginning with Chapter 38. The division is highly arbitrary. The only justification is that the first chapter sets forth some important doctrines about Tao, and the 38th chapter sets forth some important doctrines about Teh. Actually, Tao and Teh are expounded in each of the two sections. The reason is quite simple: Tao and Teh are closely related and can hardly be segregated.

In the very first chapter, Lao Tzu points out that Eternal Tao cannot be expressed in words, but he suggests that it can be attained or realized through meditation.[3] In a later chapter, Lao Tzu says:

Therefore, among people who pursue Tao,
Those tending toward Tao will identify with Tao;

92

To those identified with Tao,
Tao will gladly extend welcome.[4]

Tao, therefore, can be called the fruit of meditation. And meditation aimed at identifying with Tao is mystic meditation.

Incidentally, the above saying of Lao Tzu indicates that Tao is highly dynamic and intelligent. It moves toward its seeker just as its seeker moves toward it. There is a similar notion about God in the Bible: "Draw nigh to God, and he will draw nigh to you . . . Humble yourselves in the sight of the Lord, and he shall lift you up."[5]

What is the difference between Tao and Teh? Broadly speaking, Tao is undifferentiated, universal, and absolute, while Teh is individual, particular, and relative. After Tao is infused into the various creatures, it becomes the Teh of the individual creatures. Teh is always influenced by Tao. Lao Tzu says:

The inherent quality of Grand Virtue
Always conforms only to Tao.[6]

Consequently if one cultivates Tao, one will obtain or increase one's virtue as a matter of course. As Lao Tzu has pointed out—

Cultivate Tao in one's person,
And its virtue will be genuine;
Cultivate Tao in one's family,
And its virtue will be overflowing;
Cultivate Tao in one's village,
And its virtue will be long enduring;
Cultivate Tao in one's state,
And its virtue will be abundant;
Cultivate Tao in one's empire,
And its virtue will be pervasive.[7]

As virtue is derived from Tao, it also can be the fruit of meditation. In the *Tao Teh Ching*, Lao Tzu specifically envisages three kinds of virtue: (1) mystic virtue; (2) the virtue of noncontention; and (3) eternal virtue. And each kind yields various fruits. He who is possessed of mystic virtue will have a detached and nonchalant attitude toward success or failure, fame or ignominy, opulence or poverty. He abides by the following precepts:

> To produce things and nourish them,
> To produce but not to claim ownership,
> To act but not to presume on the result,
> To lead but not to manipulate.[8]

He is absorbed in his inner life and in the contemplation of Tao. Outside objects and interests do not particularly concern him, much less trouble him. When his mystic virtue becomes deep and far-reaching, he will be enabled to revert to his original pure nature and attain Great Concord.[9]

He who is possessed of the virtue of non-contention will have an attitude that is not at all warlike, even in wartime. He will not lose his temper even if he has to fight. He will not be pugnacious even if he has to conquer his enemies. He is adroit in using other people's strength rather than his own, taking advantage of the tendency of other people's efforts, instead of interfering with it. His life will be in accord with the supreme will of Heaven.[10] Thus he is always at peace with himself and with the world. He will not be subject to tensions and consequently will save and store up his life force.

A brief comparison of these two virtues will show that they are different only in name. He who is blessed with mystic virtue will undoubtedly also have the virtue of non-contention; for being indifferent to outward rights and privileges, he has absolutely no motive to contend with his fellow men. He too will find himself in harmony with the will of Heaven. He will also rid himself of his selfishness or egoism and will not cherish any hostile attitude toward other people.

Far, far more mysterious effects or fruits are derived from what Lao Tzu called eternal virtue. He who is always in union with eternal virtue will return to the state of the new-born babe. He whose eternal virtue is unerring will return to the Infinite. He whose eternal virtue is sufficient will return to the state of virgin wood (Tao).[11] All these tenets strongly suggest that eternal virtue will conduce to immortality.[12] First, return to the state of the new-born babe means rejuvenation, which is the very thing that renders immortality desirable. Who wants to be an immortal old man "sans teeth, sans eyes, sans taste, sans everything"?[13] Most people prefer youth and vigor and many are perhaps willing to follow the example of Dr. Faust who bartered his soul for a few years of youthfulness. Secondly, return to the Infinite is the highest destiny of man's spirit. It is no wonder that the later Taoists considered it the ultimate goal of spiritual cultivation. It clearly shows that Lao Tzu's conception of immortality is spiritual. Finally, return to Tao also suggests immortality, for Tao is eternal and immortal, and anyone who is identified with Tao may also be immortal. In fact, return to Tao is synonymous with return to the Infinite, for Tao is infinite and is symbolized by the Void.

In other contexts, Lao Tzu speaks about the mysterious and miraculous effects of Teh which, as has been noted, can be a fruit of mystic meditation. In one case, he says:

> He who is profoundly endued with virtue
> May be compared to an infant.
> Poisonous insects do not sting him;
> Wild beasts do not seize hold of him;
> Birds of prey do not pounce upon him.[14]

In another case, he says:

> He who is adept in guarding his life
> Will not come across rhinoceros and tigers,
> When travelling on land;
> And when in the armed forces,
> Will not get wounded by deadly weapons.
> In him the rhinoceros can find no place to butt,
> Nor can the tiger find any place to claw,
> Nor can the weapons find any place to injure.
> Why so? Because there is no death spot in him.[15]

These two passages have fired the imagination of many Taoists who fervently wished to prolong their life on earth indefinitely. They interpreted the passages as meaning that man's physical body can be rendered immune from injury by wild birds and beasts or by human weapons and, therefore, can be made immortal. Is their interpretation justifiable?

Let us take a close look at the two passages. The first passage does not say that the infant's body has been attacked by wild birds and beasts and poisonous insects and yet escapes being injured. It only emplies that the virtue or innocence of the infant has some taming or disarming effect on those creatures and thereby keeps them away. By no stretch of the imagination can it be interpreted to mean that the infant's body per se is not subject to injury. Incidentally, the notion that virtuous and innocent people would be spared by wild beasts is by no means unique or peculiar to Lao Tzu's philosophy. It has a long tradition and is widely circulated. It can be found in the folklore of many peoples in both the East and the West. The story of St. Francis taming and befriending the wild wolf is well known. In the poem entitled "The Little Girl Found" William Blake plays upon the same theme and tells how a little girl was protected by a lion until she was found by her parents. Hindu treatises have even claimed that in the presence of him in whom nonviolence has taken firm root, all creatures renounce their enmity. There is also an explanation given in the Bible, saying that good men and innocent children are under divine protection. Psalm 91, in part, reads:

> He shall cover thee with his feathers, and under his wings shalt thou trust: his truth shall be thy shield and buckler.
> Thou shalt not be afraid for the terror by night; nor for the arrow that flieth by day;
> Nor for the pestilence that walketh in darkness; nor for the destruction that wasteth at noonday.
> A thousand shall fall at thy side, and ten thousand at thy right hand; but it shall not come nigh thee.

The second passage expresses two views, not one. The first is that the virtuous man or the man adept in guarding his life will not encounter any tiger or rhinoceros when travelling on land. This may be because he knows how to keep out of harm's way and will not expose his body to danger. It patently cannot mean that his body is immortal and cannot be wounded, for his body has not been threatened and brought to the test. The second view says in so many words that his body has no "death spot" and that rhinoceros and tigers as well as armed men cannot injure it even if they want to do so. But can we infer from this extraordinary virtue of the physical body that man can be physically immortal? The issue is debatable. One side may say that the virtuous and innocent man, while invulnerable to attacks by wild birds and beasts and human weapons, will yet die of various diseases such as cancer, arthritis, asthma, and so on. The opposing side may retort that the man is so adept in nourishing and guarding his life that he can avoid all diseases and accidents. Obviously, then, the matter hinges on how adept he is in guarding and preserving his life. If he could indeed avoid all diseases and accidents and render his body free from any death spot, one would reasonably presume that he is physically immortal.

In Chapter 59 of the *Tao Teh Ching* Lao Tzu sets forth some almost unbelievable effects or fruits of Teh which amount to no less than invincible power. Here are the inspiring lines:

> In ruling men and serving Heaven,
> Nothing is comparable to a prudent economy.
> A prudent economy means early preparation;
> Early preparation means further accumulation of virtue;
> Further accumulation of virtue can subdue everything;
> The ability to subdue everything knows no bounds;
> Knowing no bounds (in subduing opposition)
> Can lead to the possession of a kingdom;
> Possession of a kingdom along with its Mother
> Can endure a long time.
> This is called "deep roots and strong stalks."
> It is the way to eternal life and everlasting vision.

The term "Mother" usually symbolizes Tao; but in the above passage it more specifically refers to prudence as the Tao for government. In ancient and traditional China, agriculture was the foundation of the national economy. Prudence practically means care in increasing agricultural production and in storing up grain for the rainy day. With a strong economy, the nation naturally prospers and grows and can subdue opposition. In spiritual cultivation, however, the guideline afforded by the above passage is that one should be prudent in the management of one's life force, taking care always to be profuse in its production and sparing in its expenditure so that it will grow from more to more—so that virtue or power will constantly accumulate. This is indeed like "deep roots and strong stalks" in the case of a plant, and will lead to long life or immortality.

From the foregoing exposition of Lao Tzu's teaching, it would seem reasonable to conclude that while mystic meditation may yield some significant moral virtues or powers, its major fruit is long life or immortality. Progressively the process proceeds as follows: mystic meditation conduces to union or identification with Tao; Tao manifests in man and other creatures as Teh or virtue; virtue is of various kinds; each kind produces various effects, all of which contribute, directly or indirectly, to long life or immortality.

In many chapters of the Taoist canon[16] Lao Tzu also warns people against going to the extreme limit in their endeavors, so as to make things, especially life, healthy and long-lasting. The reason is that according to the operation of Tao, once a tendency or a process reaches the climax, a reaction will set in. Those warnings, therefore, support and strengthen the hypothesis that an important purpose of the *Tao Teh Ching* is to furnish guidelines for attaining long life for the individual as well as for the state.

That Lao Tzu believes in spiritual immortality through meditation and cultivation of virtue seems hardly to be gainsaid. Such views as "return to Tao," "return to the Infinite," and "imperishable even after the disappearance of the body" may be cited as convincing evidence.

As to whether or not he believed also in physical immortality, no answer can be positive. One can only say that he did make some statements which could be construed to mean that he was inclined toward that belief.

Chuang Tzu, generally recognized as a mystic and the most brilliant exponent of Lao Tzu's teaching, has views concerning life, death, and immortality that are worthy of attention and examination, for they indicate the fruits of mystic meditation.

Both Lao Tzu and Chuang Tzu were essentially poets. While Lao Tzu developed his themes with poise and cool judgment, Chuang Tzu elaborated and embellished similar themes with wit and humor and imagination. Displaying his literary brilliance and lively style, he enlivened his conception of immortality in a number of charming parables. Here are two of them:

> Far away on the Miao-ku-che mountain, there lives an enchanting immortal. He has a milk and rose complexion and is so graceful and elegant in his manners as to seem like a virgin in her blooming youth. He does not eat cereals. He only sucks pure air and drinks dew. Yet he can drive a team of flying dragons and ride through the clouds beyond the bounds of the four seas. He can concentrate his spiritual force in such a way as to ward off evil influences from all things and he can bring on good harvests.[17]

> The Perfect Man is a spiritual being. He would not feel any heat even if the whole ocean were burnt up, nor would he feel any cold even if the rivers were frozen hard. Even if the mountains were split asunder by lightening and thunder, or the seas overturned by storms, he could not be scared. He can ride the clouds in the sky or ride astride the sun and moon and flies beyond the bounds of the four seas. Neither life nor death has any effect on him. How much the less has such a trifling thing as profit or loss![18]

In projecting such images of the immortals, Chuang Tzu undoubtedly set the later Taoists dreaming about immortality. Apart from projecting those images, he also described with great zest the method of mystic meditation which would lead to long life or immortality. Following are three parables wherein he presented the meditational techniques and procedures:

> Nieh Ch'ueh, the toothless, asked P'i Yi to tell him about Tao. P'i Yi consented and said: "If you keep your body in the proper posture and fix your inner gaze on a single center, the heavenly harmony will sooner or later take hold of you. Set aside your knowledge and concentrate your awareness on the One, and the Divine Spirit will dwell within you. Virtue will adorn your soul with its beauty, and you will abide with Tao. You will then feel as innocent as a new-born calf, simply looking at things but not wondering why." At that point, before P'i Yi finished speaking, Nieh Ch'ueh had already fallen into a trance. Highly delighted, P'i Yi went away, singing: "His body is like dried wood. His mind is like dead ashes. He now really knows the truth, no longer asking whither and wherefore.

In the gloom and obscurity, he has abstracted himself from his mind and is devoid of any design. What sort of man is he?"[19]

Huang Ti (Yellow Emperor) once went to see the Taoist master, Kuang Ch'eng Tzu, and inquired about the secret of long life and immortality. He obtained the following answer: "Be quiet and still and purify your heart. Do not weary your body. Do not sway your sperms. You will then live forever. Let your eyes see nothing. Let your ears hear nothing. Let your heart know nothing. Then your spiritual essence will preserve your body intact, enabling it to last forever. Attend carefully to your inner life. Shut out all disturbances from the outside. Much knowledge will only do you harm."[20]

Nanpo Tzu-k'uei said to Nu Yu: "You are well advanced in years, and yet you still have a baby face. How come?"

Nu Yu replied: "I have been initiated into Eternal Tao."

"Can I find Tao through study?" Tzu-k'uei asked.

"No, you can't," replied Nu Yu. "You are not the sort of person. Let me tell you the case of Pu-liang Yi. He had the potentiality of being a sage, but did not know the sagely way. I myself knew the sagely way, but did not have the potentiality. I wanted to teach him, hoping he would find fulfillment as a sage. Now, do not think it an easy task to teach the sagely way, even though to a potential sage. I had to wait patiently for the right time to begin the guidance. In three days after I began, he could detach himself from the affairs of the world. In seven more days of guidance, he could detach himself from material things. In another nine days of guidance, he could detach himself from all life. Once he could do this, his vision became clear with the light of a bright dawn. With such clear vision, he could see the One. Having seen the One, he attained the Eternal Now. Having attained the Eternal Now, he entered into the state beyond life and death, where life can neither be destroyed nor created. He then found himself in harmony with all circumstances. This is the so-called 'security in the midst of confusion,' that is, security despite or because of confusion."[21]

This last parable is strongly reminiscent of the three main stages of the mystic way as envisaged in Neo-

Platonism and later incorporated into Christian mysticism. The three stages are: the purgative, the illuminative, and the unitive. The purgative stage involves progressive detachment from layer after layer of *impedimenta* that block the mystic's spiritual progress—detachment from worldly affairs, from material things, and from all life. Afterwards he comes to the illuminative stage where he sees the One and enjoys a deep sense of joy and wonder. Finally he reaches the unitive stage where he realizes the unity and equality of all things, where the illusory dualism between subject and object is obliterated, where he is unified or interfuses with Tao.

The foregoing parables concerning immortality and mystic meditation can be interpreted in more than one way. On balance, however, they tend to support and amplify Lao Tzu's views on man's possible immortality, even physical immortality, and its attainability through mystic meditation.

Furthermore, they clearly show that Chuang Tzu had an intimate knowledge of the techniques of mystic meditation as well as the fruits such meditation was expected to yield. Though he was not explicit as to whether he himself ever practiced them, it would be strange if a wise and curious person like him would have refrained from trying them and obtaining some personal experience of the results. There is substantial circumstantial evidence to support the presumption that he must have tried them and that the fruits he obtained were not the acquirement of any miraculous power, or immunity to death, but a transcendent attitude toward life and death and a wholesome contempt for worldly success and riches and honors. Abundant evidence can be found in his works to demonstrate his transcendent frame of mind and his mystic proclivity. For instance, the King of Ch'u once sent two envoys to approach him and offer him a high post in the government. He, however, almost spontaneously declined it with unveiled contempt, saying that he would rather enjoy life and freedom like a turtle in the mud than fetter himself like a turtle to be sacrificed in a royal ancestral temple.[22]

His sane and sober attitude toward life and death is also made abundantly clear in his works. He frequently shows himself to be in favor of a free life in a transcendental atmosphere, enjoying sublime contemplation, with his spirit pure and his soul alert, untrammeled by fears and worries and other evil influences.[23] Without mincing his words, he also reveals that he liked to be "alone in communion with the spirit of Heaven and Earth *(tu yu T'ien Ti ching-shen wang-lai)*, but not haughty toward the myriad creatures."[24] The term "spirit of Heaven and Earth" may mean the Eternal Tao, or it may mean a Divine Intelligence governing Heaven and Earth. It may also correspond to the Paraclete or Holy Spirit mentioned by Jesus Christ.

That Chuang Tzu was not disturbed by the advent of death is patent from quite a number of his interesting parables or imaginary anecdotes. When his wife died, he did not shed any tears at all but sat beside the corpse and sang, convinced that she was simply undergoing a natural transformation.[25] He well knew that life and death are governed by immutable laws and considered it wise for man to understand and accept the inevitable with equanimity.[26]

In one of his parables, he compares man's fear of death to an ignorant girl's fear of marriage. He says that there was once a girl who was so afraid of marriage that she wept bitter tears on the approach of the wedding day; after the marriage, however, she felt so happy that she greatly regretted being so mournful before the event. Similarly death may turn out to be a source of joy, and man's fear of it may be wholly groundless.[27]

In another parable, Chuang Tzu actually advances the notion that life after death is much happier than life on earth. In that parable he imagines himself talking to the soul of a skull in a dream. He tried to persuade the soul to come back to earth, but the soul refused to do so, saying: "How could I give up the joys like those of a king on his throne and return to the toil of life on earth?"[28] Incidentally, this parable indicates that Chuang Tzu believed in an after life. This possibility is adumbrated in another of his parables. In it he says that he once dreamed of being a butterfly, flitting from flower to flower, never suspecting that it was he himself. On waking up, he was greatly puzzled, wondering whether or not he was in reality a butterfly, only dreaming it was he himself.[29] He thus shows himself to be rather skeptical about the reality of his mundane existence. Quite possibly, he was expecting that death would be but an awakening to a real life.

Speaking of dreams in another context, he expresses this definite view: "During their dream, people do not know they are dreaming; they know it was a dream only after they have waked up. In course of time, the great awakening will come, and we will then realize that this life is in fact a great dream."[30]

Chuang Tzu had a really wonderful mind, with a fertile imagination and a penetrating understanding. He even imagined or realized that man could travel in time, and this speculative possibility he sets forth in a fictitious anecdote involving Lao Tzu and Confucius. He imagines Confucius visiting Lao Tzu and finding the latter in a deep trance. On returning to normal consciousness, Lao Tzu is said to have told his visitor that he had travelled back to the beginning of creation and had seen Yin and Yang emerging to give birth to the ten thousand things.[31] In other words, Lao Tzu could, through mystic meditation, travel in time.

Such travel may appear incredible and impossible. But Thomas Carlyle, a literary visionary somewhat like Chuang Tzu, thought otherwise. He considered it possible through the "mystic faculties." In his witty and humorous as well as didactic work *Sartor Resartus,* he broaches the subject in the following funny way:

> Still stranger, should, on the opposite side of the street, another Hatter establish himself; and, as his fellow-craftsman made Space-annihilating Hats, make Time-annihilating! Of both would I purchase, were it with my last groschen; but chiefly of this latter. To clap on your felt, and, simply by wishing that you were *Anywhere,* straightway to be *There!* Next to clap on your other felt, and, simply by wishing that you were *Anywhen,* straightway to be *Then!* This were indeed the grander: shooting at will from the Fire-Creation of the World to its Fire-Consummation; here historically present in the First Century, conversing face to face with Paul and

Seneca; there prophetically in the Thirty-first, conversing also face to face with other Pauls and Senecas, who as yet stand hidden in the depth of that late Time![32]

If mystic meditation could really yield such fruit as the capability to travel along the long corridor of time as Chuang Tzu and Carlyle seemed to believe, it would not only gratify the Carlylean dream of conversing with the ancient saints and sages but also solve many of the crucial problems that have been for ages confronting mankind. It would, for instance, help answer the following questions posed in the Bible:

Where wast thou when I laid the foundations of the earth? declare, if thou hast understanding.

Who hath laid the measures thereof, if thou knowest? or who hath stretched the line upon it?

Whereupon are the foundations thereof fastened? or who laid the corner stone thereof;

When the morning stars sang together, and all the sons of God shouted for joy?

Or who shut up the sea with doors, when it brake forth, as if it had issued out of the womb?[33]

# References

1. Lin Yutang, *The Gay Genius*. New York: The John Day Company, 1947, pp. 233ff.

2. James M. Clark, *Meister Eckhart*. New York: Thomas Nelson and Sons, 1957, p. 164.

3. Supra, p. 23-26.

4. *Tao Teh Ching*, Chapter 23.

5. James, 4.8-10.

6. *Tao Teh Ching*, Chapter 21.

7. Ibid., Chapter 54.

8. Ibid., Chapter 10.

9. Ibid., Chapter 65.

10. Ibid., Chapter 68.

11. Ibid., Chapter 28.

12. Like the preceding chapter, this chapter also deals largely with the subject of immortality, but from a different point of view.

13. Shakespeare's phraseology in the play "As You Like It."

14. *Tao Teh Ching*, Chapter 55.

15. Ibid., Chapter 50.

16. Ibid., Chapters 9, 15, 30, and 55.

17. *Chuang Tzu*, Chapter 1.

18. Ibid., Chapter 2.

19. Ibid., Chapter 22.

20. Ibid., Chapter 11.

21. Ibid., Chapter 6.

22. Ibid., Chapter 17.

23. Ibid., Chapter 15.

24. Ibid., Chapter 33.

25. Ibid., Chapter 18.

26. Ibid., Chapter 6.

27. Ibid., Chapter 2.

28. Somewhere in his works, William Blake expresses a similar notion in an even more radical way. To him, those whom we call the living are really the dead, because they are entombed in the body. The truly living are the disembodied spirits, that is, those whom we call the dead.

29. Chuang Tzu, *op. cit.,* Chapter 2.

30. Ibid., Chapter 2.

31. Ibid., Chapter 21.

32. Toward the end of Chapter 8, Book III.

33. Job, 38.4-8.

# Chapter VI

## Mystic Meditation and Self-Discipline

Discipline is necessary for achievement in any kind of art. At first it may be keenly felt as an annoyance or an encumbrance. After being mastered and transcended, however, it will become a source of joy and freedom—true freedom. Untutored and untrained freedom is not always to be desired. Any person, for instance, can hold a violin and draw the bow all manner of ways as freely as he likes, but this is not true freedom and will only produce a cacophony of sounds highly grating to the ear. Only when the movements are in perfect accord with the laws underlying the play of the instrument can they be called truly free and can produce sweet music. Such freedom is the result of years of rigorous training and discipline.

Mystic meditation, essentially an art, cannot dispense with discipline. In fact, it needs more and stricter discipline than most other arts as it involves the reconstruction of the entire personality. A pure heart and a calm serene mind are absolutely required and therefore, both heart and mind have to be disciplined. As they are closely related to the senses, the senses also have to be disciplined.

There is a strong tendency for the senses to go outward. They are easily attracted to external things and easily become attached. They are the channels through which countless images or impressions of the outside world stream into the consciousness to agitate the heart and stimulate the mind. Unless they are controlled and disciplined, they are apt to disturb one's peace of mind and defile one's purity of heart, thereby rendering meditation difficult or even impossible.

It is common experience that images of past scenes often spontaneously recur before the mind's eye during quiet moments. This is one indication that what one sees and hears and reads about are not evanescent things without any lasting effect on the personality. Quite the contrary, they affect both heart and mind very deeply. According to the nature of the images, the heart feels joyful or sorrowful, while the mind devises ways and means to deal with the outside world so as to acquire the good and eschew the evil. Thus the sensible images may aptly be called "spiritual food," which in general is of two kinds: the wholesome and the unwholesome. Wholesome spiritual food consisting of ennobling and inspiring thoughts and ideas promotes health, beauty, and nobility and tones up the entire personality so as to render it congenial to meditation. Unwholesome spiritual food consisting of obscene sights and sounds and sensational stories about vice and violence poisons the personality and is inimical to meditation. One cannot be too careful and selective about one's spiritual food. Most people, however, seem rather careless and easy-going about this important matter. Guided usually by their curiosity, they look at and listen to everything that comes their way and read whatever appeals to their fancy, not knowing that horrid images and indecent notions remain in their subconscious mind and could even drive them to commit acts of violence and insanity.

The Chinese realized the importance of spiritual food at a very early period in their history. Before the time of Confucius (551-479 B.C.) they already practiced what was called "foetus education." A pregnant woman had to be careful about her thinking and feeling as well as her behavior and conduct. Her eyes must not see evil sights; her ears must not hear obscene sounds. She must always sit and sleep in the proper posture. She must keep up a cheerful state of mind and maintain an even tenor of life. All this, it was believed, would contribute to the health, beauty, and intelligence of her coming child.

Confucius, who is a moral teacher *par excellence,* also places strong emphasis on the importance of spiritual food. In reply to a question from his most brilliant disciple, Yen Hui, he said: "Do not see what is improper; do not hear what is improper; do not speak what is improper; do not make any move that is improper." And Yen Hui replied: "Though I am unworthy, I will act according to this teaching."[1] Thus Confucius taught his disciples to use propriety or *li* (also translated as ceremony, ritual, good form and good taste) to discipline the senses. Perhaps he should have added: "Do not think what is improper." But he apparently felt that the proper orientation of the senses would automatically condition the thinking and imaginative faculties in the proper way.

Lao Tzu shows himself to be far more severe as a disciplinarian than Confucius. He asks people to close their eyes, stop up their ears, avoid fine food and drink, and shrink from all games and sports. He disapproves of all sensual pleasures and fun-loving notions. He says:

> The five colors blind man's eyes;
> The five tones deafen man's ears:
> The five flavors vitiate man's taste;
> Racing and hunting make man's heart go wild;
> Hard-to-get articles impede man's movement.
> Thus the Sage cares for the belly, not the eye.
> Indeed, he rejects this and adopts that.[2]

These lines prove that Lao Tzu leans strongly toward asceticism as a means of discipline for the regulation of the senses and the rectification of the heart. Such asceticism is by no means unusual; in fact, even more rigorous asceticism can be found. Christians, for instance, have the notion that one should "lead a dying life; the more a man dies to himself, the more he begins to live unto God."[3] Just as Christian mysticism aims at serving God and living unto God, Lao Tzu's asceticism is not an end in itself but a means to attain Tao or at least to reach a higher level of reality and enjoy a higher form of life. It is a case of sacrificing the temporal for the eternal, or the unessential for the essential. Chuang Tzu fully endorsed the ascetic course. Said he: "Jumble up the six pitch-pipes, consign the lutes and flutes to the flames, stuff up the ears of blind Shih K'uang (symbolic representative of musicians), and each man will preserve his pristine sense of hearing. Set aside all ornaments, scramble up the five colors, glue up the eyes of Li Chu (symbolic representative of painters), and each man will preserve his pristine sense of sight."[4]

Thus both Lao Tzu and Chuang Tzu considered all sense impressions and all attachments to external things as poisonous and dangerous to the soul and hence uncongenial to mystic meditation. The obvious implication of their radical views is that one should ward off all impressions and attachments or at least reduce them to a minimum. In this regard, Lao Tzu further says:

Keep what is desirable out of sight,
So that the heart will not feel troubled.[5]

To ward off or resist desires is good and important; it is better, however, to prevent the rise of desires. All this involves the suspension of the ordinary functions of the senses. Strictly speaking, it involves the reorientation of the sensual functions or the reversal of the natural outward direction of the senses. The essential aim is not only to keep out all disturbances and distractions from the outside, but also to preserve the life force or vitality within for the cultivation of the inner life instead of squandering it in outward activities. As Lao Tzu sees it—

Much talk often leads to exhaustion.
Better concentrate on the center.[6]

Furthermore, he gives the following advice and warning:

Stop up the aperture of the vessel
And shut the doors (of the senses),
And you will not be devitalized all your life.

Open the aperture of the vessel,
And fulfill your carnal affairs,
And your whole life will be beyond salvation.[7]

Despite the serious nature of this warning, most people cannot be expected to heed it and follow it, for they are mostly fun-lovers and like to enjoy a merry sensual life. This was the case in the time of Lao Tzu, and he was fully aware of it. For instance, in Chapter 20 of the *Tao Teh Ching,* he draws a sharp contrast between himself, a lover of Tao, and the worldlings. While he himself preferred to feed on the Mother (Tao), the worldlings indulged themselves in sensual pleasure. However, though ignored by the general mass of people, his warning is undoubtedly sound from the standpoint of spiritual cultivation, for it inculcates a spirit of moderate asceticism so as to avoid outside temptations and activities and preserve inner unity.

It is, of course, wise to keep out or avoid sense images and impressions at the very outset instead of letting them in and then trying to expel them. As the saying goes, it is easier not to go into hot water than to get out of it. But every person starting meditation or a spiritual life has already gathered sense impressions and images plus numerous notions and ideas, cherished desires, aspirations, and ambitions. How to deal with these impediments to meditation? Lao Tzu suggests a thorough cathartic or purgative process. He says:

To learn, one increases day by day;
To cultivate Tao, one reduces day by day.
Reduce and reduce and keep on reducing,
Till the state of non-interference is reached.
With non-interference, then nothing cannot be done.[8]

The Hindu poet and seer Rabindranath Tagore may not have read the *Tao Teh Ching* but, perhaps influenced by the Vedas, he has expressed a view which not only is in full agreement with the above lines but even offers an explanation. He says:

In the region of nature, which is the region of diversity, we grow by acquisition; in the spiritual world, which is the region of unity, we grow by losing ourselves, by uniting. Gaining a thing, as we have said, is by its nature partial, it is limited only to a particular want; but *being* is complete, it belongs to our wholeness, it springs not from any necessity but from our affinity with the infinite, which is the principle of perfection that we have in our soul.[9]

When Lao Tzu says "Reduce and reduce" he does not point out what is to be reduced. But there seems to be no doubt that the scope of his purgative process encompasses all mental contents, including intellectual proclivities and emotional attachments as well as sense impressions and material possessions. The following is the most radical view ever expressed by him:

> Forswear wisdom, discard knowledge,
> And the people will gain a hundredfold.
> Forswear benevolence, discard righteousness,
> And the people will recover filial and parental love.
> Forswear skill, discard profit,
> And thieves and robbers will not appear.[10]

Such views cannot but shock the intellectual philistines, not only of Lao Tzu's time but also of later epochs. Though Lao Tzu was making these radical remarks concerning social life, they are even more sound for meditation and spiritual cultivation. While undoubtedly offensive especially to the Confucianists, they emphasize some deep-lying truths. In the decadent society of Lao Tzu's time, benevolence and righteousness had become empty slogans without any spiritual content. What Lao Tzu and the Taoists value is something that flows naturally and spontaneously from the heart or from the simplicity and innocence of man's true nature. As the Taoists see it, benevolence and righteousness do not have to be taught; simple people can be benevolent and righteous without knowing the concepts of benevolence and righteousness. If any virtue has to be taught and imposed from the outside, it is little more than a moral mask. As regards wisdom and knowledge, they are indeed valuable and necessary for ordinary life in the mundane world, and the same may be said of skill and profit. But Lao Tzu envisioned and glorified a much deeper dimension of life—the metaphysical and spiritual dimension. From the superior standpoint of this dimension of life, which he patently exhorted people to cultivate, ordinary wisdom has little value, while ordinary profit is just so much trash and rubbish. Even knowledge and skill are undesirable, for they both involve learning, and learning consumes time, mental energy, and the life force, all of which should be preserved for inner culture. Besides, they breed desires, and desires are always regarded as harmful to the soul because they spoil the inner unity and harmony. In this light, the meaning of the following advice given by Lao Tzu to Confucius during their historic interview stands out clearer than in the original context:

> I have heard that a clever merchant will hide his wealth of goods from view so as to make his store appear empty, and that a superior man of eminent moral excellence will behave as if he were a simpleton. Better strip yourself of your proud airs and numerous desires, your complacent demeanor and excessive ambitions. They won't do you any good. This is all I have to say to you.[11]

Chuang Tzu strongly supported this thorough-going purgative process, and has given a vivid example of it in the following imaginary conversation between Confucius and his brilliant pupil Yen Hui:

> "I am getting on," said Yen Hui to his master.
> "How so?" asked Confucius.
> "I have got rid of charity and duty," replied Yen Hui.
> "Very good," said Confucius, "but not quite perfect."
> After some time, the two met again, and Yen Hui said: "I am getting on."
> "How so?" asked Confucius.
> "I have got rid of ceremonies and music," replied Yen Hui.
> "Very good," said Confucius, "but still not quite perfect."
> Another day, Yen Hui again met his master and again said: "I am getting on."
> "How so?"
> "I can forget myself while sitting."
> "What do you mean by that?" asked Confucius, changing his countenance.
> "I have freed myself from my body. I have discarded my reasoning powers. By thus getting rid of my body and

113

mind, I have become One with the Infinite. This is what I mean by forgetting myself while sitting."

"If you have become One with the Infinite," said Confucius, "there can be no room for bias. If you have lost yourself, there can be no more hindrance. Perhaps you are really a wise one. I wish to be allowed to follow in your steps."[12]

When Yen Hui referred to "sitting," he meant sitting in meditation. Yen Hui, through meditation, emptied himself of one important thing after another till at last he emptied himself of himself. This is the height of purgation necessary for mystic attainment of Tao or Ultimate Reality.

The purgative process concerns both the discipline of the senses and that of the heart and mind. In fact, the two disciplines are closely related. The discipline of the senses inevitably facilitates and benefits the discipline of the heart and mind and vice versa, so much so that the body often reflects the inner workings of the mind.

The process, however, involves tremendous sacrifice from the worldy standpoint—not only the abandonment of one's habitual way of life but also the termination of many human ties. People who seriously take it up usually leave home and choose to stay in the forest or desert or in some cave in the mountains. Lao Tzu surely did not expect many people to detach themselves completely from outward activities and to live aloof from the busy world. He did not expect anyone to take such a drastic course all of a sudden but only gradually, if at all. For the worldly people Lao Tzu sets forth in the *Tao Teh Ching* a number of guidelines that will help them practice self-discipline, relieve them of the many worries and anxieties to which they are subject, and gradually build up a favorable mental state for meditation in case they show an interest in the practice. These guidelines, discussed in Chapter V, are relatively mild in nature. By them Lao Tzu just wants to inculcate a spirit of moderation and contentment so as to make people stay away from any keen competition for fame and power or from any intense pursuit of pleasure and excitement.

Despite prudence and contentment, people nevertheless may feel disappointed, dejected, and worried on account of inadequate understanding or lack of understanding. To help them forestall this predicament and maintain self-composure under unfavorable circumstances, Lao Tzu tells them not to worry and not to lose hope, for future developments are by no means certain. The world is in a constant flux. The vast wheel of history keeps on turning and turning. The changing situation can hardly be foreseen, much less controlled by the human intellect. Says Lao Tzu:

> Misfortune is what fortune leans on;
> Fortune is where misfortune conceals itself.
> Who can know the ultimate result?[13]

In other words, misfortune may be fortune in disguise, and vice versa.

To illustrate the wisdom of Lao Tzu's paradoxical view on human destiny, the Chinese are fond of relating the story of Sai Yung losing his horse. Sai Yung (lit., Old Man on the Frontier) was a recluse. His name was not known; but because he was old and lived in a locality near the frontier, he was given the sobriquet. He had a son who was very fond of horses. One day the best horse disappeared and his son became disconsolate. Sai Yung, with wisdom derived from his ripe experience, tried to console him and said, "You don't have to feel so sad. The horse might come back after some time. You never can tell." After a few days, the horse not only came back but even brought along some better horses from Mongolia. His son then felt very happy, and the neighbors came to offer their congratulations. Sai Yung, who remained calm, said to them, "There is no reason to feel overly happy. You never can tell what those horses will bring." Not long afterwards his son, in putting one of the fiery steeds through its paces, was rudely thrown off by the beast and broke his right leg. The neighbors came to offer their condolences. Sai Yung remained calm as usual and told them, "You can save your sympathy. I do not feel at all sad, for I know that a misfortune may turn out to be a blessing in disguise." And he was right. Before long, war broke out and all the able-bodied men were drafted into the army. His son, being a cripple, was exempted from military service and could stay home as usual with his father.

As fortune and misfortune are both as fickle as the weather, is it not unwise to be excessively sorrowful in the face of disaster, or excessively joyful at the approach of triumph?

Another paradoxical remark by Lao Tzu concerning the vicissitudes of life is as follows:

> Indeed, things sometimes benefit by an intended injury,
> And sometimes receive injury from an intended benefit.[14]

This remark did not originate with Lao Tzu, but was a quotation from *Shu Ching (Book of History)*. Its truth may not be apparent at first sight, but it is there all the same and may serve as a kind of tranquilizer for the soul. The implication is that one should not be unduly worried or angered over an injury inflicted by an enemy, nor unduly joyful over a benefit received from a friend. Conversely, one should not be too sure of the consequences when conferring a benefit to a friend or inflicting an injury on an enemy. Furthermore, there is no good reason to be envious of others' good fortune or to feel overly sorry for others' distress.

That favors or benefits may turn out to be injuries may be illustrated by the many stories about spoilt children. Parents who indulge their children often have cause for regret. On the other hand, there are also many stories about injuries and handicaps serving as a driving force toward success and victory, and about people who ploughed through difficulties and misfortunes to prosperity and glory. Mencius, the great Confucian sage, has well said: "Sorrow and trouble lead to life; security and pleasure lead to death."[15] He also says:

> When Heaven is about to assign a great task to a person, it always, first of all, harasses his mind with suffering, wearies his sinews and bones with toil, exposes his body to hunger, confronts him with poverty and difficulty, and confounds his undertakings. In so doing, it stimulates his mind, toughens his nature, and supplies his inadequacies.[16]

At first sight Lao Tzu's paradoxical guideline may seem to imply some mysterious or supernatural influence underlying the development of human events. It is, in fact, a keen satire on the limitation and imperfection of human foresight and intelligence. In order to make a correct and sound judgement, one must rely on sufficient data as well as an accurate analysis of the data. But these two conditions are not always fulfilled. If the data are incomplete or if the analysis is defective, the resultant judgment or conclusion is bound to be imperfect and unreliable. Besides, unforeseen circumstances will always occur. For this reason, people sometimes make a serious move and obtain a result altogether unintended and unexpected, as Lao Tzu has said.

As an illustration, one may refer to the anti-Communist policies and measures on the part of Japan and Nazi Germany in the 1930s. Both countries were dead set against Russia and were determined to exterminate Communism everywhere. But they either lacked the skill in analyzing the political forces then interplaying in the world or failed to comprehend or anticipate them. As a result, their anti-Communist efforts played into the hand of the Communists, and the final outcome was entirely contrary to what they had intended and expected. After World War II Russia emerged as a greater power than ever, and Communism has become far more rampant and widespread than in the 1930s in Europe and in Asia, while Nazi Germany and the Japanese empire vanished ignominiously from history.

The foregoing two paradoxical guidelines, therefore, are not random notions springing from the kindly heart of Lao Tzu. They were formulated by him apparently after deep meditation on the history and destiny of mankind, and were intended to help people form a balanced attitude toward either prosperity or adversity and preserve a calm mind in dealing with their worldly affairs. Their truth has often been uncannily reflected in the events of life, personal and national. People who understand and respect this truth will not succumb to depression when adversity frowns, nor become wild with excitement when prosperity smiles. They will always maintain equanimity of mind and tranquillity of heart. Along with Kipling, they "can meet with Triumph and Disaster and treat those two impostors just the same." They can sing with Anwari Soheili, the Persian poet—

If thou hast lost possession of a world,
Be not distressed, for it is nought;

Or hast thou gained possession of a world,
　Be not o'erjoyed, for it is nought.
Our pains, our gains, all pass away:
　Get thee beyond the world, for it is nought.

A calm and detached attitude toward the vicissitudes of life will, of course, prepare one for mystic meditation. It is the kind of attitude which Lao Tzu wished to help people cultivate and maintain, for it is conducive to a proper conditioning of the mind so that it can function properly for the development of the inner life. As can be expected, Chuang Tzu also considered it important to maintain a calm and serene state of mind. He thus advised people to be detached and dispassionate as well as virtuous. He believed that "serenity, passivity and quiescence characterize the repose of the universe, and constitute the essence of Tao and Teh." He exhorted people to enjoy repose like the Sage, saying that repose leads to ingenuousness and mellowness, and "when one is ingenuous and mellow, one will be free from fears and sorrows and other evil influences and can preserve one's character and spirit intact." He further urged people to imitate the Sage who "considers life a fleeting dream and death a rest," who "does not scheme, nor strive, nor calculate," and who "sleeps without dreams and wakes up without worries, with his spirit ever pure and his soul always alert."[17]

As has been noted, in the *Tao Teh Ching,* Lao Tzu furnishes quite a number of guidelines for self-discipline. More of these are for the discipline of the heart and the mind than for the discipline of the senses. The reason seems twofold. In the first place, the heart and the mind are more difficult to discipline. Secondly, if well disciplined, they will in turn discipline the senses; otherwise they will be seduced by the senses.

If the heart and the mind are prone to follow the lead of the senses, they are bound to be filled with desires of all sorts and will become impervious to the light of Tao, just as an opaque object is impervious to sunlight. Consequently they will indubitably venture outward to engage in the struggle for material possessions and external glories. Social contentions, conflicts, and collisions will then arise and will incline one to adopt an aggressive attitude toward one's fellow men, thereby engendering a long train of unhealthy emotions such as pride, arrogance, and avarice on the one hand, and hatred, fear and anger on the other. One's heart and mind will be embroiled in a swirl of external activities, and one's time and attention and vitality will be oriented outward. Under these conditions meditation or even relaxation will be out of the question and the inner life will be neglected and will remain undeveloped.

Therefore, one's heart and mind must lead instead of following the senses—must be their master instead of their slave. For this purpose one's heart and mind must be controlled and disciplined so as to remain sane, serene and sober. However, this is not so easy. For, after all, who or what is to control or discipline the heart and mind? In attempting to answer the question, one will inevitably find that the disciplinarian is the very entity to be disciplined! In other words, the discipline is essentially self-discipline. Here, perhaps, is where mystic meditation comes in to yield its benign and salutary effects.

As taught by Lao Tzu, mystic meditation involves concentration on the One, placid and rhythmic breathing, purification of the inner vision, habitual nonaction, assumption of the female passive role, and maintenance of equanimity. Every one of these six steps contributes to spiritual integrity, serenity and harmony, and increases inner strength and power. Progress in mystic meditation will make one less and less affected by outside disturbances and distractions, more and more detached from outside activities and temptations, and consequently better and better able to control and discipline the heart and mind as well as the senses. One's thoughts and aspirations will be more and more constantly oriented toward Tao or Supreme Good or Ultimate Reality.

Thus, while mystic meditation requires a calm heart and a serene mind and some other congenial conditions for its proper operation, it in turn fosters and promotes those conditions and effectively helps discipline the heart and mind and the senses. Moreover, mystic meditation is apt to waken and release dormant psychic powers, expand one's consciousness, deepen one's self-awareness, and enable one

119

to realize more keenly and clearly one's Higher Self, i.e., mind in its purified state, which ought to be the legitimate disciplinarian and the proper guide toward the attainment of Tao.

The reality of the Higher Self has been demonstrated by the experience of saints, sages, poets, and philosophers that have inspired mankind over a long course of human history. It is really interesting to note that they all seem to have the same inner experience but in a different manner, and consequently they express it in a different way.

In Chinese history the Higher Self is identified with the mind of Tao and the lower self with the mind of man; and the distinction was realized long before the time of Lao Tzu. In the *Shih Ching (Book of History)* it is recorded that Emperor Shun once passed on the following instruction to Yu the Great, his successor: "The mind of man is precarious. The mind of Tao is tenuous. Concentrate on the Essence and on the One. Hold fast to the Center."[18]

Lao Tzu does not expressly refer to the Higher Self in the *Tao Teh Ching*. But in setting forth his doctrines and precepts, he clearly assumes that there is in man a Higher Self that will follow those doctrines and precepts. In Chapter 33, he actually says: "He who conquers himself is valiant." The conqueror is undoubtedly the Higher Self. Similarly Confucius assumes a Higher Self in man when he says: "Conquer yourself and return to propriety."[19] More than a century later, the Confucian sage Mencius made an explicit distinction between the two selves. He said: "He who follows the Great Self is a great man. He who follows the small self is a small man."[20] He also said: "The Great Man is he who has not lost his infant heart."[21] This implies that people who *have* lost their infant heart are small men, men dominated by the lower self.

Plato has expressed similar ideas. In the *Phaedrus*, he conceives that the soul had wings while in the ideal world of Forms, but lost them on being born and invested in the body. The body is a tomb or a prison which checks its freedom. Also, the soul is like a chariot drawn by two horses, one good and one bad. If it allows the good horse to follow the bad, it will become degraded and small. On the other hand, if the bad horse follows the good one, the soul will become great and its wings will sprout again.

Later, Plotinus, the mystic philosopher, dressed some of the above Platonic ideas in a new garb in his *Enneads,* and introduced some related ideas of his own. To him the spirit or intelligence represents the Higher Self, while the body represents the lower one. He says: "Linked to lower things through the body, we are related to higher things through the intelligible essence of our being."[22] He believes that man's spiritual ascent is guided by the "daemon." He says: "If we are able to follow the daemon which is above us, we rise and in so doing we live its life. This daemon to which we are led becomes the noblest part of ourselves . . . . After it, we take another daemon for guide, and so on to the highest."[23]

Some Christian saints also realized the dual self. People who read the Bible may remember the following confession by St. Paul:

> For I do not do the good I want, but the evil I do not want is what I do. Now if I do what I do not want, it is no longer I that do it, but sin which dwells within me. So I find it to be a law that when I want to do right, evil lies close at hand. For I delight in the law of God, in my inmost self. But I see in my members another law at war with the law of my mind and making me captive to the law of sin which dwells in my members. Wretched man that I am! Who will deliver me from this body of death?[24]

What he calls "my inmost self" and "my mind" represents his Higher Self, and what he calls "my members" and "this body of death" represents his lower self. The two selves often come into conflict. The Higher Self wants to do good but the lower self opposes. The lower self wants to do evil, but the Higher Self objects.

Some centuries later, another Christian luminary, St. Augustine, experienced what St. Paul had experienced, and expressed his inner conflict in a different way. Note his own words:

> I was groaning in spirit, shaken with a gust of indigna- tion because I could not enter into Thy will, O my God, yet all my bones were crying out that this was the way

.... How did I reproach myself! with what sharp reasons did I flog my soul to make it follow me in my effort to follow Thee. And it would not; it refused and would not even make an excuse.[25]

The two foregoing quotations indicate that the Higher Self often finds it difficult to assert its legitimate rights and subjugate the lower self. As mystic meditation tends to help us realize more distinctly and frequently our Higher Self and thereby augment its power and strength, it contributes a great deal toward bringing the lower self under control; in other words, it helps self-discipline.

The realization of man's dual self on the part of the ancient saints and sages and philosophers has been confirmed by later poets and philosophers. In his famous work *Faust,* Goethe writes:

Two souls, alas! reside within my breast,
And each withdraws from, and repels, its brother.[26]

Goethe was probably influenced by the German philosopher Fichte who had advanced the doctrine of the "pure ego" *(das reine Ich)* and the "empirical ego" *(das empirische Ich).* The former is said to be transcendental, constituting a portion of the Divine Ego or God, while the latter is the mundane or practical self which belongs to the realm of matter and death.

Ralph Waldo Emerson, the distinguished American transcendentalist, became aware of the dual self early in his life, as indicated in the following passage:

I recognize the distinction of the outer and inner self; the double consciousness that within this erring, passionate, mortal self sits a supreme, calm, immortal mind, whose powers I do not know; but it is stronger than I; it is wiser than I; it never approved me in any wrong; I seek counsel of it in my doubts; I repair to it in my dangers; I pray to it in my undertakings. It seems to me the face which the Creator uncovers to his child.[27]

The English poet Browning, noted for his optimism, expresses his inner experience in the following lines:

Truth is within ourselves. It takes no rise
From outward things, whate'er you may believe.
There is an inmost centre in ourselves
Where truth abides in fulness; and to know
Rather consists in finding out a way
Whence the imprisoned glory may escape
Than by effecting entrance for a light
Supposed to be without![28]

More supporting citations are available, but it is not necessary to add them here. In fact, it is quite common for people now and then to experience an inner conflict between reason and the passions, or between the spirit and the flesh, or between the understanding and the appetites. The Higher Self is represented by reason, spirit, and understanding, and the lower self by passions, the flesh, and the appetites. Now mystic meditation promotes a keener and sharper realization of the Higher Self as meditation progresses. Consequently it makes a votary more and more disposed to follow the dictates of the Higher Self. With the Higher Self enthroned as sovereign ruler and director of his whole being, the discipline of his senses and lower desires and appetites will become easy, effective, and successful, and his life may reasonably be expected to sail along serenely toward the Good, the True, and the Beautiful—nay, toward the holy and divine.

When a man is always occupied with the cravings of desire and ambition, and is eagerly striving to satisfy them, all his thoughts must be mortal, and, as far as it is possible altogether to become such, he must be mortal every whit, because he has cherished his mortal part. But he who has been earnest in the love of knowledge and of true wisdom, and has exercised his intellect more than any other part of him, must have thoughts immortal and divine, if he attain truth, and in so far as human nature is capable of sharing in immortality, he must be altogether immortal; and since he is ever cherishing the divine power, and has the divinity within him in perfect order, he will be perfectly happy.[29]

# References

1. *The Analects,* Book XII, Chapter 1.

2. *Tao Teh Ching,* Chapter 12.

3. Thomas A. Kempis, *The Imitation of Christ,* tr. Aloysius Croft and Harold Bolton. Milwaukee: The Bruce Publishing Company, 1940, p. 81.

4. *Chuang Tzu,* Chapter 10.

5. *Tao Teh Ching,* Chapter 3.

6. Ibid., Chapter 5.

7. Ibid., Chapter 52.

8. Ibid., Chapter 48.

9. Rabindranath Tagore, *Sadhana.* New York: The Macmillan Company, 1916, p. 155.

10. *Tao Teh Ching,* Chapter 19.

11. Ssuma Ch'ien, "Biographical Essay on Lao Tzu," *Shih Chi.*

12. *Chuang Tzu,* Chapter 6.

13. Ibid., Chapter 58.

14. Ibid., Chapter 42.

15. *Mencius,* Book VI, Part II, Chapter 15.

16. Ibid.

17. *Chuang Tzu,* Chapter 15.

18. *Shu Ching (Book of History),* "Ta Yu Mu" (Plan of Yu the Great).

19. *The Analects,* Book XII, Chapter 1.

20. *Mencius,* Book VI, Part I, Chapter 15.

21. Ibid., Book IV, Part II, Chapter 12.

22. Emile Brehier, *The Philosophy of Plotinus,* tr. Joseph Thomas. The University of Chicago Press, 1958, pp. 54-56.

23. Ibid.

24. Romans, 7.19-24.

25. James M. Gillis, *Favorite Texts from The Confessions of St. Augustine.* Washington D.C.: National Council of Catholic Men, 1941, p. 29.

26. *Zwei Seelen wohnen, ach! in meiner Brust,*
   *Die eine will sich von der andern trennen.*

27. Quoted in Arthur Cushman McGiffert, ed., *Young Emerson Speaks.* Boston: Houghton Mifflin, 1938, p. 200.

28. From the poem "Paracelsus."

29. Plato, *Timaeus,* in *The Dialogues of Plato,* tr. B. Jowett. Oxford: Oxford University Press, 1931, III, p. 513.

道德經

## Part Two

*Translation of*
*The Tao Teh Ching*
*with comments*

# 1
## REALIZATION OF TAO
## T'i Tao

*The Tao that can be stated is not the Eternal Tao.*[1]
*The name that can be named is not the Eternal*
  *Name.*
*The Unnameable is originator of Heaven and*
  *Earth.*[2]
*The Nameable is mother of the ten thousand*
  *things.*[3]
*Therefore,*
*Always be desireless, so as to discern Tao's*
  *wonderful essence;*
*Always have some desire, so as to discern its*
  *manifestations.*[4]
*These two come out from the same source,*
*But are different in name.*
*Their identical nature is a mystery.*
*Mystery of mysteries—*
*That is the gate of all wonderful essence.*

In this first chapter Lao Tzu expresses his notion of Eternal Tao and sets forth the two general principles of meditation as the way for its realization.

An exposition of this chapter is presented in Part One, Chapter I.

---

1. Cf. also Chapter 81 for similar idea.
2. Cf. also Chapters 14, 25, 40.
3. Cf. also Chapters 4, 34.
4. This and the preceding line are faithful to the original Chinese both in sense and in expression; nevertheless they may cause some misunderstanding. People may say: "How can one be always desireless and always have some desire?" What should be pointed out is that the word *always* does not necessarily mean *constantly*. Sometimes the sense of the word is limited to the time of action. For instance, it is correct to say: "One always feels happy when meeting a good friend, and always feels somewhat sad when saying good-bye to him."

# 2
## SELF-CULTURE
# Yang Shen

*When all the world knows beauty as beauty,*
*Then ugliness comes into being;*
*When all the world knows goodness as goodness,*
*Then evil comes into being.*
*Therefore,*
*Being and Non-Being condition each other;[1]*
*Difficult and Easy give rise to each other;*
*Long and Short set off each other;*
*High and Low contrast each other;*
*Tone and Voice harmonize each other;*
*Front and Rear succeed each other.*
*Thus the Sage handles affairs non-assertively,[2]*
*And imparts his teaching without words.*
*The ten thousand things grow apace,*
*But he does not let them down.*
*He produces but does not claim ownership;*
*He acts but does not presume on the result;[3]*
*He achieves success but does not take the credit.[4]*
*For the very reason that he takes no credit,*
*Credit does not separate from him.*

This chapter follows the preceding one in a proper sequence. While the preceding chapter deals with the absolute aspect of Tao, this chapter speaks of its relative aspect. In terms of the *I-Ching,* which may very well have influenced the thinking of Lao Tzu, the first chapter is about the *T'ai Chi* or Supreme Ultimate, while the second chapter concerns the emergence of the world of dualism polarized between the two cosmic principles, Yin and Yang, which are derived from the *T'ai Chi* and in turn give rise to pairs of opposites such as high and low, large and small, strong and weak, good and bad, and so on.

In such a relative world, how does the Sage conduct himself? As a moral and spiritual personality, he acts naturally and spontaneously, as if expressing some inherent tendency in his being. He manifests a detached attitude and does not care about the beneficent results of his actions. He is interested in cultivating his inner life and sets little value on external things. As all standards are relative, he feels there is not much sense in making claims and asserting himself.

130

Even in teaching, he prefers to maintain silence, and this apparently for two reasons. First, cultivation of the inner life requires preservation of the breath, which is considered very precious. Secondly Tao cannot be taught or transmitted by words, but only by the subtle influence of personality. Ch'an or Zen Buddhism strongly supports this view. According to a legend, the Lord Buddha transmitted the experience of enlightenment to his disciple Maka-Kasyapa by silently holding up a flower in the course of a sermon. When Maka-Kasyapa, alone among the audience, smiled, the Buddha knew that his enlightening experience had hit the mark. This was the beginning of Zen Buddhism.

Silence is the way the Sage transmits his spiritual influence, and this is how he benefits the ten thousand creatures. The latter in the course of growth expect wise guidance from him and he never disappoints them.

1. Wing-Tsit Chan renders this line thus: "Being and non-being produce each other." One is inclined to think that this translation may be misleading. In Chapter 40 of the *Tao Teh Ching*, Lao Tzu says that Being is derived from Non-Being, not *vice versa.*

2. Cf. also Chapters 3, 10, 29, 37, 38, 47, 48, 57, 64.

3. Cf. also Chapters 10, 34, 51.

4. Cf. also Chapter 77.

# 3
## PEACE TO THE PEOPLE
## An Min

*Do not exalt the worthy,*
*So that the people will not contend.*
*Do not treasure hard-to-get objects,*
*So that the people will not become thieves.*
*Keep what is desirable out of sight,*
*So that their heart will not get excited.*[1]
*Therefore, in ruling the people the Sage*
*Empties their hearts,*
*Fills their bellies,*
*Weakens their aspirations,*
*Strengthens their bones.*
*He always makes them guileless and desireless,*[2]
*And makes the guileful ones afraid to interfere.*
*Practice non-interference,*[3]
*And there will never be any misrule.*

This chapter, addressed to a prince or ruler, treats the subject of Wu Wei in a very cogent and coherent manner. Wu Wei is a cardinal tenet taught in the *Tao Teh Ching*. It recurs in various versions in quite a number of later chapters in the Taoist canon. It connotes nonaction in the sense of nonassertion or noninterference. Essentially it means following Tao or doing things in conformity with Tao. The point seems to be that if we would conform our will to Tao, we could accomplish more and with greater ease than by our own volitional efforts, just as a boat will proceed more swiftly and gracefully by adjusting its sails to the direction of the wind than by laborious human rowing.

Now, underlying every action or assertion or interference, there is a desire. So Lao Tzu says that a wise ruler, a Sage, tries to make the people guileless and desireless and at the same time makes the guileful ones afraid to interfere.

But how to eliminate desire or make the people desireless? Fundamentally, by not arousing their desire. Hence the ruler should not exalt the worthy, so that the people will not desire to gain fame or honor. Similarly, he should not treasure hard-to-get objects, nor should he let the people see any desirable objects, so that the hearts of the people will remain calm instead of being agitated by greed and avarice. He should help the people serve the necessities of nature. Above all, he should see to it that the people can satisfy their hunger.

Lao Tzu considers interference in the affairs of the people as the basic cause of misrule; so he recommends Wu Wei to the ruler, saying: "Practice non-interference and there will never be any misrule."

---

1. Cf. also Chapters 12, 19, 34, 57.
2. Cf. also Chapter 65.
3. Cf. also Chapters 2, 10, 29, 37, 38, 47, 48, 57, 64.

# 4
## SOURCE NON-EXISTENT
## Wu Yuan

*Tao is hollow, yet its utility*
*Seems unlikely to reach the limit.*[1]
*Profound indeed it is;*
*It seems to be the fount of all things.*[2]
*It blunts the sharp;*
*It unravels the tangled;*
*It harmonizes with the light;*
*It mingles with the dust.*[3]
*Calm like a deep pool it seems to remain.*
*I do not know whose son it is.*
*It apparently antecedes the Creator.*[4]

In this chapter, Lao Tzu sets forth an essential characteristic of Tao as he conceives it; Tao is hollow and yet is so useful that its utility is practically inexhaustible. This is a great mystery. Though hollow, Tao is pregnant with potentialities and possibilities. It is the fount of the myriad things and antecedes even the Creator, indicating that it is probably what gave birth to the Creator. The Creator created Heaven and Earth and is usually regarded as another name for God. Thus, in a sense, Lao Tzu may be said to believe in God; but, as he sees it, God is not self-creating but originates from Tao. But whence came Tao? Lao Tzu confesses that he does not know. He does not know "whose son it is."

Since Tao is hollow, it is also considered to be humble and non-assertive; therefore, it always tends toward harmony by adapting itself to all circumstances—by rounding off sharp angularities, smoothing away incongruities, harmonizing the various shades of light, and mingling with the barren dust.

Water is one of Lao Tzu's pet symbols for Tao. But the calm of deep water is a more distinct symbol, for it suggests mystery and quiescence. And Tao is profoundly mysterious and essentially quiescent.

---

1. Cf. also Chapters 5, 6, 11, 35.
2. Cf. also Chapters 1, 25.
3. Cf. also Chapter 56.
4. This line shows that Lao Tzu did believe in a Creator.

# 5
## THE UTILITY OF HOLLOWNESS
### Hsu Yung

*Heaven and Earth are not kindly;*
*They equate the ten thousand things with straw*
*  dogs.[1]*
*The Sage is not kindly;*
*He equates the people with straw dogs.*
*The space between Heaven and Earth,*
*Is it not like a bellows?*
*It is hollow, yet it never fails to supply.[2]*
*The more it is worked, the more it gives forth.*
*Much talk often leads to exhaustion.*
*Better concentrate on the center.*

Wang Pi, whose commentary on the *Tao Teh Ching* is the earliest and commands the respect of later commentators, has this to say on this chapter: "Heaven and Earth follow Nature; there is no (purposeful) action and no (purposeful) creation. Each of the myriad

134

things takes care of itself. There is, therefore, no mercy." This view anticipates the modern concept of scientific law which is impersonal, inexorable and immutable, hence impartial and no respecter of particular persons or things. It is also similar to the Christian view: God "maketh his sun to rise on the evil and the good, and sendeth rain on the just and the unjust." (Matt., 5:45)

Impartiality or inexorability may appear merciless, but may be interpreted as truly merciful. Hence Chuang Tzu's remark: "Absolute mercy is not merciful." A similar paradox appears in another well-known Taoist work, the *Yin Fu Ching*: "Heaven's greatest mercy is without mercy." How so? For instance, if Heaven and Earth suspend their laws in favor of the good or to the detriment of the bad—if Nature's laws function one way one day and another way another day—then the universe will be in a state of chaos or anarchy, and man cannot know what will happen from moment to moment and consequently has nothing to rely on for making steady plans for steady progress.

The Sage or Ruler, who follows Tao, acts the same way as Heaven and Earth and treats all people impartially and unemotionally, just as he treats straw dogs. His laws thus constitute a reliable guidepost for the people in their daily activity.

It is rather difficult to make out a coherent meaning for this whole chapter as the chapter seems divided into two or three portions out of context with each other. If there is any coherent meaning, it may be as follows: There are immutable laws operating in the universe—in the hollow between Heaven and Earth. They are observed by the Sage and other wise men. They constitute an infinite source of power. The more they operate, the more things they produce and the more changes they make. Amidst these incessant changes, men should hold on to some central principle instead of being distracted like a rudderless ship driven by the changing winds and waves.

The two lines ending "the more it gives forth" are reminiscent of the Christian teaching: "Ask, and it shall be given you; seek, and ye shall find; knock, and it shall be opened unto you." (Matt., 7:7)

The last two lines embody some important instruction on Taoist meditation and yoga. The breath is considered very precious and should not be wasted in idle talk. During meditation, one should concentrate on one of the seven key centers, most of which are located along the spine.

---

1. Straw dogs were used as sacrifices in some ancient Chinese ritual. After the ritual, they were thrown away. They thus symbolize something cheap and undesirable.

2. Cf. also Chapters 4, 6, 11, 35.

135

# 6
## PERFECTION OF THE SYMBOL
## Ch'eng Hsiang

*The Spirit of the Valley never dies.*
*Hence comes the name Mysterious Female.*[1]
*The gateway of the Mysterious Female*
*Is the root of Heaven and Earth.*
*Continuous like a thread it seems to exist;*
*Its utility is inexhaustible.*[2]

This chapter is highly important as it concerns spiritual cultivation as well as Lao Tzu's conception of Eternal Tao.

An exposition of this chapter is presented in Part One, Chapter II.

---

1. These first two lines are often translated thus: "The Spirit of the Valley never dies. It is called the Mysterious Female." This does not seem to be quite right. For Spirit is the active male cosmic principle. It should not be called the Mysterious Female.

2. Cf. also Chapters 4, 5, 35.

# 7
## Dimming the Light
## T'ao Kuang

*Heaven is eternal, Earth is durable.*
*The reason why they are eternal and durable*
*Is that they do not exist for themselves.*
*This is why they can long endure.*
*Therefore, the Sage putting himself behind,*
*Finds himself in front;*
*And placing himself beyond his concern,*
*Finds himself well preserved.*
*Is this not because he is unselfish?*
*For the very reason that he is unselfish,*
*He is able to find Self-fulfilment.*

This chapter highlights the virtue of selflessness or self-denial or effacement of the lower self.

The first four lines clearly hint that self-denial may lead to long life, if not also immortality.

The remaining lines point out the almost miraculous effects of self-denial—miraculous in the sense of being contrary to common sense and usual expectation. Ordinary people are generally of the opinion that one has to compete and struggle in order to get to the top. But the Sage of Lao Tzu, following and sharing the selflessness of Heaven and Earth, can go to the front by placing himself behind, and can preserve himself by nonconcern about himself.

This kind of teaching is not peculiar to Lao Tzu. Christ supports Lao Tzu beautifully, as indicated in the following quotations:

"For whosoever will save his life shall lose it: and whosoever will lose his life for my sake shall find it." (Matt., 16:23-25.)

"If any man desire to be first, the same shall be last of all, and servant of all." (Mark, 9:35.)

This chapter also implies the virtue of humility and the value of Wu-Wei or noninterference which is closely related to humility.

---

1. Cf. also Chapters 34, 61, 66, 67.

# 8
## YIELDING NATURE
## I Hsing

*A man of the superior type resembles water,*
*Whose goodness lies in benefiting all things without*
  *contention,*[1]
*And staying in places detested by the masses.*[2]
*This makes him closely akin to Tao.*
*The goodness of his abode is its low location.*[3]
*The goodness of his heart is its cavern-like*
  *hollowness.*
*Benevolence is the goodness of his offerings.*
*Sincerity is the goodness of his speech.*
*The goodness of his rule means peace.*
*The goodness of his dealings means competence.*
*His moves are good because timely.*
*As he is not disposed to contend,*
*He causes little resentment.*

This chapter shows that Tao inspires noncontention, which is akin to humility or nonassertion or noninterference.

Whoever reads the *Tao Teh Ching* will know that water is one of Lao Tzu's symbols for Tao. Now, a man of the superior type is decidedly a man of Tao, so he also is very much like water, especially in the sense that, while rendering beneficent services to mankind in numerous ways, he is not at all contentious. This is an important point, for it runs counter to the common view, that one must contend and struggle aggressively in order to achieve success.

How does a man of the superior type conduct himself in the world and serve his fellow men? The answer is given in the latter major portion of the chapter, beginning with the fifth line. The Sage in tune with Tao manifests goodness in his life spontaneously, follows the right virtue in every situation, and lives in harmony with his fellow men.

A low abode is symbolic as well as literal in meaning. It is good in the sense that it approaches nearest to the water, which always seeks the lowest level and which is essential to life, to the cultivation of flowers, and to the growth of civilization. Patently a low abode also suggests humility. The same may be said of the notion of a hollow heart *(hsu-hsin)*, which frequently appears in Chinese literature and conversation to mean humility. It is also an important goal in spiritual cultivation which, according to Lao Tzu, requires constant reduction of the mental contents (Cf. Chapter 48). It is only when the heart is hollow that Tao can operate therein with maximum power.

With his hollow heart, the superior man always acts in consonance with Tao. His gifts or offerings spring spontaneously from his innate benevolence and are untainted by any selfish desire for cheap publicity, for vainglory, or for decreasing the tax payment. Similarly he is true to himself and offers no deceits. As violence is contrary to Tao, he as a ruler favors peace as the highest good and places a premium on competence in handling his affairs. In Chapter 49, Lao Tzu says that the heart of the Sage mirrors the heart of the people. The moves of the Sage, therefore, cannot fail to be timely, for they will be in full accord with the conscious or subconscious aspirations of the people.

Far from causing any resentment, the Sage or man of the superior type will inspire goodwill and contentment all around.

---

1. Cf. also Chapters 22, 66, 68, 81.
2. Cf. also Chapter 78.
3. Cf. also Chapters 61, 66.

# 9
## PRACTICE OF PLACIDITY
### Yun Yi

*To hold and fill a vessel to brimful*[1]
*Is not so good as to stop before the limit.*
*Hone a tool to its sharpest state,*
*And its keenness cannot be long preserved.*
*A hall filled with gold and jade*
*Can hardly be safeguarded.*
*To show pride in one's wealth and high rank*
*Is to pave the way for one's own doom.*
*Retire after achieving success and winning*
*    renown!*[2]
*This is the Way of Heaven.*

This chapter warns against going to the limit and, what is worse, going to excess, in one's endeavors. It counsels people to eschew pride and vanity and practice contentment and moderation or the Golden Mean.

139

All the phenomena in the universe are in a state of constant flux and everything, in accordance with Tao, will undergo a setback or re-action after reaching the utmost limit. A vessel brimful with water is ready to be emptied; a bent bow is apt to break; a sharp knife or a sharp pencil will soon become blunt. A man of wealth, especially if vain and proud, will be a target for robbers, kidnapers, murderers, and slanderers. The same may be said of a man of high rank.

Yet most people, impelled by pride and vanity and ambition, want to push things to the limit or even to excess. They know how to advance but not to retreat. They seldom think that retreat rather than advance sometimes constitutes the better part of wisdom.

So Lao Tzu teaches them that it is better to stop before going to the limit, to retire after achieving success and winning renown. He considers this the Way of Heaven, that is, Tao.

This chapter also contains some teachings similar to those of Christianity. The two lines ending "safeguarded" remind one of a saying by Christ: "Lay not up for yourselves treasures upon earth, where moth and rust doth corrupt, and where thieves break through and steal." (Matt., 6:19.) The two lines ending "doom" correspond in sense to another saying by Christ: "How hard it is for the wealthy to enter the Kingdom of God." (Luke, 18:24.)

The last two lines of the chapter suggest to some prosaic critics that the Taoists are like worldly Utilitarians, because they also want to achieve success and win renown. Those critics fail to see that the Taoists are different from the Utilitarians in both objective and method. The Taoists aim at the attaining of Tao and the diffusion of Tao, not the making of money or the winning of phony honors. Furthermore, the Taoists follow Tao and practice Wu Wei, while the Utilitarians follow the competitive and aggressive ways suggested by Darwin and Nietzsche. However, for Utilitarians as well as Taoists, the teaching that one should practice moderation and stop before reaching the limit seems to be sound, only the Utilitarians may be slow to follow it, if at all.

---

1. The Chinese verb *ying* (here translated "fill") does not apply to a bow, as some translators think. The verb applicable to a bow is *chang*, meaning "extend" or "stretch." Cf. Chapter 77.

2. Cf. also Chapters 15, 29, 30, 32, 55.

# 10
## It Can Be Done
## Neng Wei

*In harmonizing your* hun *and* p'o *to embrace the
  One,*[1]
*Can you concentrate without deviating?*
*In attuning your breath to induce tenderness,*
*Can you become like a new-born babe?*[2]
*In cleansing and purifying your Mystic Mirror,*
*Can you make it free from all stain?*
*In loving the people and ruling the state,*
*Can you practice non-interference?*[3]
*When the Heavenly Gate opens and closes,*
*Can you play the part of the Female?*
*When your light shines forth in all directions,*
*Can you ignore it with perfect equanimity?*
*To produce things and nourish them,*
*To produce but not to claim ownership,*
*To act but not to presume on the result,*[4]
*To lead but not to manipulate,—*
*This is called Mystic Virtue.*

This chapter deals essentially with meditation and yoga. A detailed exposition of the chapter is presented in Part One, Chapter III.

---

1. *Hun* and *p'o* are two Chinese words, meaning respectively the active (yang) and the passive (yin) aspect of the human soul.
2. Christ says: "Except ye be converted, and become as little children, ye shall not enter into the kingdom of heaven." (Matt., 18:3.)
3. Cf. also Chapters 2, 3, 29, 37, 38, 47, 48, 57, 64.
4. Cf. also Chapters 2, 34, 51.

# 11
## UTILITY OF NON-BEING
# Wu Yung

*Thirty spokes converge on the nave of a wheel:*
*It is where there is non-being (hollow space)*
*That the usefulness of the wheel lies.*
*Clay is molded into a vessel:*
*It is where there is non-being*
*That the usefulness of the vessel lies.*
*Doors and windows are hewn out to make a room:*
*It is where there is non-being*
*That the usefulness of the room lies.*
*Therefore, while being is valuable,*
*It is non-being that is useful.*[1]

This chapter reveals Lao Tzu's keen observation and right understanding. People usually see the concrete aspect of the wheel, the vessel, or the room, not realizing that utility or usefulness lies in their hollowness. Hollowness symbolizes Tao or Non-Being.

Inferentially, man's mind should be hollow in order to function properly and efficiently, i.e., to be useful. This is why Chuang Tzu suggests that it is good for man to sit in meditation with a "blank mind." Lao Tzu also teaches that in spiritual cultivation man should clear his mind not only of cobwebs and garbage but even of knowledge and learning. In Chapter 48 he says: "To learn, one increases day by day. To cultivate Tao, one reduces day by day."

A hollow mind is most apt to encounter Tao; put differently, Tao manifests or operates best in a hollow and pure mind.

---

1. Cf. also Chapters 4, 5.

# 12
## Examination of Desires
## Chien Yu

*The five colors blind man's eyes;*[1]
*The five tones deafen man's ears;*[2]
*The five flavors vitiate man's taste;*[3]
*Racing and hunting make man's heart go wild;*[4]
*Hard-to-get articles impede man's movement.*
*Thus the Sage cares for the belly, not the eye.*
*Indeed, he rejects this and adopts that.*

The five colors and the five tones represent respectively the sights and sounds of the world. The five flavors represent the varieties of food. Racing and hunting are representative of all kinds of sports and other intense outward activities.

All the above four categories are related to the senses and constitute man's sensual life. Lao Tzu patently looks upon them as inimical to the life of the spirit or to the cultivation of Tao. He also shows contempt for hard-to-get objects, which he regards as impediments to the spiritual freedom of man.

Lao Tzu knows well that the worldlings are fond of sensual pleasures (Cf. Chapters 20 and 35). While he does not expressly denounce their folly and ignorance, he is positive that the Sage and other wise men will choose cultivation of inner peace and serenity in preference to the gratification of the senses.

The belly is the symbol for inner life, while the eye is symbolic of sensual life. This is because the eye, wanting to see lots of things, is, therefore, a fertile source of distractions. It is a centrifugal force, tending to draw the mind and the life force outward. The belly, however, is a centripetal force, tending to withdraw man's attention inward. It is also relatively easy to satisfy; and once satisfied, it becomes a source of strength and vitality. Thus Wang Pi, the born metaphysician, says: "The belly nourishes oneself by receiving inward material things. The eye enslaves oneself by directing one's attention outward to material things. The Sage, therefore, cares little for the eye."

---

1. The five colors are red, yellow, blue, white, and black.
2. The five tones in ancient Chinese music are *kung, shang, chueh, chih, yu*, corresponding to *do, re, mi, sol, la,* or C, D, E, G, A of the key of C major.
3. The five flavors are sweet, sour, bitter, salty, and hot (like pepper).
4. Cf. also Chapters 3, 19.

# 13
## ABHORRENCE OF SHAME
## Yen Ch'ih

*Favor and disgrace both seem startling.*
*Honor is great trouble if identified with the self.*
*What does it mean by saying*
*That favor and disgrace both seem startling?*
*Favor descends from superior to inferior.*
*The recipient seems startled upon getting it;*
*He seems no less startled upon losing it.*
*This is what it means by saying*
*That favor and disgrace both seem startling.*
*What does it mean by saying*
*That honor is great trouble if identified with*
*   the self?*
*The reason why I have great trouble*
*Is that I have a self;*
*If I am selfless and unselfish,*
*What trouble do I have?*
*Therefore, he who feels honored*
*In offering himself for the world,*[1]
*Can be assigned the rule of the world;*
*He who loves to offer himself for the world,*
*Can be trusted with the world.*[2]

In this chapter, Lao Tzu dwells on the subject of honor and favor, and points out some frailties of human nature together with their cause. Honor or favor is indeed given by the superior to the in-

144

ferior, that is to say, from the king or prince or president to the common people. Now, kings or princes or presidents themselves are often insecure. As Goldsmith has well said in his famous poem, "The Deserted Village":

> Princes and lords may flourish, or may fade—
> A breath can make them, as a breath has made.

Even if they are secure, they may be fickle-minded. Today they may smile and confer favor or honor, tomorrow they may frown and take away what they have conferred. Ordinary people, therefore, often find themselves in a harassing predicament. Before obtaining honor or favor, they are anxious about it. After they have obtained it, they are afraid to lose it. And when they do lose it, they feel bitter at heart. In Shakespeare's play *Henry VIII*, the following lines are found in the soliloquy of Wolsey:

> Vain pomp and glory of this world, I hate ye!
> I feel my heart new-opened. Oh! how wretched
> Is that poor man that hangs on princes' favors!

Long before Shakespeare and Goldsmith, the Confucian sage, Mencius, cherished the same view, and suggested that it is better to obtain true honor ("good honor") by developing one's own faculties or talents than to obtain it from external sources. He says: "To desire to be honored is the common mind of men. And all men have in themselves that which is truly honorable. Only they do not think of it. The honor which men confer is not good honor. Those whom Chao, the Great, ennobles he can make mean again." (James Legge's translation.)

Lao Tzu anticipates all the above three authors when he writes the first seven lines of the chapter under consideration. He also points out the reason why ordinary people are so often tormented when receiving or losing honor or favor. The reason is that they are selfish and deviate from Tao. They are eager to inflate their ego and afraid to deflate it, instead of cultivating and following Tao and facing the vicissitudes of fortune with equanimity. They are, in his opinion, not fit to be rulers. Only people who are attuned to Tao and identified with the universal interest of humanity can rise above considerations of honor and disgrace and can be entrusted with the rule of the world.

---

1. That is to say, he who is glad to serve the world unselfishly.
2. Cf. also Chapter 78.

# 14
## In Praise of the Mysteries
### Tsan Hsuan

*What is invisible when looked at is called yi;*
*What is inaudible when listened to is called hsi;*
*What is elusive when grabbed at is called wei.*
*These three are not amenable to investigation;*
*Therefore, they mingle as One.*
*On rising, the One does not become bright;*
*On falling, it does not become dark.*
*Unnameable it goes on and on,*[1]
*And again reverts to Non-Being.*
*This is called shape of the shapeless,*
*And form of the formless.*
*This is called winking-waning, as in a dream.*[2]
*On greeting it, one cannot see its front;*
*On following it, one cannot see its back.*
*Taking hold of the Tao of antiquity*
*To cope with the problems of the present*
*Could make one know the ancient origins.*
*This is called the unbroken strand of Tao.*[3]

This is a chapter difficult to understand, and no wonder, for it is about the mystery of Tao. In the very first chapter of the *Tao Teh Ching*, Lao Tzu has definitely stated that Tao cannot be expressed in words. Yet in this and other chapters, he does attempt in various ways to hint and suggest its mystery.

Tao cannot be seen, nor heard, nor touched. So it cannot be investigated, much less experimented upon. It becomes all One. A good way to understand this abstruse metaphysical concept is perhaps to consider it as universal Being before its differentiation among varied concrete forms. As such it cannot be contacted by our senses. Consequently we cannot assign any attribute to it such as brightness or darkness. It is indeed unnameable. Yet it exists and "goes on and on." Eventually it "reverts to Non-Being." It is clear, then, that Being and Non-Being alternate. This shows beyond doubt that Lao Tzu is here speaking of cyclic reversion which, in Chapter 40, he calls the movement of Tao.

Non-Being is a puzzling concept. Wang Pi, the boy wonder in philosophy and metaphysics, has this to say about it: "Is it nothing? Yet the myriad things are derived from it. Is it

146

something? Yet we cannot see it." It may perhaps be regarded as Tao in its hidden state—in its essence, hence "shape of the shapeless, and form of the formless." To our senses, it appears elusive and evasive. It seems to wink at us and straightway wanes. It seems like things seen in a dream. It has neither "front" nor "back." In other words, it has no beginning and no ending, or rather it ends at the beginning and begins at the ending—another symbol of cyclic reversion.

The last four lines, too, refer to cyclic reversion but in a different way. The term "Tao of antiquity" is misleading. For Tao is the same eternally and is indivisible into ancient and modern. However, as Lao Tzu points out in Chapter 1, it has two aspects: essence and manifestations. And these two aspects alternate and revert to each other. The last four lines, therefore, may reasonably be interpreted as follows: If we study the manifestations of Tao in former times and apply them to tackle problems of the present, we will find the cyclic movements of Tao, for Tao pervades the universe and moves in cycles continuously and eternally.

---

1. Cf. also Chapters 1, 41.
2. Cf. also Chapter 21. The two Chinese words *huang* and *hu* are usually regarded as meaning "elusive and evasive." This is substantially correct, for things in the process of rapid change, especially from light to darkness and vice versa, always appear elusive and evasive. Here the two words are translated "winking-waning" just to make the meaning a little more vivid.
3. Tao has continuity as well as unity.

VIRTUE REVEALED
# Hsien Teh

*The good scholars of ancient times*
*Were keen, astute, mysterious, and intuitive.*
*They were so profound as to be incomprehensible.*
*Since they show themselves incomprehensible,*
*They must be depicted in some arbitrary way:*
*They were cautious as if fording a stream in*
    *winter,*
*Hesitant as if afraid of the neighbors around,*
*Dignified as if in the role of a guest;*
*They were easy-going, like ice about to melt,*
*Unpretentious, like wood in its virgin state,*
*Open-minded, like a valley,*
*And murky, like turbid water.*
*Who, being like turbid water, can remain calm,*
*So that quiescence will gradually lead to clarity?*
*Who can stay relaxed for a long while,*
*So that an impulse will gradually lead to Life?*
*He who conserves this Tao does not go to the*
    *limit.*[1]
*For the reason that he does not go to the limit,*
*He can wear well and does not need renewal.*

Although Lao Tzu does not expressly say so, there is no doubt that "the good scholars of ancient times" practiced spiritual cultivation and followed Tao. They were like Tao in many respects. In the first place, they were mysterious (*hsuan*), which is the typical characteristic of Tao. Then they are said to be easy going, unpretentious, open-minded, "murky, like turbid water." All these characteristics are virtues derived from Tao. For Tao is easy-going, i.e., tending toward harmony (Cf. Chapter 4). It is unpretentious, i.e., manifesting spontaneously and naturally, and is like virgin wood in simplicity (Cf. Chapters 19 and 32). It is also open and hollow like a valley (Cf. Chapter 6), and exists like the calm of deep water (Cf. Chapter 4).

    The good ancient scholars are also said to be cautious, hesitant, and dignified. It is easy to understand that they were dignified, for all gentlemen worthy of the name assume some dignity. But why were they also "cautious as if fording a stream in winter" and "hesitant as if afraid of the neighbors around"? The reason would seem to be that they were following Tao and practicing Wu Wei or non-interference. They did not like to disturb the natural trend whether within their own being or within their neighbors', and they took great care not to do so.

The last seven lines clearly refer to meditation and yoga, which will not only lead to mental clarity but also "turn on" some impulse within one's being. This will be followed by the cyclic reversion of Tao. So, in order to avoid the setback, or reaction that will inevitably set in, wise people will not allow it to develop to the limit.

---

1. Cf. also Chapters 9, 29, 30, 32, 55.

# 16
## Return to the Root
## Kuei Ken

*Empty the mind to the utmost extent.*
*Maintain quiescence with the whole being.*
*The ten thousand things are growing with one impulse,*
*Yet I can discern their cyclic return.*[1]
*Luxuriant indeed are the growing things;*
*Yet each again will return to the root.*
*Returning to the root means quiescence;*
*Quiescence means renewal of life;*
*Renewal of life means in tune with the Immutable.*
*Knowing the Immutable brings enlightenment.*
*Not knowing the Immutable causes disaster.*
*Knowing the Immutable, one will be broad-minded;*
*Being broad-minded, one will be impartial;*
*Being impartial, one will be kingly;*
*Being kingly, one will attain the Divine;*
*Attaining the Divine, one will merge with Tao,*
*And become immortal and imperishable,*
*Even after the disappearance of the body.*[2]

This is another important chapter from the standpoint of spiritual cultivation, inasmuch as it sets forth some important Taoist ideas about long life and immortality. An exposition of the chapter is presented in Chapter IV in Part One of this work.

---

1. Cf. also Chapters 25, 40, 65.
2. Cf. also Chapters 33, 50, 52, 59.

## 17
### THE ATMOSPHERE OF SIMPLICITY
## Ch'un Feng

*The best rulers are not known to the people;[1]*
*Then come those who are loved and praised;*
*Then those who are held in awe;*
*And lastly those who are despised.*
*When one's faith is inadequate,*
*It will not evoke faith from other people.[2]*
*(Wise rulers) are wary and treasure their words.*
*When their task is accomplished and their work*
  *done,*
*All the people would say: "We did it of our free*
  *will."*

This chapter furnishes a good illustration of Wu Wei or noninterference, although the word is not mentioned.

Four kinds of rulers are pointed out. The best are those who practice Wu Wei to such an extent as to be unknown to the people. This does not mean that they do nothing at all. Whatever they do, however, harmonizes with the wishes of the people. It is done with little noise and fuss and involves little interference with ordinary life. The people, far from having suffered any tyrannical pressure, would actually feel that they are free and enjoying self-government.

---

1. Cf. also Chapter 58.
2. Cf. also Chapter 23.

# 18
## Social Decadence
## Su Po

*The Great Tao having been abandoned,*
*There arise benevolence and righteousness.*
*With the emergence of wit and wisdom,*
*There comes into being monstrous hypocrisy.*
*When the six relatives fail to live in harmony,[1]*
*There arise filial piety and parental love.*
*When the state falls into darkness and disorder,*
*There come into existence loyal ministers.[2]*

In this chapter, Lao Tzu dwells on the importance and power of
Tao, though somewhat indirectly. The central idea implicit in the
whole chapter is that when Tao prevails, goodness or morality will
flow spontaneously from the human heart. People will do the right
thing and will be benevolent to each other as a matter of course—
even without any notion about benevolence and righteousness.

However, after Tao has been eclipsed, then wit and wisdom arise
and lead to hypocrisy. All such virtues as benevolence,
righteousness, filial piety, compassion, and loyalty are created by
the intellect to remedy some unpleasant deteriorating situation.
They are not natural expressions of internal goodness. They do not
spring out of Tao. So Lao Tzu and other Taoists consider them objectionable.

---

1. Husband and wife, parents and children, younger and elder
brothers.
2. Cf. also Chapters 19, 38.

RETURN TO INNOCENCE
## Huan Ch'un

*Forswear wisdom, discard knowledge,*
*And the people will gain a hundredfold.*
*Forswear benevolence, discard righteousness,*
*And the people will recover filial and parental love.*
*Forswear skill, discard profit,*
*And thieves and robbers will not appear.*
*These three steps are inadequate for culture.*
*They, therefore, have to encompass some others,*
*Such as: Display plainness, embrace simplicity,*
*Reduce selfishness, and decrease desires.*[1]

This chapter contains some very radical ideas. In essence, it shows that Lao Tzu sets a high value on the simplicity and innocence of man's original nature and takes a very dim view of artificial morals and intellectual conceptions.

The chapter is generally regarded as a direct frontal attack on Confucian morals. It should be noted, however, that the attitude of the Taoists toward the Confucian virtues is different from that of the Confucians themselves. The latter do not consider their morals or virtues as artificial creations. They do believe that their virtues are natural manifestations of the heart and are utterly sincere. For instance, Mencius says: "What belongs by his nature to the superior man are benevolence, righteousness, propriety, and knowledge. These are rooted in his heart." (*The Mencius*, Book VII, Part I, Chapter 21. James Legge's translation.) In the Confucian classic, *Chung Yung*, it is also said: "It is only he who is possessed of the most complete sincerity that can exist under heaven who can give its full development to his nature." (Chapter XXII. James Legge's translation.) Lao Tzu and his disciples, however, regard the Confucian virtues as artificial creations. They, therefore, look upon them with contempt.

It should be noted also that at the time Lao Tzu was writing, the Chou dynasty was in its declining stage and moral culture was at a low ebb especially among the officials. Virtues like benevolence and righteousness had lost their spiritual content and become masks for hypocrisy. This is another reason why Lao Tzu wanted to abolish them. In his opinion, only a radical change of the human heart or a return to the simplicity of Tao can heal the political and social evils of his day. Thus at the end of the chapter he urges people to display plainness, embrace simplicity, reduce selfishness, and decrease desires.

---

1. Cf. also Chapters 3, 34, 57.

# 20
## DIFFERENT FROM THE MADDING CROWD
## I Su

*Forswear learning, and vexation will vanish.*
*Between an abrupt "Yes" and a gentle "Yea,"*
*How much is the difference?*
*Between the good and the bad,*
*How much is the difference?*
*What others fear, one should also fear—*
*What a silly notion! Whither will it lead?*[1]
*Merrily, merrily, the multitude is rejoicing,*
*As if feasting after the Great Sacrifice,*
*As if mounting the Terrace of Love.*
*I alone remain indifferent and show no emotion,*
*Like an infant as yet unable to smile.*
*Wandering aimlessly, I look like a homeless*
*    tramp.*
*The multitude all have enough and to spare;*
*I alone seem to be left on the wayside.*
*Oh, my mind is indeed like that of an idiot!*
*So dull, so dull I feel.*
*The worldlings are bright and cheerful;*
*I alone feel gloomy and dismal.*
*The worldlings are smart and self-confident;*
*I alone feel disgusted and depressed.*
*Restless like the sea,*
*I drift along as if never able to settle down.*
*The multitude all have some worthy employment;*
*I alone am stubborn and worthless.*
*I alone differ from other people,*
*And love to draw nourishment from the Mother.*[2]

This chapter is highly autobiographical in nature. It furnishes a sharp contrast between Lao Tzu or the man of Tao and the common herd of worldlings, or between life rooted in Tao and life steeped in sensual gratification.

The common herd loved sensual pleasures and enjoyed material things. They knew little about Tao and cared less. They were able to earn their living and appeared bright and smart and joyful. Lao Tzu, however, enjoyed the contemplation and experience of Tao and cared little for material things and sensual pleasures. He appeared to other people like a stupid bumpkin or a penniless and homeless tramp. In all this, there is much in common between him and Christ. For Christ loved and enjoyed hardly anything except doing the will of his Father in Heaven, and was destitute, even lacking some of the necessities of life. Note his own words: "Foxes have holes, and birds of the air have nests; but the Son of man hath not where to lay his head." (Luke, 9:58.)

Another personage resembling Lao Tzu was Yen Hui, the most perceptive disciple of Confucius. As recorded in the *Analects*, Confucius once said of his favorite disciple: "A sage indeed was Hui. With only a wicker vessel for his rice and only a gourd as his water-cup, he lived in a tumble-down lane. Such misery could hardly be endured by other people, yet it did not alter Hui's happiness." About fifteen centuries later, some Neo-Confucian masters raised the question "What was Yen Hui so happy about?" It would not be wide of the mark to reply that like Lao Tzu he found happiness in Tao. Such inner joy, according to Buddhism and Hinduism, usually occurs to the soul when it is completely free from worldly attachments and recovers its pristine purity.

1. The man of Tao will not conform to the ways of the multitude.
2. "Mother" is the symbol for Tao. As such, it ranks with water and the new-born babe.

## 21
### HOLLOW HEART
### Hsu Hsin

*The inherent quality of Grand Virtue (Teh)*
*Always conforms only to Tao.*
*Tao is something dreamily winking and waning.*[1]
*Waning, winking, it embodies forms;*
*Winking, waning, it embodies things.*
*It may seem receding afar and darkening,*
*Yet within it there is an essence.*
*This essence is very real.*
*Inside is something invariably vital.*
*From hoary antiquity to the present time,*
*Its effect has never gone awry,*
*And serves as witness to the Creator of all things.*
*How do I know the way of the Creator?*
*Through this (witness).*

In this chapter, Lao Tzu again tries to suggest the mysterious nature of Tao. His central idea appears to be that while Tao itself is so subtle and profound as to elude the grasp of our intellect, its effect on the myriad things in the universe can be perceived and serves as witness to its existence.

Tao and Teh or virtue are closely related. Tao informs all things in the universe, and having done so it becomes the Teh of each individual thing. Teh is particular, while Tao is universal. Teh makes each individual thing what it is. As Teh is derived from Tao, it naturally conforms only to Tao. It is from Tao that Teh draws any meaning. It follows also that from Teh the existence of Tao can be deduced.

Tao in its universal and undifferentiated state, however, is profoundly mysterious. It is elusive and evasive not only to our senses but to our intellect also. Yet Lao Tzu knows that it contains forms and things in their potentiality. It also seems fugitive and darkening, yet Lao Tzu knows that it contains an essence which is very real and possessed of something invariably vital. How did Lao Tzu come to know all this? By noting the manifestations of that vital reality which since time immemorial has been manifesting its effect and has never gone wrong or ceased operation. This vital reality underlies every phenomenon in the universe and serves as

155

witness to the way as well as existence of Tao. It is apparently this witness that made Lao Tzu Tao-conscious.

---

1. The two Chinese words *huang* and *hu* are usually taken to mean elusive and evasive. This is correct. In order to make the meaning somewhat more vivid, the two words are here translated as "winking-waning."

## 22
### STRENGTH TO THE HUMBLE
### I Ch'ien

*To be crooked is to become perfect;*
*To be bent is to become straight;*
*To be hollow is to become full;*
*To be worn out is to be renewed;*
*To have little is to receive more;*
*To have plenty is to be perplexed.*
*Therefore, the Sage embraces the One,*
*And serves as model for the world.*
*As he does not like to show off, he is enlightened;*
*As he is not prone to be self-righteous, he is*
  *distinguished;*
*As he does not blow his own horn, he acquires*
  *merit;*
*As he does not extol himself, he is fit to be a*
  *leader.*[1]
*And it is precisely because he does not contend,*
*That no one under heaven can contend with him.*[2]
*The ancient saying "To be crooked is to become*
  *perfect"*
*Surely is not an empty remark.*
*The world goes to him who is truly perfect.*

The first six lines of this chapter dramatize the view that Tao always tends toward harmony and balance. The Sage who follows Tao, therefore, embraces the One which represents unity, balance, and harmony. Consequently he is free from selfish thoughts and words and deeds, and does not contend with anybody about anything. He has no motive to show off his accomplishments or to justify his actions or to otherwise brag about himself. As he does not stoop to do those vulgar things, he gains credit and prestige without expecting them.

Much of the teaching in this chapter is paralleled in the Christian Bible. It is really surprising that a passage in the Old Testament almost duplicates the first six lines of the chapter: "Prepare ye the way of the Lord, make straight in the desert a highway for our God. Every valley shall be exalted, and every mountain and hill shall be made low: and the crooked shall be made straight, and the rough places plain." (Isaiah, 40:3-4.) The first five lines of the chapter also remind us of the first four of the Eight Beatitudes enunciated by Christ. (Cf. Matt., 5:3-6.)

---

1. Cf. also Chapter 24.
2. Cf. also Chapters 8, 66, 68, 81. These two lines are similar in sense to the following saying by Christ: "Take my yoke upon you, and learn of me; for I am meek and lowly in heart: and ye shall find rest unto your souls." (Matt., 11:29.)

# 23
## EMPTINESS AND NON-BEING
## Hsu Wu

*Nature is brief in its speech.*[1]
*Thus a tempest does not last a whole morning,*
*Nor does a rainstorm last a whole day.*
*What is it that causes the wind and rain?*
*It is Heaven and Earth.*
*Even Heaven and Earth cannot be long in their*
*    outbursts.*
*How much the less can man in his!*[2]
*Therefore, in the pursuit of Tao,*
*Those tending toward Tao will identify with Tao;*
*Those tending toward virtue will identify with*
*    virtue;*

*Those tending toward failure will identify with*
  *failure.*
*To those identified with Tao,*
*Tao will gladly extend welcome;*[3]
*To those identified with virtue,*
*Virtue will gladly extend welcome;*
*To those identified with failure,*
*Failure will gladly extend welcome.*
*When one's own faith is inadequate,*
*It will not evoke faith from other people.*[4]

Lao Tzu gives some important lessons in this chapter not only for spiritual cultivation but also for the daily life in general.

The first line clearly indicates that Nature prefers silence or quiescence to noisy expression; quiescence is the rule while noisy expression is the exception. This interpretation is supported by the last line of Chapter 45, which reads: "Purity and quiescence are the norms of the universe."

While Lao Tzu mentions only tempests and rainstorms, other noisy manifestations of Nature, notably earthquakes and volcanic eruptions, are also brief in duration. They are aberrations or departures from the norm and cannot last long.

Men, especially those interested in spiritual cultivation, should imitate Nature and maintain silence as a rule, while noisy talk and heated arguments and emotional outbursts should be avoided as much as possible. Breath literally means life and is very precious, especially in view of the fact that the supply is limited and cannot sustain any violent outburst for long. It should be preserved for the maintenance of health, physical and spiritual. As Lao Tzu says in Chapter 5: "Much talk often leads to exhaustion. Better concentrate on the center."

Faith is of paramount importance. One will be what one has faith to be, and will get what one has faith to get, whether Tao or virtue or failure. If one is a man of little faith, he cannot make others have faith in him and he will not obtain what he wants. On the other hand, if he has strong faith, he will most likely succeed in his endeavors. Christ seems to have the same idea, for he says: "If thou canst believe, all things are possible to him that believeth." (Mark, 9:23.)

---

1. Cf. also Chapter 45.
2. Cf. also Chapter 5.
3. "Draw nigh to God, and he will draw nigh to you." (James, 4:8.)
4. Cf. also Chapter 17.

# 24
## Bitter Favors
## K'u En

*He who stands on tip-toe will totter;*
*He who takes long strides is a poor walker.*
*He who likes to show off is not enlightened;*
*He who is prone to be self-righteous is not*
*   distinguished;[1]*
*He who blows his own horn will acquire no merit;*
*He who extols himself is not fit to be a leader.[2]*
*From the standpoint of Tao, it can be said:*
*"Eating excessive food or to walk with a burden*
*May be disgusting to creatures."*
*People possessed of Tao, therefore, reject them.*

In the light of Lao Tzu's teaching humility is prized, while pride and vanity are objectionable. They become doubly objectionable when gratified by means of stunts or redundant efforts.

To the Taoists, such self-assertive and self-aggrandizing efforts are like eating excessive food or walking with a load on one's back. They are utterly inconsistent with Tao, and will only defeat one's purpose, just as excessive food or burdensome walking will spoil one's health and waste one's vitality.

The chapter may be taken as a satire on pride and vanity. All vain and proud people want to be admired and respected as enlightened and distinguished leaders, but their nauseating haughty airs produce contrary results.

---

1. This line is reminiscent of the following saying by Christ: "Ye are they which justify yourselves before men; but God knoweth your hearts." (Luke, 16:15.)

2. Cf. also Chapters 22, 69.

## 25
### Symbol of the Great Origin
# Hsiang Yuan

*There is something formless and perfect,*
*Ever-existing, even before birth of Heaven and*
  *Earth.*
*How still it is! How quiet!*
*Abiding alone and unchanging,*
*It pervades everywhere without fail.*[1]
*Well may it be the mother of the world.*[2]
*I do not know its name,*[3]
*But label it Tao,*
*And arbitrarily name it Great.*
*Great means going incessantly;*
*Going incessantly means reaching far;*
*Reaching far means completing the cycle.*[4]
*Therefore, Tao is Great;*
*Heaven is Great;*
*Earth is Great;*
*Kingliness is Great.*
*In the cosmos there are four Greats,*
*And Kingliness constitutes one of them.*
*Man patterns after Earth;*
*Earth patterns after Heaven;*
*Heaven patterns after Tao;*
*Tao patterns after Innate Freedom.*

This chapter represents another version of Tao as conceived by
Lao Tzu. In the first half of the chapter he sets forth three main
ideas: Tao is ineffable Non-Being, the source of Heaven and Earth;
Tao has an immutable essence; Tao goes far but in a circular man-
ner, eventually returning to the starting point. In expressing these
ideas, Lao Tzu reiterates in a different fashion what he has said in
Chapters 1, 4, and 21, and anticipates what he is going to say in
Chapter 40.

In the latter half of the chapter the four "Greats" in the cosmos
which he mentions are probably not his original idea. That Heaven,
Earth, and Man are the three great Powers (*san ts'ai*) of the cosmos
seems to be quite ancient in Chinese thought and has been frequently referred to by later scholars. In the Confucian classic

*Chung Yung* for instance, it is said: "Able to assist the transforming and nourishing powers of Heaven and Earth, he (who is possessed of the most complete sincerity) may with Heaven and Earth form a triad." (James Legge's translation.) Lao Tzu, however, improves upon the ancient idea by substituting "Kingliness" for man and adding Tao as another Power or "Great." He apparently considers Kingliness as the perfection of man. In his opinion, not every man constitutes the copartner of Heaven and Earth, but only the man who has a kingly character.

The last line of the chapter deserves some special attention. It shows that Tao is not the ultimate in Lao Tzu's thought but that Innate Freedom (*tsu ran*, lit. self-so) is also an important notion. It is synonymous with Wu Wei or non-action in the sense of non-interference or non-assertion of the self. The self with its efforts and actions is regarded as an obstruction to Innate Freedom. When one transcends or forgets the self, then Innate Freedom will manifest and one can do things effortlessly and beautifully—one can even create. This is why artists in the course of creative activity are often so absorbed as to be self-forgetful. A poem by the famous poet Su Tung-po about his friend, an expert bamboo-painter, will perhaps illustrate the point. The poem may be translated as follows:

> When Yu K'o is engaged in bamboo-painting,
> He is fully aware of the bamboo,
> But unaware of men, no matter who,
> Nay, he even forgets his own being.
> When his being fuses with the bamboo,
> There's an endless flow of pure creation.
> As the world no longer has a Chuang Tzu,
> Who can understand such concentration?

---

1. Cf. also Chapter 21.
2. Cf. also Chapters 1, 4.
3. Cf. also Chapter 1.
4. Cf. also Chapters 16, 40, 65.

# 26
## GRAVITY AS A VIRTUE
## Chung Teh

*Heaviness is the root of lightness;*
*Quiescence is the master of hastiness.*
*Thus the Sage traveling all day*
*Will not stay away from his loaded cart.*[1]
*Though glorious prospects are in view,*
*He remains serene in a transcendental atmosphere.*
*For what reason should it be*
*That a weighty person like the lord of ten*
*    thousand chariots*
*Would consider himself lighter than worldly*
*    vanities?*
*In making light of himself, he loses his ministers;*
*In being hasty, he loses his kingly command.*

The first line of this chapter may refer to seriousness or gravity versus levity or frivolity, indicating that the former can keep the latter under control. It may also have the literal meaning that light things are rooted in heavy things or come from heavy things; for instance, steam comes from water and the leaves of a tree are supported by the trunk.

The general purport of the chapter is that the lord of a big and powerful country should not be frivolous and hasty in his personal conduct or in the handling of affairs; otherwise he will lose his position and power. He should imitate the Sage who will not only keep close to his belongings but also retain his gravity and self-composure and is not distracted by the glittering sights of the world.

The chapter also has some significance from the standpoint of yoga and meditation. It suggests that any person interested in spiritual cultivation should avoid levities and frivolities and should not let his even tenor be disturbed and distracted by the glorious sights and sounds of the world or by prospects of wealth or honor. He should rather constantly care for his inner life and retain his self-composure so that he may remain serene in a transcendental atmosphere always.

---

1. The term "loaded cart" has a metaphorical as well as a literal meaning. Metaphorically it means seriousness or gravity.

# 27
## SKILLFUL APPLICATION
## Ch'iao Yung

*A good walker leaves no traces behind;*
*A good speaker leaves no blemishes for criticism;*
*A good counter does not use counting chips;*
*A good lock has no bolt, yet cannot be opened;*
*A good knot has no string, yet cannot be untied.*
*Thus the Sage (in his silent and subtle way)*
*Is always good in saving people,*
*Thereby leaving no people unsaved;*
*And always good in saving things,*
*Thereby leaving nothing unsaved.*
*This is called "Passing the light."*[1]
*Hence the good man is the teacher of the bad,*
*And the bad is object lesson for the good.*
*He who does not honor his teacher,*
*Nor loves any object lesson,*
*Is lost in a great maze, clever though he may be.*
*Such is called Significant Subtlety.*

The theme of this chapter is *shan*, meaning good in the sense of skillful, expert, or adept.

The first few lines about the various skills are rhetorical remarks leading up to the statement that the Sage too has an adept way of saving people and things, so that nobody nor anything is rejected. He wants to spread the light all around so that all people and all things may inherit and share it.

It is patently unwise to reject anybody because he is bad, for a bad man can turn good and even serve some good purpose. From the doings of a so-called bad man and their consequences, one may learn a lesson or even find a way to turn bad into good. One should honor the teacher and love the object lesson.

---

1. In other words, let others inherit the light *(hsi ming).*

## 28
### RETURN TO SIMPLICITY
### Fan P'u

*He, who knows the Male*
*And yet holds on to the Female,*
*Becomes the ravine of the world.*
*Being the ravine of the world,*
*He is always in union with Eternal Virtue,*
*And returns to the state of the new-born babe.*
*He, who knows the white (Yang)*
*And yet holds on to the black (Yin),*
*Becomes a model for the world.*
*Being a model for the world,*
*His Eternal Virtue becomes unerring,*
*And he returns to the Infinite.*
*He, who is aware of glory*
*And yet holds on to ignominy,*
*Becomes the valley of the world.*
*Being the valley of the world,*
*His Eternal Virtue becomes sufficient,*
*And he returns to the state of virgin wood*
*(simplicity).*
*The virgin wood, on being cut up, is used as*
*implements.*
*Sages, who make use of the implements,*
*Become high officials and leaders.*
*The Supreme Ruler uses the wood without cutting it.*

In this chapter, Lao Tzu hints that man can become immortal spiritually by cultivating Eternal Virtue. "New-born babe," "Infinite," and "virgin wood," mentioned in the chapter, are all symbols for Tao. Return to Tao means attainment of immortality, for Tao is immortal.

How to cultivate Eternal Virtue in order to attain spiritual immortality? Mainly by maintaining harmony between Yin and Yang: between male and female, between white and black, and between glory and ignominy. Man is apt to incline toward Yang and away from Yin. So Lao Tzu warns that Yin must not be neglected.

Tao, as symbolized by virgin wood, could still serve some useful purpose when differentiated or cut up. But it functions best when remaining intact. People with various virtues (individualized Tao) will become high officials. The Supreme Ruler, however, uses Tao in its integral perfection.

# 29
## Non-Action
## Wu Wei

*One might wish to get hold of the world,*
*And wilfully interfere with it.*
*In my view, this is bound to fail.*
*The world is a Divine Vessel.*
*It cannot be interfered with.*
*He who interferes with it spoils it;[1]*
*He who grasps it loses it.*
*For among the creatures of the world,*
*Some are leaders, some are followers;*
*Some tend to condone, some to condemn;*
*Some are strong, some are weak;*
*Some are forward-looking, some are downcast.*
*The Sage, therefore, eschews the excessive,*
*Eschews the extravagant, and eschews the*
*       extreme.[2]*

This chapter dealing with Wu Wei or non-action in the sense of noninterference or nonassertion of the self contains a clear warning against interference with the natural state of things. Special attention should be paid to the two lines: "The world is a Divine Vessel. It cannot be interfered with." The term "Divine Vessel" (*Shen ch'i*, translated as here by D. T. Suzuki and Paul Carus, and as "God's own vessel" by Lin Yutang) indicates that Lao Tzu does believe in the existence of God. Another such indication appears in Chapter 4, where Tao is supposed to antecede "the Creator."

Since the world is a vessel fashioned by God, puny man whose intelligence is far from divine should not interfere with it. He will only make a mess of things but never can succeed in his venture.

The world as fashioned by God contains all kinds of creatures: some are bold leaders, some meek followers; some are easy-going, some are captious; some are strong, some are weaklings; some are optimistic, some pessimistic. Each creature is born with an inherent pattern for its personality, which should be given an opportunity to grow and mature. To interfere with it and try to mold all creatures, whether human or subhuman beings, into a common mass according to the dictates of a single individual is as tragic and deplorable as it is futile and impossible.

Thus the Sage who respects and follows Tao avoids what is excessive, extravagant, or extreme, for all this involves interference of some sort and deviates from Tao. The movement of Tao is cyclic reversion. Followers of Tao refrain from pushing things to the limit to avoid the inevitable setback or reaction.

---

1. Cf. also Chapters 2, 3, 37, 38, 43, 47, 48, 57, 64.
2. Cf. also Chapters 9, 15, 30, 32, 55.

## 30
### MODERATE USE OF FORCE
### Chien Wu

*He who uses Tao to assist the ruler of a people*
*Will not employ armed force to dominate the*
*    world.*
*For such a scheme is apt to boomerang.*
*Where armies are quartered,*
*Briers and brambles abound.*
*After a great war, famine inevitably happens.*[1]
*Therefore,*
*A good-natured man attains his objective and*
*    stops;*
*He dares not grab by violence.*
*He wants to attain his objective,*
*But does not extol it,*
*Nor brag about it, nor take pride in it.*
*He attains his objective as if it could not be*
*    helped,*
*And does not use it to practice violence.*
*For things, after their prime, will begin to decay.*
*Decay indicates disregard of Tao.*[2]
*Whatever disregards Tao soon vanishes.*

Lao Tzu or any Taoist is a pacifist, for Tao patterns after Innate Freedom and signifies Wu Wei or noninterference. In other words, Taoism is essentially pacifism.

In Lao Tzu's opinion, the best thing is to banish war altogether, for war is a positive evil. It is as disastrous to the victor as to the vanquished. Directly and indirectly it causes immense loss of human lives and treasures.

Human nature being what it is, however, total abolition of war will not be possible for a long time to come. Lao Tzu must have been aware of this deplorable situation. So he goes on to exhort rulers to practice moderation in the conduct of war. He urges them to stop the war as soon as the war aims have been attained and to refrain from continuing violent measures against the enemy.

Finally he raises the warning against pushing any war to the limit or beyond the scope of necessity. Hence he refers again to the cyclic reversion of Tao. Decay or defeat is the result of disregarding Tao by taking excessive measures. He who wants to avoid decay or eventual defeat must practice moderation.

---

1. Cf. also Chapter 31.
2. Cf. also Chapters 9, 15, 29, 32, 55.

# 31
## BANNING THE USE OF FORCE
### Yen Wu

*Fine weapons are inauspicious instruments.*
*They are probably detested by the people.*
*Therefore, he who is possessed of Tao rejects them.*
*The superior man honors the left in time of peace;*
*In time of war he honors the right.*
*Weapons are inauspicious instruments;*
*They are not instruments for the superior man.*
*He uses them only under dire necessity,*
*And in this case priority is given to moderation.*
*He does not consider victory a fine thing.*
*Those who consider victory a fine thing*
*Are those who delight in slaughtering people.*
*Those who delight in slaughtering people*
*Can never gratify their ambition to win the world.*[1]

*Therefore, the left is favored for felicitous*
    *occasions;*
*For mournful occasions, the right is favored.*
*The second-in-command stands on the left,*
*While the commander-in-chief stands on the right;*
*For according to funeral rites are they treated.*
*Mass slaughter is to be bewailed with grief and*
    *sorrow.*
*Victory is to be mourned with funeral rites.*[2]

This chapter may be taken as an extension of the preceding one, as it is also a version of Lao Tzu's pacifist ideas.

According to Chinese tradition, the left is the side of honor and the symbol of fortune, while the right is the side of lowliness and symbol of misfortune. The left is favored for happy or felicitous occasions, while the right is favored for mournful occasions. Thus in time of war, the right becomes the side of honor instead of the left, for war is a tragic and unfortunate thing. This also explains why the commander-in-chief stands on the right side, while the second-in-command stands on the left.

The term *chia ping* in the first line of the Chinese text may mean either fine weapons or fine soldiers. But there is no doubt that both are considered by Lao Tzu as inauspicious instruments, for both are used for killing people.

The general theme of the chapter is that war is an evil and, if or when unavoidable, should at least be prosecuted with moderation. In developing the theme, Lao Tzu advances the rather novel notion that victory should be treated like a funeral. This may appear bizarre at first blush, but it is really quite consonant with reason. For war often claims a vast number of human lives besides causing tremendous desolation and destruction. Victory is better than defeat, but usually the victor also suffers considerable casualties and losses. Why should not this sad and mournful state of affairs be bewailed with grief and sorrow? Is it not sensible that the good-natured man will not extol or glorify victory?

It is not unjust to say that he who loves war and glorifies victory delights in mass slaughter. In Lao Tzu's opinion such a wicked man cannot realize his ambition in the world. History seems to have confirmed this opinion.

---

1. Cf. also Chapters 30, 76.
2. The last seven lines were thought by some critics to be comments by Wang Pi, not part of the text.

# 32
## Holy Virtue
## Sheng Teh

*Tao is eternal and has no name.*[1]
*Though P'u (Simplicity) may appear puny,*
*Yet the world dare not dominate it.*
*If kings and nobles can preserve it intact,*
*The ten thousand things will gladly pay them*
*    homage.*
*Heaven and Earth unite in harmony*
*To pour down showers of sweet dew,*
*To benefit all mankind graciously and evenly.*
*Institutions once begun, names come into being.*
*Names having come into being,*
*One should know where to rest.*[2]
*To know where to rest is to forestall peril.*
*Tao differentiated in the world (will return to One),*
*Like streams and rivers flowing to the sea.*

In this chapter, Lao Tzu likens Eternal Tao to *p'u* or virgin wood, a symbol of simplicity or original nature. He also dramatizes its mysterious mystic power.

*P'u* may be small in size, yet potent in essence. As symbol of Tao, it is the prime source of all things and cannot be subordinated to anything in the world. If rulers and government officials could preserve it as their original nature instead of losing it through forgetfulness or neglect, they would be able to work for the welfare of the people and command love and respect. They would even influence Heaven and Earth to enter into harmony and send down seasonable rain and dew to prosper agricultural production for the nourishment of mankind.

In the latter part of the chapter, Lao Tzu warns of the danger of neglecting or forgetting *p'u* or Tao as man's ultimate end. Tao itself has no name; but after its differentiation into phenomena, it is given all sorts of names. Amidst the infinite variety of names or phenomena, man is apt to get engrossed in the manifestations of Tao and forget its essence. So Lao Tzu exhorts people to rise above the manifestations at some suitable time and return to Tao's essence wherein they should rest; otherwise they will find themselves in peril.

The last two lines serve to illustrate the view that like streams and rivers flowing ceaselessly until they finally reach the ocean, so all creatures will ultimately return to Tao and identify with Tao.

In passing, it may be worthwhile to note that the three lines ending with the words "graciously and evenly" are reminiscent of Christ's remark: God "maketh his sun to rise on the evil and the good, and sendeth rain on the just and the unjust." (Matt., 5:45.)

---

1. Cf. also Chapters 1, 25.
2. Cf. also Chapters 9, 15, 29, 30, 55.

# 33
## DISCRIMINATING VIRTUE
### Pien Teh

*He who knows others is wise;*
*He who knows himself is enlightened.*
*He who conquers others is strong;*
*He who conquers himself is valiant.*
*He who knows contentment is rich;*
*He who acts with determination has high aims.*
*He who has not lost his proper abode endures;*
*He who dies and yet does not perish becomes*
    *immortal.*[1]

This chapter indicates that Lao Tzu believes in spiritual immortality. The last two lines clearly show that if a man can abide in Tao and preserve the innocence and purity of his original nature, he may die *(ssu)* and yet will not perish *(wang)*. The two Chinese words, *ssu* and *wang*, are usually regarded as synonymous; but *ssu* seems to apply to corporeal things, while *wang* to incorporeal as well. The belief in immortality is also presented in several other chapters, and appears to be a favorite subject with Lao Tzu.

The first six lines of the chapter suggest that such virtues as self-knowledge and self-conquest together with contentment and determination are essential for spiritual enlightenment and immortality. To know others is not the same as to know oneself. Any person who has some rich experience and some degree of empathy can know others. To know oneself, however, requires high intelligence and deep meditation. The difference amounts to the difference between wisdom and enlightenment. Similarly, to conquer others is not the same as to conquer oneself. Any person with considerable muscular strength can conquer others. But to conquer oneself requires a high degree of moral and spiritual strength, as indicated in a proverb in the Bible: "He that is slow to anger is better than the mighty; and he that ruleth his spirit than he that taketh a city." (Proverbs, 16:32.)

It is not difficult to understand that "he who acts with determination has high aims," for the high aims serve as a strong incentive to action and tend to strengthen the determination. For instance, a scholar who aims at emancipating himself and his fellow men from ignorance and vulgarity is bound to be determined to work hard. But why is it that "he who knows contentment is rich?" Here the word "rich" *(fu)* is used in a higher sense than material wealth. He who knows contentment knows that money is merely a means to an end. He knows there are things more precious than material wealth. Some of these wonderful things may already be in his possession. In this sense, he is rich.

---

1. Cf. also Chapters 16, 50, 52, 59.

## 34
### NATURAL PERFECTION
## Ren Ch'eng

*The Great Tao is all pervasive;*
*It could be on your right or on your left.*
*The ten thousand things depend on it for growth,[1]*
*And it never lets them down.*
*It achieves success but is not possessive.*
*It enfolds and nourishes the ten thousand things,*
*Yet it does not claim ownership.[2]*
*Always desireless and covetous of nothing,*
*It could be termed small.*
*But as the ten thousand things return to it,*
*And it does not care to be their lord,*
*It could be termed great.*
*Thus the Sage never in life tries to be great,*
*And for this very reason becomes truly great.[3]*

171

In this chapter, Lao Tzu gives another version of his conception of Tao: Tao is both transcendent and immanent—it is *in* everything but not *of* anything. It fosters the growth of the myriad things but is detached from them. Lao Tzu demonstrates the idea in a vivid and paradoxical fashion. The greatness of the Tao lies in its transcendence or transcendental nature. It is absolutely selfless so far as its relation to the world is concerned. Though it helps all things to grow and protects and nourishes them, all this does not spring from any selfish motive but is simply the result of its spontaneous manifestation. The Tao thus inspires such virtues as unselfish love or charity as well as humility and meekness.

The Sage, who is attuned to Tao, also maintains a detached attitude toward his achievements and his gifts to mankind and thus appears to be humble and unselfish. His indifference to greatness in the world is conducive to his attainment of true greatness in the transcendent empyrean.

---

1. Cf. also Chapters 1, 4. The line reminds one of Christ's remark: "Consider the lilies of the field, how they grow; they toil not, neither do they spin." (Matt., 6:28.)
2. Cf. also Chapters 2, 10, 51.
3. Cf. also Chapters 7, 61, 66, 67.

# 35
## VIRTUE OF BENEVOLENCE
### Ren Teh

*Hold fast to the Great Form,*
*And wherever in the world you go,*
*You will meet with no harm,*
*But enjoy security, peace, and well-being.*
*Where there is music with good food,*
*The passers-by will pause and linger.*
*But Tao, on being set forth orally,*
*Is insipid and tasteless.*[1]
*It is invisible when looked at,*
*And inaudible when listened to,*
*Yet its utility will never come to an end.*[2]

The term "Great Form" patently means Tao. It appears also in Chapter 41 wherein it is said: "The Great Form has no sign."

The present chapter sets forth a contrast between the spiritual benefaction of Tao and sensual delectation. He who follows Tao closely and manifests its effect in his conduct and activity will be free from danger and will find lasting peace and happiness; for Tao, though imperceptible to our senses, is infinite in its utility. Because of its imperceptible spiritual nature, however, Tao is hardly felt by the worldlings who only relish sensual delights such as good food and sweet music.

In preferring Tao to sensual enjoyment, Lao Tzu is very much like Aristotle who preferred the life of reason to an ordinary life. He says: "Indeed, if reason is divine in comparison with the rest of human nature, then the life of reason is divine in comparison with ordinary life." (Aristotle, *Nicomachean Ethics,* tr. M. S. Everett, Bk. X, p. 1177.)

---

1. "The kingdom of God is not meat and drink, but righteousness and peace, and joy in the Holy Ghost." (Romans, 14:17.)
2. Cf. also Chapters 4, 5, 20.

# 36
## Faint Light
## Wei Ming

*Wishing to restrict anything,*
*One must first expand it;*
*Wishing to weaken anything,*
*One must first strengthen it;*
*Wishing to abolish anything,*
*One must first set it up;*
*Wishing to take from anything,*
*One must first supply it.*
*This is called Faint Light.*
*The soft conquers the hard;*
*The weak conquers the strong.*[1]
*Fish should not break forth from the deep;*
*Deadly weapons of the state must not be shown*
  *off.*

The first eight lines of this chapter may be interpreted various ways. They may be regarded as suggesting dark designs or subterfuges of the Machiavellian type. They may also be regarded as warnings to those who are at the peak of power or wealth, reminding them that a setback will inevitably follow. Thirdly, they may be taken as statements of simple common sense. For instance, if a person is already as poor as a church mouse, how can one further impoverish him or take anything from him? Is it not reasonable to say that he should be enriched first?

"Faint Light" means a slight sign or a little hint, from which a wise man can already discern or foresee further and more serious development. As is taught in the *I Ching* or *Book of Changes,* from the faint or minute it is possible to know the manifest. A little tendency to expand, for instance, may indicate a future tendency to restrict.

That the soft could conquer the hard and the weak could conquer the strong is a peculiar doctrine of the *Tao Teh Ching* and has recurred frequently in other chapters. It seems intended to teach people that it is wiser to be meek and gentle than otherwise.

The last two lines have the same tenor. They serve to exhort people not to show off. If fish break forth from the deep and come to the surface of the sea, they will surely get caught. Similarly, formidable weapons of the state should be kept safe in secret places.

---

1. Cf. also Chapters 43, 78.

## 37
### THE WAY OF GOVERNMENT
## Wei Cheng

*Tao is eternal and devoid of action,[1]*
*Yet there is nothing it does not do.*
*If kings and nobles can preserve it intact,*
*The ten thousand things will reform of themselves.*
*If after the reform they desire to be active,*
*I shall calm them with the Nameless Simplicity*
　　*(p'u),*
*The Nameless Simplicity will induce desirelessness,*
*Desirelessness will tend to quiescence,*
*And the world will set itself on the right course.*


This chapter dwells on the same theme as that of Chapter 32, only with stronger emphasis on Wu Wei or noninterference as a way of government. It not only shows the salutary effect of noninterference, but also points out the way leading to noninterference by attaching basic importance to simplicity, an essential characteristic of Tao and symbolized by *p'u* or wood in its virginal state. Simplicity will induce desirelessness, desirelessness will bring about quiescence, and quiescence will lead to noninterference. Human reason is not always reliable for it is fallible. Better, therefore, just let Tao prevail, and everything will then work out its destiny correctly and the world will set itself on the right course. "Practice noninterference, and there will never be any misrule." (Cf. Chapter 3.)

Wu-wei, in a sense, may be considered a sort of divine power. The concept is by no means peculiar to Lao Tzu's philosophy. For instance, in his unfinished play *The Suppliants* the ancient Greek poet Aeschylus (524-456 B.C.) writes:

> God striveth not, nor straineth;
> His thought performs His will
> Straightway, while quiet he reigneth
> In His holy Heaven still.

If the word "God" is changed into "Tao", the lines still make sense and reflect Lao Tzu's key teaching.

---

1. Cf. also Chapters 2, 3, 10, 29, 38, 43, 47, 48, 57, 64.

# 38
## DISCOURSE ON VIRTUE
## Lun Teh

*Superior virtue is not virtue-conscious,*[1]
*Therefore it has virtue.*
*Inferior virtue never forgets virtue,*
*Therefore it has no virtue.*
*Superior virtue does not interfere,*[2]
*And has no motive to interfere.*
*Inferior virtue interferes,*
*And has a motive to interfere.*
*Superior benevolence interferes without motive;*
*Superior righteousness interferes from motive;*
*Superior propriety interferes,*
*And failing to evoke any response,*
*Lifts its arm and resorts to violence.*
*Therefore, after the loss of Tao, virtue appears;*

*After the loss of virtue, benevolence appears;*
*After the loss of benevolence, righteousness*
    *appears;*
*After the loss of righteousness, propriety appears.*[3]
*Propriety is a mere veneer of loyalty and sincerity,*
*And constitutes the prime cause of confusion.*
*Traditional knowledge is the flower (outward show)*
    *of Tao,*
*And has become the origin of folly.*
*Therefore, men of the heroic type abide by depth,*
*And stay away from shallowness;*
*Abide by the fruit and stay away from the flower.*
*Forsooth, they reject this and adopt that.*

This chapter has been regarded as the first chapter of a separate discourse on Teh or virtue. While such a division of the *Tao Teh Ching* into two parts is rather meaningless (for Tao and Teh are dealt with throughout the entire work), this chapter does set forth Lao Tzu's basic view on virtue. According to this view, superior or true virtue is and should be natural, spontaneous, and straight from the pure human heart; inferior virtue, on the other hand, is studied and affected and requires memory and effort.

In a sense, this chapter once more stresses the merit of Wu Wei or non-interference, which is used as a criterion to judge the various virtues. Like Chapters 18 and 19, it may be taken as a serious swipe at the Confucian virtues and morals. But Confucius himself and his disciple Mencius both assert that benevolence, righteousness and related virtues are not artificial creations but spring from the pure human heart. Mencius says: "The feeling *(hsin,* lit., heart) of commiseration is the principle *(tuan,* lit., root or starting point) of benevolence. The feeling of shame and dislike is the principle of righteousness. The feeling of modesty and complaisance is the principle of propriety. The feeling of approving and disapproving is the principle of knowledge." (James Legge's translation.)

---

1. All the abstract concepts in this chapter, such as virtue, benevolence, righteousness and propriety, are personified, as in the English expression: When poverty comes in by the door, love flies out through the window.
2. Cf. also Chapters 2, 3, 10, 29, 37, 43, 47, 48, 57, 64.
3. Cf. also Chapters 18, 19.

# 39
## FOUNDATION OF THE LAW
## Fa Pen

*Since antiquity, these have possessed the One[1]—*
*Heaven in possession of the One has become clear;*
*Earth in possession of the One has become steady;*
*Spirits in possession of the One have become*
*    divine;*
*Valleys in possession of the One have become full;*
*Creatures in possession of the One have become*
*    alive;*
*Kings and nobles in possession of the One have*
*    become exemplary.[2]*
*All the above became what they are in the same*
*    way.*
*Heaven without the One to make it clear*
*Is apt to crack;*
*Earth without the One to make it steady*
*Is apt to quake;*
*Spirits without the One to make them divine*
*Are apt to cease operation;*
*Valleys without the One to make them full*
*Are apt to become dry;*
*Creatures without the One to make them alive*
*Are apt to become extinct;*
*Kings and nobles without the One to make them*
*    exemplary*
*Are apt to lose their prestige and eminence.*
*Forsooth, the honorable is rooted in the humble,*
*And the high is founded on the low.*
*So kings and nobles call themselves orphaned,*
*    lonely, and unworthy.*
*Does not this indicate that the honorable is rooted*
*    in the humble?*
*Indeed, if a chariot is taken apart,*
*There will no longer be any chariot.[3]*
*Desire not to be like polished jade,*
*But rather to be like rough rocks.*

The word "One" is sometimes considered to be another name for Tao, but this view does not seem to be sound. In Chapter 42, Lao Tzu clearly says that Tao gives birth to One. When Tao began to differentiate, One was the first to emerge and in turn gave and still gives birth to other things. It may well be called the Creator. To substantiate this point, it is helpful to consider the Chinese word for One, which is a continuous horizontal line (—). In the *I Ching* such a line represents Yang, the active or creative cosmic principle, while a broken line (--) represents Yin, the passive cosmic principle. It is reasonable to interpret One as the Yang principle which underlies the existence not only of the myriad things but also of Heaven and Earth and makes them what they are.

This creative and vitalizing power of One or Yang also furnishes a clue to the tenor of the short latter portion of the chapter, which may appear inconsistent with the tenor of the major first portion. Why is the honorable rooted in the humble, and the high founded on the low? It is because those who are humble or stay low will attract the Yang principle to them and receive some mystic power. The same may be said of people who can preserve or recover their Simplicity.

The last four lines of the chapter clearly convey the sense that a chariot or any other thing has a virtue or power inherent in its integral entity and must not be taken apart or otherwise interfered with. Hence rough rock is to be preferred to polished jade which has lost its natural simplicity through interference with its natural state.

---

1. Cf. also Chapter 42.
2. This and the preceding line are reminiscent of Christ's remark: "And ye shall know the truth, and the truth shall make you free." (John, 8:32.)
3. For the One or its integrity has been lost.

# 40
## MOVEMENT AND FUNCTION
### Ch'u Yung

*Cyclic reversion is Tao's movement.*[1]
*Weakness is Tao's function.*[2]
*All things in the universe are derived from Being.*[3]
*Being is derived from Non-Being.*[4]

Though the shortest in the *Tao Teh Ching,* this chapter is replete with significance. It is highly metaphysical and rather difficult of comprehension. Every one of the four lines states a truth. The truth stated in the first line was set forth in the ancient classic, the *I Ching,* which existed long before Lao Tzu's time. In the *I Ching,* it is taught that when a thing reaches its extreme point of manifestation, it will inevitably turn around *(wu chi pi fan),* i.e., revert to its opposite. Lao Tzu recognizes this truth and calls it movement of Tao.

"Weakness is Tao's function," appears rather abtruse. But Lao Tzu has ingeniously demonstrated it in Chapter 78, wherein he likens Tao to water which, though weak, can wear away hard and strong things.

Some commentator links the first and second truths together and expresses the view that water or any weak thing, after attacking and conquering the hard and strong, will become hard and strong itself and will in its turn be attacked and conquered by something weak. This view is not sound. Water after attacking the hard and strong does not become hard and strong itself. It remains water.

There is also a comment that the law of cyclic reversion, even if true, is "useless" and "impracticable." Such comment seems a little short-sighted. The law or theory of cyclic reversion could produce very beneficent effects on the health of mankind, especially at a time when the life ideal of most people is to work, struggle, compete, and go to extremes to reach their goal with feverish speed. Such a way of life may be very harmful and lead to some very serious diseases. Furthermore, when the inevitable reaction sets in, they are prone to become downcast and depressed and may suffer from psychosomatic ailments. People who listen to Lao Tzu will practice moderation and will be free from nervous tension and stress. And when the inevitable reaction or setback eventually arrives, they will accept it with equanimity, well knowing that it is the result of an immutable law. To be contented and to be able to accept the inevitable philosophically will enable one to face life with poise and composure and to enjoy health as well as peace of mind.

In the last two lines, Lao Tzu states his theory of cosmogony in metaphysical terms. The term Non-Being is often misunderstood as meaning "nothing" in the general sense. This is incorrect. Broadly speaking, Non-Being may be taken to mean what is spiritual, abstract, and beyond human sensation and ideation, while Being means what is material, concrete, and within human sensation and ideation. Non-Being corresponds to the unnameable Eternal Tao, and Being corresponds to Heaven and Earth. It is thus clear that Lao Tzu is here reiterating what he has said in

Chapter 1. "All things in the universe are derived from Being" is another way of saying "The Nameable is mother of the ten thousand things." And "Being is derived from Non-Being" is only another version of "The Unnameable is originator of Heaven and Earth."

---

1. Cf. also Chapters 16, 25, 65.
2. Cf. also Chapters 8, 78.
3. Paul Carus and D. T. Suzuki translate this line thus: "Heaven and Earth and the ten thousand things come from existence." With all respect to the two venerable scholars, their translation in this case does not seem to be quite correct. In Chapter 1, Lao Tzu says that the Unnameable (Non-Being) is originator of Heaven and Earth.
4. Cf. also Chapters 1, 25.

# 41
## SIMILARITY AND DIFFERENCE
## T'ung I

*The first-rate scholar, on hearing Tao,*
*Is diligent in practicing it;*
*The second-rate scholar, on hearing Tao,*
*Wavers between faith and forgetfulness;*
*The third-rate scholar, on hearing Tao,*
*Bursts into loud laughter.*
*If not laughed at, it would not be Tao!*
*Hence the following proverbs—*
*He who understands Tao seems confounded by it.*
*He who advances toward Tao seems retreating*
    *from it.*
*He who follows plain Tao seems treading on*
    *rugged ground.*
*Superior virtue appears to be hollow.*
*Perfect purity appears to be tainted.*
*Vast virtue appears to be inadequate.*
*Solid virtue appears to be infirm.*
*Genuine substance appears to be spurious.[1]*
*Vast space is devoid of corners.[2]*
*Great talent is late in maturing.*
*A high note can hardly be heard.*
*The Great Form has no sign.*
*Tao is hidden and has no name;[3]*
*Yet only Tao excels in contributing to achievement.*

This chapter serves to convey the peculiar impression Tao gives to people in general. Tao is understood and practiced only by the first-rate scholars. The second-rate already harbor some doubts about it. The third-rate apparently consider it a stark crazy thing. The non-scholars may have some even worse notion about it. All this is because Tao usually manifests itself in such a way as to be at odds with common sense. Indeed, the manifestation is so misleading as to give a contrary impression: people who are advancing toward Tao seem to be retreating from it, perfect purity seems to be tainted, and genuine substance seems to be fake or spurious. People may think a high note is very loud, but actually it is inaudible. They may think the Great Form is very striking, but actually it has no sign. Lastly, though Tao is excellent in helping people achieve success, it is usually hidden and as a result people may think that it does not exist at all.

Tao's nature being such, people with spiritual insights do not judge merely by outward appearance and behavior but always try to see through the surface to the reality beyond.

---

1. Cf. also Chapter 45.
2. This may be Lao Tzu's notion of infinite space, of which the center is everywhere but the circumference nowhere.
3. Cf. also Chapters 1, 14.

# 42
## TAO AND TRANSFORMATION
### Tao Hua

*Tao gave birth to One;*
*One gave birth to Two;*
*Two gave birth to Three;*
*Three gave birth to the ten thousand things.*
*The ten thousand things carry Yin and embrace*
*    Yang.*
*The two primordial breaths blend and produce*
*    harmony.*
*To be orphaned or lonely or unworthy[1]*
*Is what all people detest;*
*Yet kings and nobles apply those terms to*
*    themselves.*
*Indeed, things sometimes benefit by an intended*
*    injury,*

*And sometimes receive injury from an intended*
    *benefit.*[2]
*What others teach, I shall also teach:*
*"The strong and violent will die an unnatural*
    *death."*
*This will serve as my chief lesson.*

The first four lines of this chapter are among the most enigmatic in the *Tao Teh Ching*. Arthur Waley's explanation is as follows: "Tao gave birth to the One; One gave birth successively to two things, three things, up to ten thousand." This is not much of an explanation; it almost repeats the text verbatim or simply paraphrases it.

Those four lines represent another version of Lao Tzu's theory of cosmogony. As has been discussed in the comment for Chapter 39, "Tao gave birth to One," means Tao gave birth to Yang. "One gave birth to Two" means "—" (Yang, or Spirit, or Heaven) gave birth to "--" (Yin, or Matter, or Earth). In case this interpretation may seem rather odd, it should be noted that the Bible states that God made woman (Yin) from man (Yang). This can reasonably be regarded as equivalent to saying that Yin was originally derived from Yang, or Earth from Heaven.

How to explain "Two gave birth to Three"? "Three" symbolically means "☰", i.e. one long stroke plus two short ones; it means Yin and Yang together and united.

"Three gave birth to the ten thousand things" means that the union or the interplay of Yin and Yang produced and still produces all the diverse things in the world. This is why, immediately afterwards, Lao Tzu says: "The ten thousand things carry Yin and embrace Yang. The two primordial breaths blend and produce harmony." In other words, each creature is produced through the interplay of Yin and Yang, and embodies both principles.

Chapter 42, as interpreted above, thus gives a more adequate version of Lao Tzu's theory of cosmogony than elsewhere in the *Tao Teh Ching*. For instance, Chapters 1 and 25 only say that Tao is originator of Heaven and Earth, giving the impression that Heaven and Earth came out at the same time. But Chapter 42 makes the stages of creation amply clear.

The latter part of the chapter implies that Yin and Yang always tend toward balance and harmony and that cyclic reversion is the movement of Tao. According to these truths, it is decidedly advantageous to stay low rather than high, for the low tends to rise or to be exalted while the high tends to fall or to be laid low. Thus "things sometimes benefit by an intended injury, and sometimes receive injury from an intended benefit." Wise kings and nobles, therefore, prefer to consider themselves lowly and unworthy. The

182

strong and violent, on the other hand, are likely to meet with a violent death. All this indeed constitutes an important lesson for Lao Tzu who consequently favors peace and opposes violence.

---

1. Cf. also Chapter 39.
2. Cf. also Chapter 58.

## 43
### UNIVERSAL APPLICATION
### Pien Yung

*The softest things in the world*
*Can match and overcome the hardest.*[1]
*Non-being penetrates even the crackless.*
*Thus the value of non-interference is clear to me.*[2]
*The teaching without words,*
*And the virtue of non-interference,*
*Can hardly be matched in the world.*

We may infer the greatest conqueror is Non-being, for it ranks even below the weakest and softest thing. It is not surprising, therefore, that Non-being can penetrate even the crackless. From all this, Lao Tzu deduces the value and power of wordless teaching and non-action or noninterference.

The power of Non-being appears to be corroborated by science, as indicated in the following report which appeared in a San Francisco newspaper on December 31, 1978:

> Scientists from Western Washington University disclosed that they had carried out the first successful demonstration that neutrinos—mysterious nuclear particles that have neither electric charge nor mass—can be used to carry messages through the seas and the earth itself.

From the standpoint of common sense, neutrinos may be said to resemble Non-being most closely.

---

1. Cf. also Chapters 36, 40, 78.
2. Cf. also Chapters 2, 3, 10, 29, 37, 38, 47, 48, 57, 64.

# 44
## Self-Imposed Abstinences
## Li Chieh

*Which is more dear: Fame or health?*
*Which is more valuable: Health or wealth?*[1]
*Which is more baneful: Gain or loss?*
*Excessive love is bound to cause great expense.*
*Immense hoarding is bound to end in heavy loss.*
*He who knows contentment is free from disgrace;*[2]
*He who knows when to quit will be free from peril.*
*He can endure a long time.*

The prime purport of this chapter is to teach people that they should take a realistic look at the various values in life and make an intelligent choice or calculation. The didactic note obviously stresses the importance of life and health, and warns against achieving fame or wealth at the expense of life and health. Consequently, it praises the virtue of contentment and the wisdom of retreat at the right moment. It plainly states that contentment is essential to long life.

Christ offers practically the same teaching when he says: "For what is a man profited if he shall gain the whole world, and lose his own soul?" (Matt., 16:26.)

---

1. Cf. also Chapters 50, 75.
2. Cf. also Chapter 46.

# 45
## GRAND VIRTUE
### Hung Teh

*Great perfection seems imperfect;*
*Its utility will never deteriorate.*
*Great fullness seems hollow;*
*Its utility will be inexhaustible.*[1]
*The most straight appears to be bent;*
*The most skillful appears to be awkward;*
*The most eloquent appears to be stammering.*[2]
*Hastiness subdues cold;*
*Quiescence subdues heat.*
*Purity and quiescence are the norms of the*
*    universe.*

Like Chapter 41, this chapter shows that the appearance of Tao is misleading from the standpoint of common sense, though its utility is perennial. Consequently we must not judge things or people merely by their outward appearance. A fellow may appear dumb but may turn out to be very bright and intelligent. What appears to be an adverse turn of fortune may in fact be a key to prosperity. The wisdom of Tao does not always correspond to the wisdom of men. This somehow reminds one of the following statement by St. Paul:

> The foolishness of God is wiser than men; and the weakness of God is stronger than men. God hath chosen the foolish things of the world to confound the wise; and God hath chosen the weak things of the world to confound the things which are mighty. (I Cor., 1:25, 27.)

The last three lines of the chapter would seem to indicate that Yin and Yang always tend toward balance and harmony. When in harmony, they constitute the normal state of the universe. The harmony will lead to purity and quiescence.

---

1. Cf. also Chapters 4, 11.
2. Cf. also Chapter 41.

# 46
## MODERATION OF DESIRE
## Chien Yu

*When the world goes in accord with Tao,*
*Horses are used for hauling manure.*
*When the world is out of keeping with Tao,*
*Horses are reared in the suburbs for war.*
*No sin is greater than yielding to desires;*
*No misfortune greater than not knowing*
    *contentment;[1]*
*No fault greater than hankering after wealth.*
*Therefore, know contentment!*
*He who knows contentment is always content.[2]*

The general purport of this chapter is the importance of Tao to the world. When Tao prevails in the world, men and beasts and natural resources are used for the production of food and other necessities of life for the welfare of the people. When Tao is eclipsed, they are wasted in warfare with all its disastrous consequences.

What are the factors that cause the eclipse of Tao? They are inordinate desires, discontent, and greed, especially of the rulers. They are, therefore, denounced by Lao Tzu as sin, misfortune, and grievous fault—all contrary to Tao. On the other hand, contentment is a blessing. It is an antidote to human greed and ambition and will lead to peace.

Christ expresses the same wisdom when he says: "Take heed and beware of covetousness: for a man's life consisteth not in the abundance of things he possesseth." (Luke, 12:15.)

---

1. Cf. also Chapter 44.
2. Cf. also Chapter 33. There are two Chinese words with the sound of *chih,* one meaning *know,* the other indicating the possessive case, like the English *of.* Some versions of the *Tao Teh Ching* translate the word in the former sense, and some in the latter. The former sense is adopted here.

# 47
## FAR SEEING
## Chien Yuan

*Without going out of doors,*
*One can know the world;*
*Without looking through the window,*
*One can realize the Way of Heaven.*
*The farther one goes,*
*The less one knows.*
*Therefore, the Sage knows without going out,*
*Discriminates without seeing,*
*And accomplishes without action.*[1]

In these modern days of radio, television, newspapers, and magazines, it is evident that one can know much of the world without going out of doors. But in Lao Tzu's time, there were none of those media of communication. The first and immediate impression one receives from this chapter, therefore, is that it deals with occult powers such as clairvoyance and clairaudience. This may be a correct impression and may lead to a right interpretation.

But other interpretations, even of a scientific nature, are possible. The first two lines are certainly true of theoretic physics. Many truths, not only of the world but even of the universe, were originally theories. The most famous is, of course, Einstein's theory of relativity, which was worked out by the great scientist long before it was verified by experiment.

The third and fourth lines also state a fact. Philosophers can realize the Way of Heaven or Divine Will by inner philosophizing and contemplation, while mystics usually do so through meditation as well as contemplation.

The fifth and sixth lines are susceptible of two interpretations. First, they mean that the farther one goes outward and gets entangled in external activities, the less one knows about Tao. Secondly, they may refer to one's scope of knowledge. Some people want to know something about everything, and the farther they expand their scope the more superficial they become. On the other hand, some people want to know everything about something, and the more they stay within their scope the more expert they become.

The last three lines apply especially to people like Einstein and Thomas Edison. From truths already known, they can deduce other truths or create something new without going out of their office or laboratory. Such a faculty may appear incredible but it is well known. The Confucians recognized it a long time ago, and attributed it to sincerity. "Sincerity is the way of Heaven. The attainment of sincerity is the way of men. He who possesses sincerity is he who, without an effort, hits what is right, and apprehends without the exercise of thought."[2]

1. Cf. also Chapters 2, 3, 10, 29, 37, 38, 48, 57, 64.
2. *Chung Yung (Doctrine of the Mean),* Chapter 20. James Legge's translation.

## 48
### FORGETTING KNOWLEDGE
## Wang Chih

*To learn, one increases day by day;*
*To cultivate Tao, one reduces day by day.*
*Reduce and reduce and keep on reducing,*
*Till the state of non-action is reached.*[1]
*With non-action there is nothing that cannot be*
    *done.*
*Therefore, he who wins the world*
*Always resorts to non-action.*
*Once he resorts to action,*
*He will not be qualified to win the world.*

This chapter is very important for spiritual cultivation or the cultivation of Tao. Lao Tzu contrasts such cultivation with the process of learning. Learning aims at gathering more and more knowledge and experience, while the cultivation of Tao is a thorough cathartic process and requires constant unlearning or reducing of knowledge and experience as well as desires and impressions which obstruct the flow or manifestation of Tao. Non-action practically means the spontaneous flow of Tao or absence of human wilful efforts.

In a sense this teaching bears a strong resemblance to the well known sixth Beatitude advanced by Christ: "Blessed are the pure in heart, for they shall see God."

1. Cf. also Chapters 2, 3, 10, 29, 37, 38, 47, 57, 64.

# 49
## TRUST IN VIRTUE
### Ren Teh

*The Sage has no fixed state of mind;*
*His reflects the state of mind of the people.*
*To the good, I show goodness;*
*To the not good, I also show goodness.*[1]
*Hence goodness is realized.*
*To the sincere, I show sincerity;*
*To the insincere, I also show sincerity;*
*Hence sincerity is realized.*
*While in the world, the Sage is very anxious*
*To harmonize his mind for the harmony of the world.*
*To him all the people turn their eyes and ears;*
*He treats them all alike as children.*

The first two lines of this chapter are strongly reminiscent of the following statements in the *Shu Ching (Book of History)*: "Heaven sees as the people see, and hears as the people hear." This shows that the Sage possesses perfect virtue and is well versed in the way of Heaven. He treats all people alike with impartiality and even-handed justice. In so doing, he benefits other people but meets with no harm himself, for he is in a position to influence and not to be influenced. Since he is perfect in virtue, good people cannot add to his goodness and bad people cannot detract from it, while he himself can make bad people good and good people better, thereby fulfilling or realizing his own goodness. The same may be said of his relation with sincere and insincere people. He is anxious to harmonize his mind so that he can bring into harmony the various kinds of people in the world. He is therefore well liked by the people, for he treats them with love.

The last line may cause some misunderstanding. Some readers may think the Sage adopts a condescending attitude toward the people, considering them as immature. But in the *Tao Teh Ching* children are considered a symbol of Tao and therefore should be treated with love and affection.

It may be worthwhile to point out that the third to the eighth lines are similar in tenor to the following remark by Christ: "Love your enemies, bless them that curse you, do good to them that hate you, and pray for them which despitefully use you and persecute you." (Matt., 5:44.)

---

1. Cf. also Chapter 63.

# 50
## IMPORTANCE OF LIFE
# Kuei Sheng

*As life emerges, death enters.*
*The agents of life are thirteen;*
*The agents of death are likewise thirteen;*
*The thirteen also may make men move in a death*
*    spot.*
*Why so? Because life is lived in too intense a*
*    manner.*[1]
*I have heard that—*
*He, who is adept in guarding his life,*
*Will not come across rhinoceros and tigers,*
*When travelling on land;*
*And when in the armed forces,*
*Will not get wounded by deadly weapons.*
*In him the rhinoceros can find no place to butt,*
*Nor can the tiger find any place to claw,*
*Nor can the weapons find any place to injure.*
*Why so? Because there is no death spot in him.*[2]

The first part of this chapter is highly enigmatic. The enigma lies around the Chinese phrase: *shih yu san,* which may mean three out ten, or ten plus three. The latter meaning was adopted by Han Fei Tzu (d. 233 B.C.), a founder of the Legalist school of philosophy. His commentary on the *Tao Teh Ching* is the earliest, as he lived closer to the time of Lao Tzu than any other commentator. Also, he had a keen mind, so his choice is followed here.

The first line of the chapter appears somewhat absurd, but actually embodies a truth. Birth is the beginning not only of life but also of death. As his life progresses, man daily approaches nearer and nearer the grave.

According to Han Fei Tzu, "thirteen" represents the four limbs and the nine exterior orifices of the human body. These thirteen are considered by Lao Tzu, not without reason, as channels of death as well as of life. They are also channels whereby men are made to "move in a death spot," i.e., to make life a living death. This term may seem self-contradictory, but nevertheless makes sense. As some philosophers, notably Plato and Aristotle, have taught, life should be spent in the exercise of its highest faculties. When men devote their lives to frivolous activities and neglect their highest

190

faculties, their lives may be termed a living death. Of course, when a man suffers from certain diseases and is unable to exercise his faculties, his life may also be termed a living death. In either case, the thirteen appendages act as the channels of the evil influence.

As the title of the chapter indicates, Lao Tzu considers it important to improve and preserve one's life instead of merely letting it end in death or degenerate into living death. Though in other passages he suggests that immortality is only spiritual, in the latter part of this chapter he virtually says that life can be made immortal, physically as well as spiritually. The last line is definitive. Man's body can be rendered free from death spots.

---

1. Cf. also Chapters 44, 75.
2. Cf. also Chapters 16, 33, 52, 59.

## 51
### NOURISHING VIRTUE
## Yang Teh

*Tao produces all things;*
*Teh (virtue) rears them;*
*Material elements shape them;*
*Environmental forces perfect them.*
*That's why of the ten thousand things,*
*None does not honor Tao and exalt Teh.*
*Tao is honored and Teh is exalted,*
*Not in obedience to anyone's command,*
*But always in accord with Innate Freedom.*
*Thus while Tao produces things, Teh rears them,*
*Brings them up, develops them, perfects them,*
*Matures them, feeds them, and shelters them.*
*To produce but not to claim ownership,*
*To act but not to presume on the result,*
*To lead but not to manipulate—*
*This is called Mystic Virtue.*[1]

191

This chapter says, in effect, that the whole universe and all things therein are the spontaneous manifestation of Tao, produced without anything resembling human calculation or ulterior motive. Hence it appears utterly indifferent to its own creations, making no effort to own them or make use of them. This brings to mind the following passage in the Christian Gospel: "Behold the fowls of the air: for they sow not, neither do they reap, nor gather into barns; yet your heavenly Father feedeth them." (Matt., 6:26.)

Tao and Teh are essentially the same thing. Teh comes from Tao. When Tao is differentiated among the myriad creatures, it becomes Teh of the individual creatures. Teh, therefore, is what makes each creature what it is. Every creature, conscious of its origin, thus has a natural and intimate kinship with Tao and Teh and, of its free accord, honors and exalts them. Such spontaneous manifestation and beneficence of Tao are expressive of its Mystic Virtue.

---

1. Cf. also Chapters 2, 10, 34.

# 52
## RETURN TO THE ORIGIN
## Kuei Yuan

*The world has a beginning as its mother.*
*Having got hold of the mother,*
*Know her children;*
*And having known the children,*
*Further hold on to the mother,*
*And you will survive the disappearance of the body.*[1]
*Stop up the aperture of the vessel (tui),*
*And shut the doors (of the senses),*
*And you will not be devitalized all your life.*
*Open the aperture of the vessel,*
*And fulfill your carnal affairs,*
*And your whole life will be beyond salvation.*
*To be able to see the minute is to have keen vision;*
*To be able to remain docile is to be strong.*
*Make use of the light,*
*Withdraw its brilliance inward,*
*Cause no injury to your body—*
*This is called "Abide by the Immutable."*

Apart from mystic meditation and yoga, this chapter has little meaning or significance. Those intellectuals who do not believe in mysticism or meditation may be hard put to figure out its coherent purport.

The whole chapter deals with inner cultivation. The essential idea is the reversal of the natural physiological process, that is to say, turning upward or sublimating the life force instead of letting it go downward as is natural, and withdrawing from outward life so as to concentrate on the inward. The next few lines speak of the danger of indulging in the sensual life and the benefits of checking and restraining it.

*Tui* is one of the eight trigrams of the *I Ching:* ☱. It is a symbol for mouth and for a vessel or organ with an opening, such as the genital organ.

The whole chapter may be summed up in the following words of St. Paul: "For if ye live after the flesh, ye shall die: but if ye through the Spirit do mortify the deeds of the body, ye shall live." (Romans, 8.13)

A partial exposition of this chapter is presented in Chapter IV of Part One of this work.

---

1. Cf. also Chapters 16, 33, 50, 59.

# 53
## INCREASING EVIDENCE
## I Cheng

*If I were determined, with the knowledge I have,*
*To walk along the Great Highway,*
*My only fear would be to stray from it.*
*The Great Highway is very safe and plain;*
*Yet people prefer the bypaths.*[1]
*While the Court is very magnificent,*
*The fields have become very barren,*
*And the granaries have become very empty;*
*Yet officials are dressed in gorgeous garments,*
*Carry sharp swords,*
*Gorge themselves with sumptuous food and drink,*
*And possess a superabundance of precious articles.*
*Such patent robbery is the usher of other*
*robberies.*[2]
*Verily it goes contrary to Tao.*[3]

In this chapter, Lao Tzu stresses the importance of following unswervingly the Great Highway, Tao, and laments the reprehensible tendency of deviating from it, especially on the part of rulers and officials.

It is plain that the Great Highway for rulers and officials is to work for the interest and welfare of the people, which eventually will redound to their own interest and welfare. But they are prone to deviate into the bypaths and pursue their selfish interests to the detriment of the people. Hence while the fields are lying fallow and the people are suffering on the verge of starvation, the Court is full of splendor, and the officials have good food and drink and fine clothes and precious articles in their homes. The entire situation is obviously wrong. Though the official facade is glittering and imposing, the state is corrupt at the very core. All this is because the officials give top priority to the decoration of the outward appearance and not to the consolidation of the state by promoting the welfare of the people. Their statecraft is wholly unworthy of the name. It practically degenerates into robbery. This is bad enough but, what is worse, it will induce the people to resort to robbery also, for the people always follow the example of the officials above them.

---

1. Cf. also Chapter 70.

2. This line is largely a free translation of the two Chinese words: *tao u* (lit., tao flute). In his treatise on Lao Tzu, Han Fei Tzu (d. 233 B.C.) points out that *u* is a leading voice or instrument whose melody has to be followed or harmonized by other voices or instruments. *Tao u* is, therefore, here taken as meaning robbery that will lead to, or usher in, other robberies, i.e., lesser robberies on the part of the people who usually follow the example set by the officials.

3. Cf. also Chapters 41, 77.

# 54
## RECTIFYING VIEWPOINTS
## Hsiu Kuan

*Those adept in establishing themselves*
*Cannot be plucked up;*
*Those adept in the act of embracing*
*Cannot be made to relax their hold.*
*They are worshipped for generations in a row.*
*Cultivate Tao in one's person,*
*And its virtue will be genuine;*
*Cultivate Tao in one's family,*
*And its virtue will be overflowing;*
*Cultivate Tao in one's village,*
*And its virtue will be long enduring;*
*Cultivate Tao in one's state,*
*And its virtue will be abundant;*
*Cultivate Tao in one's empire,*
*And its virtue will be pervasive.*
*Therefore,*
*By one's person, one sizes up other persons;*
*By one's family, one sizes up other families;*
*By one's village, one sizes up other villages;*
*By one's state, one sizes up other states;*
*By one's empire, one sizes up other empires.*
*How do I know this is so with the empire?*
*By this.*[1]

A dominant note of this chapter is the close relation between Tao and Teh. Tao can be cultivated by man, and once obtained it becomes Teh. The word "cultivate" *(hsiu)* indicates that Tao or the seed of Tao is inherently implanted in man, only it is often neglected. It therefore has to be cultivated before it can shoot up and blossom and bear fruit. In other words, it has to be cultivated before it can shine forth as the sterling character of man. A man of sterling character is invulnerable to outside temptations and unshakable in his uprightness. He is firm and adept in establishing and embracing what is good and will enjoy the fruits of his virtue indefinitely.

Tao can be cultivated not only in one's person, but also in various social units, either by the head of each unit or by all members. It follows that each person or each social unit, after possessing Teh, can serve as a model or standard for sizing up other persons or other social units of the same kind.

1. This phrase is uncertain in meaning. It may mean "by Tao."

## 55
### THE MYSTIC CHARM
## Hsuan Fu

*He who is profoundly endowed with virtue*
*May be compared to an infant.*
*Poisonous insects do not sting him;*
*Wild beasts do not seize hold of him;*
*Birds of prey do not pounce upon him.*[1]
*Weak in bone and soft in sinews,*
*He yet has a firm grip.*
*Though ignorant of intercourse between the sexes,*
*His genital organ is yet firm and strong,*
*Indicating the plenitude of his vital essence.*
*He may scream all day,*
*Yet his voice does not become hoarse,*
*Indicating the plenitude of his inner harmony.*
*To know harmony is to accord with the*
*    Immutable;*
*To accord with the Immutable means*
*    enlightenment.*
*Improvement in health is a good omen;*[2]
*Mental control of the breath means strength.*[3]
*Things begin to decay after reaching the prime.*[4]
*Decay indicates disregard of Tao.*
*Whatever disregards Tao soon vanishes.*

In this chapter, Lao Tzu idealizes and glorifies the infant as a symbol of Tao. The third, fourth, and fifth lines may sound strange but can be explained in various ways. First, the perfect innocence of the infant will not arouse the hostile intent on the part of the dangerous creatures. Secondly, the infant may be under divine protection, like the followers of Moses in their exodus from Egypt. Thirdly, the infant may be possessed of some mystic power which could ward off dangers and prevent injuries. It will be remembered that in sending his disciples forth to proclaim the Kingdom of

Heaven, Jesus said to them: "Behold, I give unto you power to tread on serpents and scorpions, and over the power of the enemy: and nothing shall by any means hurt you." (Luke, 10:19.)

The last few lines of the chapter refer to the cyclic reversion of Tao (Cf. Chapter 40) and warn people against disregarding it; decay and decline will surely set in if the warning is not heeded. They also touch on the subject of yoga, indicating that inner harmony may lead to enlightenment and that mental control of the breath is conducive to good health.

---

1. Cf. also Chapter 50.
2. Note the term *pu hsiang* (ill omen) in Chapter 78.
3. The word *ch'iang* (strength) appears also in Chapters 33, 52.
4. Cf. also Chapters 9, 15, 29, 30, 32.

# 56
## MYSTIC VIRTUE
## Hsuan Teh

*Those who know do not speak;*
*Those who speak do not know.*
*Stop up the aperture of the vessel,*
*Shut the doors of the senses,*[1]
*Blunt the sharp,*
*Unravel the tangled,*
*Harmonize with the light,*
*Merge with the dust,—*[2]
*This is called Mystic Assimilation.*
*Men with this attainment, therefore, are*
*Above endearment or estrangement,*
*Above enrichment or impoverishment,*
*And above exaltation or degradation.*
*Therefore they are highly honored by the world.*

The first two lines of this chapter are perhaps the most memorable ones in the *Tao Teh Ching,* and consequently are most often quoted. Indeed, if in a party or any meeting there is a talkative fellow who would spew out of each corner of his mouth a long and tortuous torrent of words, it may be a good idea to quote the two lines with tongue in cheek in order to check him by mocking him.

Some people, in fact, may think that Lao Tzu mocked himself. Consider, for instance, the following poem by Po Chu-i, one of the famous poets of the T'ang dynasty:

Those who speak do not know;
Those who know do not speak.
This is what Lao Tzu told us.
If we believe that he himself was the one who knew,
Why, then, did he write as many as five thousand words?

Would Lao Tzu indeed have mocked and discredited himself? Hardly likely. A proper interpretation would seem to be that the first two lines serve as a prelude to what is said in the succeeding lines where Lao Tzu speaks about some yoga practice and gives hints as to its effect. The purport of the first two lines may be this: Those who have experienced and known the yoga effect do not speak about it, while those who speak about it really do not know and do not have the experience.

The third and fourth lines of the chapter also appear in Chapter 52, and the four lines beginning with "Blunt the sharp" appeared in Chapter 4. They all are related to the practice of yoga and spiritual cultivation. The main purpose is to shut off outside distractions or, failing that, to neutralize them and adapt to them, so that they will not disturb one's inner peace and serenity. A person who succeeds in doing that will have some profound and transcendental experience which is beyond the expressive power of human speech. Such a person has a higher or different scale of values and is not influenced by such worldly values as wealth or fame or honor or even affection. He is truly the glory of the world and deserves to be highly honored, for he personally demonstrates that man is capable of a higher stage of evolution.

The Confucian sage, Mencius, has more or less the same conception of a great or honorable man. Following is one of his best known remarks: "He who cannot be prostituted by riches and honors, nor deflected from the right course by poverty and lowliness, nor made crooked by the high and mighty—such is what is called a great man."

---

1. Cf. also Chapter 52.
2. Cf. also Chapter 4.

# 57
## ATMOSPHERE OF INNOCENCE
# Ch'un Feng

*Use justice to rule a country;*
*Use strange tactics to conduct battles;*
*Use non-assertion to win the world.*[1]
*How do I know this should be the case?*
*By this—*
*When the world abounds in prohibitions,*
*The people will become impoverished.*
*When men have plenty of weapons in hand,*
*The state will be in great confusion.*
*When men have plenty of techniques and skills,*
*Queer articles will crop up in abundance.*
*When laws and decrees are numerous and*
    *manifest,*
*Bandits and robbers will increase and multiply.*
*Therefore, the Sage has said—*
*I practice non-interference,*[2]
*And the people reform themselves;*
*I love to be quiescent,*[3]
*And the people become upright;*
*I do not assert myself,*
*And the people become wealthy;*
*I cherish no desires,*[4]
*And the people become simple and innocent.*


It is generally agreed among scholars that the *Tao Teh Ching* was intended for the edification of the prince or ruler. This chapter, especially, may be taken as a typical political sermon.

The first three sentences are statements of principle.

The middle portion is negative in character, for it sets forth what a ruler ought not do, namely, interfere in the life of the people. It should be noted that Lao Tzu is not against prohibitions, nor against weapons, nor against techniques and skills, nor against laws and decrees, but against an excess or overabundance of those things. In his opinion, such an abundance only defeats the purpose and will only make the people poor and desperate and cause confusion and disorder in the state.

The last portion is positive in character. It sets forth what Lao Tzu thinks the ruler ought to do, namely, the practice of Wu Wei. Noninterference, quiescence, nonassertion, and desirelessness are all peculiar characteristics of Wu Wei, and they have the merit of making the people upright, wealthy, innocent, and able to reform themselves.

Lao Tzu does not say in this chapter what he considers to be strange tactics. In Chapter 69, he expresses some views on the matter, and they are all consistent with Wu Wei.

---

1. Cf. also Chapter 63.
2. Cf. also Chapters 2, 3, 10, 29, 37, 38, 47, 48, 64.
3. Cf. also Chapters 26, 37, 45, 61.
4. Cf. also Chapters 3, 19, 34.

# 58
## TRANSFORMATION WITHOUT FRICTION
## Shun Hua

*When the government is shrouded in gloom,[1]*
*The people will be simple and honest.*
*When the government is sharp and officious,*
*The people will get disgusted and discontented.*
*Misfortune is what fortune leans on;*
*Fortune is where misfortune conceals itself.[2]*
*Who can know the ultimate result?*
*Is there no justice?*
*Anyway, justice will become injustice again,*
*And good will turn into evil once more.*
*Mankind has been thus deluded for a long time.*
*That's why the Sage acts four-square,*
*But does not "cut" people to his own shape;*
*He has a high sense of integrity,*
*But is not offensive to people.*
*He is upright and straightforward,*
*But does not push people around;*
*He is bright and brilliant,*
*But does not outshine people.*

This chapter serves as another commendation of Wu Wei or noninterference, although the word is not mentioned. The first two lines indicate the good effects of a noninterfering government, while the next two lines indicate the evil effects of an interfering one.

The passage from the 5th to the 11th line amounts to an explanation as to why interference should be avoided. It says that human reason or foresight is fallible for things are constantly in a state of change and there may be unforeseen circumstances beyond human calculation and expectation. Consequently, both fortune and misfortune may be misleading and deceptive. Hence the two oft-quoted lines about fortune and misfortune. Their truth is perhaps the source of the following Japanese proverb: "Pleasure is the seed of pain; pain is the seed of pleasure." *(Raku wa ku no tane; ku wa raku no tane.)*

The last portion of the chapter idealizes the Sage as the person who eschews interference in the affairs of the people but simply cultivates himself as a model for the people to follow. He teaches through silence, without words. Possibly he also radiates beneficent vibrations which would influence the people and impel them to do good.

---

1. Cf. also Chapter 17.
2. Cf. also Chapter 42.

# 59
## ADHERENCE TO TAO
## Shou Tao

*In ruling men and serving Heaven,*
*Nothing is comparable to a prudent economy.*
*A prudent economy means early preparation;*
*Early preparation means further accumulation of*
*    virtue;*
*Further accumulation of virtue can subdue everything;*
*The ability to subdue everything knows no bounds;*
*Knowing no bounds (in subduing opposition)*
*Can lead to the possession of a kingdom;*
*Possession of a kingdom along with its Mother*
*Can endure a long time.*
*This is called "deep roots and strong stalks."*
*It is the way to eternal life and everlasting vision.*[1]

---

1. Cf. also Chapters 16, 33, 50, 52.

This chapter symbolically furnishes a lesson in yoga. A partial exposition of it is presented in Chapter V of Part One of this work.

## 60
### MAINTAINING ONE'S POSITION
### Chu Wei

*Ruling a big country is like frying a little fish.*[1]
*When Tao is made to prevail in the world,*
*Evil spirits will lose their supernal power.*
*Not that they lose their supernal power,*
*But rather that the supernal power does no harm*
*    to people.*
*Not only the supernal power does no harm to*
*    people,*
*The Sage (Ruler) also will do no harm.*
*As both do not mutually cause any harm,*
*Virtue reverts to all parties respectively.*

The first line of this chapter is a favorite one for quotation. One wonders how it will appeal to the leadership in Peking, or the White House in Washington, or the Kremlin in Moscow. Would they be curious to know the secret? Let them note what Lao Tzu practically says: When Tao prevails in the world, ruling a big country will be easy. Why? Because when Tao prevails, neither evil spirits nor the rulers can or will hurt the people, and the supernal power cannot be employed to hurt the people. The people will be free from molestation and exploitation and will live a happy and contented life. In fact, all will be right with the world, for all parties and all beings will enjoy what they have received from Tao, namely, their individual virtue.

The first care of a ruler is to cultivate Tao and make it prevail in his state.

1. That is, without taking out the entrails and scratching off the scales, as when frying a big fish; in other words, without any interference. This chapter may serve as another lesson in Wu Wei.

# 61
## VIRTUE OF HUMILITY
## Ch'ien Teh

*A great country should assume a low position.[1]*
*Being the hub of the world,*
*It should play the part of the Female.[2]*
*The Female always employs quiescence*
*To subdue the Male, and takes a low position.*
*Therefore, a big country, stooping low,*
*Will win over a small country;*
*And a small country, staying low,*
*Will win over a big country.*
*Therefore, some stoop low to conquer,*
*And some stay low to conquer.*
*What a big country wants is merely*
*To absorb and support more people;*
*What a small country wants is merely*
*To enter a big country to offer services.*
*For each of the two to get what it wants,*
*The big country, therefore, should be lowly.*

As its title indicates, this chapter is an expatiation on the wonderful virtue of humility. This virtue is important not only for interpersonal relations but also for international relations.

The low position for the Female, signifying docile surrender to the Male, may give the impression of weakness but actually it leads to the quiet conquest of the Male by winning and shaping his heart. The title of Oliver Goldsmith's famous play, "She Stoops to Conquer," may serve to illumine the point.

Lao Tzu implies that humility is also sound and salutary as a principle of international policy. By showing humility or a conciliatory attitude in its diplomacy, a big country will win over a small country and *vice versa*, and each will satisfy what it wants. The big country preferably should take the initiative and assume a low position. On this point, one is reminded of the first sentence of Chapter 66, which reads: "That rivers and seas can be kings of all valleys is because they are adept in staying low."

Christ provides the same kind of teaching when he says: "Whosoever therefore shall humble himself as this little child, the same is greatest in the kingdom of heaven." (Matt., 18:3-4.)

---

1. Cf. also Chapters 7, 34, 66, 67.
2. Cf. also Chapter 10.

## 62

## Practicing Tao
## Wei Tao

*Tao is a mystery within all things.*[1]
*It is a treasure to the good men;*
*To the bad men it gives protection.*
*Fine words may be shown at the market place;*
*Noble deeds may serve as gifts to people.*
*Some people may not be good,*
*But why should any of them be discarded?*
*Therefore, when an emperor is enthroned,*
*Or when the three chief ministers are installed,*
*Though they may have fine pieces of jade*
*Respectfully presented before the team of horses,*
*There is nevertheless nothing better for them*
*Than to sit (in meditation) and advance in Tao.*
*For what reason did the ancients prize this Tao?*
*Did they not say: "With Tao one finds what one*
    *seeks,*
*And can get pardoned for one's offenses"?*
*Hence Tao is highly prized by the world.*

The first line of this chapter is another version of what has been said in Chapter 42: "All creatures carry Yin and embrace Yang."

In a mysterious way Tao is inherent in the constitution of every creature. Good men regard it as a treasure and try to follow it and stay tuned to it. Bad men may lack the will power to act up to it but nevertheless are protected by it. No creature can depart from the beneficent and vitalizing effect of Tao entirely.

The fourth and fifth lines have two slightly different Chinese versions. One version is translated as in the above text. The other may be translated as follows: "Fine words may be traded for honor. Fine deeds may serve as gifts to people." The essential idea underlying both versions is the same, namely, the transforming effect of Tao. Fine words stemming from Tao may be shown like merchandise in the market place for the people to see and select. Noble deeds stemming from Tao may serve as models or examples for the people to follow, thereby becoming their property like gifts. In either case, the people will be influenced—good people will become better and bad people will become good. There is, then, no reason to discard any of the bad people. Thus, as Lao Tzu has said in

Chapter 27, "the Sage is always good in saving people, thereby leaving no people unsaved."

With Tao a person will find and follow the right course. Even if he makes a mistake, he can repent and redeem himself. This is why the ancients prized Tao so highly.

The first care of an emperor or a king or any ruler and his ministers should be to practice meditation and cultivate Tao and make it prevail in the world. Here one is reminded of the tenor of Chapter 60 wherein Lao Tzu practically says that when Tao prevails, all will be right with the world.

The line "to sit (in meditation) and advance in Tao" in the text of the present chapter is a translation of the Chinese text: "*tso chin tz'u Tao.*" These four words literally mean either "sit advance the Tao" or "sit to present the Tao." Some commentators adopt the latter meaning and contend that the full purport is that "one should sit down and present Tao as a gift to the emperor and his ministers." This interpretation seems rather inept. In presenting things to superiors, politeness requires that one should be standing up, not sitting down. Furthermore, it is highly improbable that Tao can be presented from one person to another. If this could be done, Lao Tzu should have presented Tao to his king or emperor and saved the latter's dynasty from decline and fall.

---

1. Cf. also Chapter 1.

# 63
## ORIGIN OF FAVORS
## En Shih

*Practice non-interference.*[1]
*Assert non-assertion.*[2]
*Taste the tasteless.*
*Regard small as great, little as much.*
*Requite evil with virtue.*[3]
*Tackle difficult tasks while they are easy;*
*Perform great tasks while they are small.*
*Difficult tasks must be begun when yet easy;*
*Great tasks must be begun when yet small.*[4]
*That's why the Sage, to the end of his days,*
*Does not have to tackle great tasks,*
*And for this very reason achieves greatness.*[5]
*Promises lightly made show little good faith;*

*Duties neglected are bound to become difficult.*
*That's why the Sage assumes things to be difficult,*
*And never in life incurs any difficulty.*

Lao Tzu seems never tired of eulogizing Wu Wei or noninterference. But in this chapter, he goes a step further than in previous chapters. The important remark is: "Requite evil with virtue." This is different from the Confucian teaching: "Requite a grievance with justice." It shows that even when another person does something evil to you, you nevertheless should practice noninterference and assume a nonchalant attitude. Such teaching is essentially identical with that given by Christ when he says: "Love your enemies, do good to them who hate you." (Luke, 6:27.)

Noninterference does not mean doing nothing. It means spontaneously following the flow of Tao, that is, doing things without much volitional effort. This is why the whole chapter is practically an earnest exhortation to do things when they are at an early and easy stage, for things at such a stage can be dealt with easily, with little effort. This is what the Sage does, and consequently he will meet with no difficulties in achieving success and greatness.

Promises lightly made may be the result of misunderstanding a difficult task as easy, and so are apt to be broken. Duties neglected will become greater in scope as time goes on and consequently involve more difficulties.

---

1. Cf. also Chapters 2, 3, 10, 29, 37, 38, 47, 48, 57, 64.
2. Cf. also Chapter 57.
3. Cf. also Chapters 49, 62.
4. Cf. also Chapter 64.
5. Cf. also Chapter 34.

# 64
## Shou Wei

*What is secure can be easily maintained.*
*What is yet unmanifest can be easily tackled.*
*What is brittle can be easily broken.*
*What is puny can be easily scattered.*
*Act before any trouble starts.*
*Enforce order before disorder arises.*
*A big tree, whose girth fills a man's embrace,*
*Springs from a tender shoot.*
*A terrace nine stories in height*
*Rises from a heap of earth.*
*A journey one thousand miles long*
*Begins with the first step.*[1]
*He who interferes will fail;*
*He who grasps will lose.*[2]
*Therefore, the Sage does not interfere,*[3]
*And incurs no failure;*
*He does not grasp,*
*And suffers no loss.*
*People in handling their affairs*
*Often fail when within an ace of fulfilment.*
*Be circumspect at the end as at the beginning,*
*And there will be no failure.*
*Therefore the Sage desires what is not desired*
    *(by others),*[4]
*And does not treasure hard-to-get objects.*
*He learns what is not learned (by others),*
*And restores what the multitude has skipped.*
*He assists the natural trend of all things,*
*But dares not venture to tamper with it.*

In essence, this chapter is the same in tenor as the preceding one. It again stresses the wisdom of noninterference and the folly of interference. It gives examples of great things developing from small beginnings, and again suggests that duties or tasks should be attended to when they are at the initial easy stage or, better still, before they arise.

The chapter once more praises the Sage because he does not interfere in the natural trend of things and consequently meets with no failure or disaster.

One novel piece of advice given in this chapter is "Be circumspect at the end as at the beginning." In other words, once tackling a task at the early easy stage, one should continue to tackle it as it gradually develops until it is done. One should follow the example set by the Sage who does not skip any stage which appears undesirable or is difficult.

---

1. Cf. also Chapter 63.
2. Cf. also Chapter 29.
3. Cf. also Chapters 2, 3, 10, 29, 37, 38, 47, 48, 57, 63.
4. Cf. Chapter 8 wherein Lao Tzu says: "He (the Sage) stays in places detested by the multitude." Cf. also Chapter 78.

## 65
### Virtue of Innocence
Ch'un Teh

*The ancients who were adept in following Tao*
*Used it not to develop the people's intelligence,*
*But to keep the people simple-minded.*[1]
*People are difficult to rule,*
*Because they have too much knowledge.*
*Therefore, to use knowledge to rule a country*
*Inflicts a curse on the country;*
*Not to use knowledge to rule a country*
*Confers a boon on the country.*
*He who is aware of these two rules*
*Also sets a standard pattern (as the ancients did).*
*Awareness of the standard pattern is called*
*    Mystic Virtue.*
*As Mystic Virtue goes deep and reaches far,*
*And leads creatures to revert to their origin,*[2]
*Then Great Concord will prevail.*

This chapter is highly provocative, perhaps even offensive to many readers, perhaps even in previous centuries. The offensive idea is that the people should be kept simple-minded and that ruling a country with knowledge inflicts a curse on the country.

Ever since civilization began, knowledge has been generally considered necessary to life and important to government. In this light, Lao Tzu's anti-intellectual viewpoint is radically revolutionary, but this does not mean it makes no sense. It only shows how greatly different is Tao from knowledge and how far apart is Tao from the life of the ordinary people.

In Chapter 48, Lao Tzu frankly states that "to learn, one increases day by day; to cultivate Tao, one reduces day by day." This shows that Tao and knowledge are mutually incompatible. This is a great truth, endorsed by later philosophers and religious leaders. Nowhere, however, is it better dramatized than in the Old Testament of the Bible, where the story is told that Adam and Eve lost their state of original blessedness after eating of the tree of knowledge.

Lao Tzu, therefore, takes a very dim view of knowledge and sings the praises of Tao. In so doing, he may have been influenced not only by his own spiritual attainment but also by Chinese history. There was a Golden Age in the hoary past, when both the ruler and the ruled were simple-minded and lived a simple life in harmony with Tao. Lao Tzu may have adored that sort of paradise; but Lao Tzu lived in a very troubled period when the Chou dynasty was falling apart and tottering toward its downfall. The social and intellectual atmosphere was in a muddle and the people were contentious and difficult to rule. In these historical circumstances, it was highly probable that there lingered in Lao Tzu's mind a sharp contrast between the benign effects of Tao and the evil effects of knowledge—knowledge not in the form of what is now called scientific facts or truths but in the form of political notions, ideas, and isms. Such knowledge is positively divisive and detrimental to social unity and harmony. It is understandable, then, why Lao Tzu favored the ancient Taoists' position that the people should be kept simple-minded and that to use knowledge to rule a country would inflict a curse on the country.

Of course keeping the people simple-minded only for selfish reasons is an abuse of Lao Tzu's teaching. For him, the aim of keeping the people simple-minded is not merely to make them easier to rule but also to dispose them toward spiritual cultivation so that they may enjoy a higher happiness than is afforded by knowledge. In the latter part of this chapter Lao Tzu defines Mystic Virtue as awareness of the difference between the rule by knowledge and the rule by Tao; and says that when Mystic Virtue eventually leads people to revert to their original innocence, then Great Concord will prevail.

To ordinary people, happiness means the enjoyment of power and the gratification of desires. As knowledge is a key to power and can both create desires and find means to gratify them, it is highly prized by people. But Lao Tzu's conception of happiness is the enjoyment of Tao and the preservation of one's pristine purity and innocence through spiritual cultivation. In Chapter 20, he makes himself quite clear. He does not reprove the people for their love of creature comforts, but he does want and exhort the Ruler to lead and guide the people toward Tao.

In passing, one feels inclined to say that quite apart from Lao Tzu's philosophy and even from a Utilitarian standpoint, knowledge is not always a desirable thing. Just consider the wars and other conflicts in human history. Did not knowledge contribute to their horror and inhumanity?

It is also relevant to ask: Should life be spent in pursuing knowledge? Chuang Tzu says: "My life has a limit, but knowledge has no limit. To use the limited to pursue the unlimited is perilous."

There is also this question: Is knowledge always conducive to happiness? The great philosopher Kant gave a negative answer. In his *Fundamental Principles of the Metaphysic of Morals,* he says: "Knowledge may turn out to be a sharper eye to reveal to man the more horribly the evils now hidden from him but unavoidable and to intensify his desires which already cause him great concern." Kant may have been influenced by what is said in the Bible: "For in much wisdom is much grief: and he that increaseth knowledge increaseth sorrow." (Eccles., 1:18.)

An intellectual giant, therefore, is not necessarily a happy or a likable person unless he also has a high degree of moral or spiritual culture. In his *De Profundis,* Oscar Wilde reminds us: "When one has weighed the sun in the balance, and measured the steps of the moon and mapped out the seven heavens star by star, there still remains oneself. Who can calculate the orbit of his own soul?"

In pondering the above questions, one perhaps will find that the revolutionary anti-intellectual attitude of Lao Tzu is after all not so objectionable as it at first may seem.

---

1. Cf. also Chapters 3, 19.
2. Cf. also Chapters 16, 25, 40.

## 66

## APRES VOUS
## Hou Chi

*That rivers and seas can be kings of all valleys*
*Is because they are good in staying low.*[1]
*That's why they can be kings of all valleys.*
*Thus the Sage wishing to be above the people*
*Always speaks as if he were inferior to them;*
*And wishing to lead the people,*
*Always places himself behind them.*[2]
*So when the Sage occupies a high position,*
*The people do not feel any oppression;*
*And when he occupies a leading position,*
*The people do not receive any harm.*
*Therefore the world is glad to support him,*
*And never gets tired of doing so.*
*Because he does not contend,*[3]
*No one in the world can contend with him.*

The tune of this chapter is familiar, but the song is somewhat different. Here Lao Tzu gives another version of his pet subject, namely, humility and its merits. Once more he points to the Sage as a model of humility, inevitably receiving beneficent effects from that important virtue. In this chapter, however, Lao Tzu employs different observations and illustrations.

What are now rivers and seas were originally valleys. Because they lay lower than other valleys, they received water flowing out of those valleys and in course of time became what they are. The Sage also practices lowliness or humility in his relation with the people. Though he may be occupying a high position, he will neither harm nor oppress the people. With his non-contentious attitude, he would win their trust and support and become their leader.

Christ also teaches humility but in his own way. He says: "Whosoever will be great among you, let him be your minister; and whosoever will be chief among you, let him be your servant." (Matt. 20:26-27.)

In case anyone may think that humility could be used as a deceptive social strategy to attain power or prominence, it should be noted that humility must be genuine in order to produce the good effects. Fake or spurious humility, such as that practiced by

Uriah Heep in Dicken's novel *David Copperfield,* may have some temporary advantages, but in the long run it will not work. Besides, it is injurious to spiritual cultivation.

---

1. Cf. also Chapter 61.
2. Cf. also Chapters 7, 34, 61, 67.
3. Cf. also Chapters 8, 22, 68, 81.

# 67
## THREE TREASURES
## San Pao

*All the world says I am great*
*But rather odd and different from the ordinary.*
*Be it noted that greatness itself is the very reason*
*Why it appears rather odd and different from the*
  *ordinary.*
*If it had resembled the ordinary,*
*It would have become pettiness long ago.*
*I have three treasures.*
*Keep them and treasure them.*
*The first is compassion;*
*The second is frugality;[1]*
*The third is: Dare not be first in the world.[2]*
*Because compassionate, a person can be*
  *courageous;*
*Because frugal, he can expand his scope;*
*Because he dare not be first in the world,*
*He can develop his gifts of leadership.*
*Nowadays people are courageous without*
  *compassion,*
*Expand their scope without frugality,*
*And assume leadership without being humble.*
*They are doomed!*
*Compassion is invincible in offense,*
*And in defense invulnerable.*
*When Heaven wants to deliver a person from*
  *harm,*
*It grants him compassion as a protective charm.*

This chapter has some historical and autobiographical value, and resembles Chapter 20 in tenor and nature. It throws some bright gleams of light on the life of Lao Tzu and on the social conditions of his time.

The first two lines would seem to indicate that Lao Tzu was widely known in his time both as a person and for his teaching. People called him great, but considered him rather odd and his teaching incongruous with the current social trends.

Lao Tzu, however, points out that greatness necessarily involves incongruity with current social trends. Apparently as an illustration, he presents his three precious virtues—compassion, frugality, and humility—sets forth their merits, and clearly hints that they constitute his principal teaching as well as his greatness. He laments the fact that those three precious virtues ran counter to the social tendencies of his time, that the people were reluctant to practice them and consequently brought about their own doom.

Like so many other chapters, this chapter contains some teachings similar to Christ's. Following are two of the eight Christian Beatitudes: "Blessed are the meek: for they shall inherit the earth." "Blessed are the merciful: for they shall obtain mercy." (Matt., 5:5, 7)

Of the three treasures, compassion seems especially precious to Lao Tzu. It is also noteworthy that he prefers the word *tz'u* (here translated "compassion") to the word *ren* (benevolence) which is preferred by Confucius. *Tz'u* essentially means motherly love. As Lao Tzu glorifies the female and often uses *mother* as a symbol for Tao, it is understandable that the word *tz'u* better suits his taste.

---

1. Cf. also Chapter 59.
2. Cf. also Chapters 7, 34, 61, 66.

# 68
## HARMONY WITH HEAVEN
### P'ei T'ien

*A good warrior is not warlike;*
*A good fighter does not lose his temper;*
*A good conqueror is not pugnacious;*
*A good leader of men is humble.*
*This is called the virtue of non-contention,*[1]
*Also called the use of other's strength,*
*Also called harmony with Heaven's Eternal*
   *Supreme Will.*

This chapter dramatizes the virtue of noncontention which is closely related to humility and noninterference. The first four lines give vivid examples of all the three related virtues.

In reference to noninterference, the chapter points out another feature, namely, "use of other's strength." To illustrate, if a person throws a punch at you, it is less effective to force it back with some effort than to pull the other fellow's fist in the direction it is going. This will make him fall headlong on the ground—with his own strength.

The last line means harmony with Tao.

---

1. Cf. also Chapters 8, 22, 66, 81.

## 69
### MYSTIC APPLICATION
### Hsuan Yung

*Military strategists have said—*
*I dare not be the host,*
*But prefer to be the guest.*
*I dare not advance one inch,*
*But prefer to retreat a foot.*
*This is called—*
*Marching as if without motion;*
*Brandishing arms as if having none;*
*Attacking as if without enmity;*
*Seizing as if without weapons.*
*No disaster is greater than belittling the enemy.*
*Belittling the enemy almost ruins my treasures.*[1]
*Therefore, when two armies encounter each other,*
*The side that laments war will win.*[2]

This chapter is similar in general purport to the preceding one. It may be looked upon as a vivid illustration of Wu Wei or doing things with minimum effort as if spontaneously following Tao. Perhaps apprehensive lest noninterference be misunderstood to mean belittling the enemy, Lao Tzu seriously warns against this haughty or arrogant way of treating the enemy, calling it the greatest disaster. Why? Because it is contrary to his three treasures: compassion, frugality, and humility. In other words, one should practice the three virtues even in dealing with one's enemy in war, for the side that shows compassion will win.

---

1. Cf. also Chapters 22, 67.
2. Cf. also Chapters 31, 76.

# 70
## DIFFICULT TO UNDERSTAND
## Chih Nan

*My teaching is very easy to understand,*
*And very easy to carry out.*
*Yet the world is incapable of understanding it,*
*And incapable of carrying it out.*[1]
*My teaching has an ancient source,*
*My practices have a ruling principle.*
*As people are ignorant of this,*
*So they fail to understand me.*
*When those who understand me are few,*
*Then I am distinguished indeed.*[2]
*That's why the Sage wears a coarse cotton robe,*
*To conceal the jade ornament worn on his bosom.*

In this chapter, Lao Tzu speaks candidly of his own teaching. In writing the first two lines, he may have felt the same way as Christ did when he said: "My yoke is easy and my burden is light." (Matt., 11:30.) But Lao Tzu goes on to deplore the ignorance of the people who were unable to understand his teaching, much less carry it into practice. He knows, however, the reason why. His teaching is based on an ancient source, and his practices are governed by a principle. But the people were ignorant of the ancient source and the principle; so they did not understand him. He consoles himself, however, by noting that the fewer the people who understand him, the more distinguished he becomes. In a sense, this is indeed true. A recent case in point is Einstein. His theory of relativity is understood by so few people that Einstein himself, as well as his theory, is highly respected and honored.

Lao Tzu does not say what is the ancient source of his teaching or the ruling principle of his practices. If one may venture an opinion, the former is probably the *I Ching* or *Book of Changes* which had been in existence long before Lao Tzu was born; the latter is almost certainly Tao.

215

The last two lines are sometimes interpreted as indicating humility or modesty, without any self-display or show-off. But such interpretation does not quite fit into the meaning of the preceding lines. In the light of those lines, the reason why the Sage conceals his jade ornament beneath a cotton robe is that he wants only a few people to see it so that it will become precious and sought after by arousing more curiosity.

The same two lines may also have some sarcastic overtone. They are tantamount to saying "What is the use of casting pearls before swine?"

---

1. Cf. also Chapter 53.
2. Another possible translation of this Chinese sentence is: When those who understand me are few, then the few who follow me are distinguished. This also makes sense.

# 71
## KNOWING THE DISEASE
## Chih Ping

*He who knows what he does not know is superior.*
*He who does not know what he knows is diseased.*
*Only when a disease is recognized as a disease*
*Can the disease cease to be disease.*
*The Sage is free from disease;*
*He recognizes a disease as a disease,*
*Therefore he is free from disease.*

The underlying moral of this chapter seems to be: Be true to yourself; do not be vain and pretend to know anything when you are in fact ignorant of it. Confucius also warns against vain pretension to knowledge. He does not call it a disease but he suggests that it is better to be honest. Note his interesting and well-known remark: "Knowing is knowing. Not knowing is not knowing. That's knowing."

The way the human mind works is rather mysterious. Sometimes a person may sincerely think he knows something about something, but actually he does not. On the other hand, sometimes a person may indeed know something but he is not aware of his knowledge. Note, for instance, the following Arab maxims:

He who knows not, and knows not that he knows not, is a fool. Avoid him. He who knows not, and knows that he

216

knows not, is simple. Teach him. He who knows, and
knows not that he knows, is asleep. Wake him. But he who
knows, and knows that he knows, is a wise man. Follow
him.

Lao Tzu would read the above maxims with an approving smile.

# 72
## Self-Respect
## Ai Chi

*When people no longer fear authority,*
*Great Authority will come to them.*
*Do not pen them up in narrow surroundings;*[1]
*Do not make them weary of life.*
*Only when they are not wearied,*
*Will they cease to be weary.*
*That's why the Sage has self-knowledge,*
*But does not display himself;*[2]
*He maintains his self-respect,*
*But does not feel high and mighty.*
*Forsooth, he rejects this and adopts that.*

This chapter shows Lao Tzu ranging himself on the side of the people and warning the government officials against resorting to
repressive measures. The first two lines are susceptible of two interpretations. One meaning is that when the people are no longer
afraid of the government authorities and are ready to rebel, the
sovereign power of state will come into their possession. The other
possible interpretation is that when the people no longer fear the
authorities, they will be visited with the wrath of Heaven (Great
Authority). The first interpretation seems to fit into the context
better. Lao Tzu had the making of a rebel in him. He wanted to
change the status quo.

The last few lines of the chapter were intended as an exhortation to the officials to imitate the Sage who is humble and does not
even try to outshine the people, much less dominate the people and
interfere with their lives.

---

1. Metaphorically, this means: Broaden their outlook on life.
2. Cf. also Chapters 22, 24.

# 73
## Natural Action
# Ren Wei

*Courage in daring leads to slaughter;*
*Courage in daring not leads to life.*
*Either may have its advantage or disadvantage.*
*When Heaven detests anything,*
*Who can know the reason why?*
*Thus even the Sage feels some difficulty here.*
*Heaven's way does not contend, yet excels in*
*winning;*
*It does not speak, yet excels in making response;*
*It receives no summons, yet would come of itself;*
*It is patient and easy-going, yet excels in*
*planning.*[1]
*The net of Heaven spreads far and wide;*
*Though its meshes are large,*
*Yet it allows nothing to slip through.*

In this chapter, Lao Tzu shows it is difficult for the finite human mind to know or understand the reason behind Heaven's way. He first points out two kinds of courage. Courage in daring is easy to understand. But courage in daring not is paradoxical and rather puzzling. Perhaps it should be likened to pacifist courage. Bertrand Russel once said that it required more courage to be a pacifist than to be a soldier. Lao Tzu favors this kind of courage and says it leads to life. But he also says that either kind of courage has its advantage or disadvantage. This is probably what makes him ask: "When Heaven detests anything, who can know the reason why?"

There are things objectionable to Heaven, and this implies there are also things agreeable to Heaven. But why does Heaven like some things and dislike others? Even the Sage among men can hardly find out.

Lao Tzu then proceeds to explain why it is difficult to find out the reason behind Heaven's way. In the latter part of the chapter, he gives illustrations to show that Heaven's way seems to have superhuman intelligence and can do things silently and efficiently without what human beings call action or effort. This is Wu Wei or non-interference par excellence. This is also why it is difficult to find out the reason behind Heaven's way, for Heaven's way manifests itself so spontaneously as to seem devoid of any motive or reason.

At the same time, the latter part of the chapter sets forth a serious warning against doing evil. The warning indicates there is such a thing as retributive justice. Though seemingly easy-going, Heaven plans so well that nothing can escape its notice. Though silent, Heaven responds to good or evil deeds with precision and accuracy, and it arrives at the scene without being summoned. And it always wins. All this points to the moral that good deeds will be rewarded and evil ones punished. Like the Hindus, the Chinese believe in karma. The last three lines of the chapter, therefore, have become a household proverb in China through the centuries.

Christ has his own peculiar version of the same teaching when he says: "Are not five sparrows sold for two farthings, and not one of them is forgotten before God?" (Luke, 12:6.) This is to say that God knows everything and will make the proper response.

---

1. Cf. also Chapters 3, 28, 37, 47. 48.

# 74
## SUBDUE DELUSION
### Chih Huo

*When the people are not afraid of death,*
*What avails it to scare them with death?*
*Assuming that they often do fear death,*
*And that any pervert can be seized and killed,*
*Who dares to do the killing?*
*It is the job of the Director of Death to kill.[1]*
*To take over the job of the Director of Death*
*Is like wielding the hammer for the master-builder.*
*He who wields the hammer for the master-builder*
*Seldom escapes wounding himself in the hand.*

219

In this chapter, Lao Tzu strikes a new note regarding Wu Wei and stresses the demerits of interference. The height of interference is reached in putting people to death. Lao Tzu, therefore, seriously warns government officials against resorting to that practice. He sternly asserts that killing people will have a boomerang effect on the killer.

He points out that people are not always afraid of death. The social situation confronting the people may be so hopeless and so oppressive and so fraught with evil that the death penalty will lose its sting. Then they will take the law into their own hands and rise in rebellion which, history shows, often leads to the overthrow of the powers that be. Rulers and government officials, therefore, should indeed consider carefully before putting people to death if they want to maintain social peace and avoid popular upheaval. They should also heed the warning raised by Christ: "All they that take the sword shall perish with the sword." (Matt., 26:52.)

---

1. The Director of Death is said to have, as its agents or agencies, various calamities such as pestilence, famine, lightning, earthquakes, and so on.

# 75
## THE HARM OF GREED
### T'an Sun

*The reason why the people are starving*
*Is that the officials "eat their taxes" too much.*
*That's why the people are starving.*
*The reason why the people are difficult to rule*
*Is that the authorities resort to interference.*
*That's why the people are difficult to rule.*
*The reason why the people make light of death*
*Is that they are too eager for high living.*
*That's why the people make light of death.*
*Those who have nothing to make life pleasurable*
*Are worthier than those who value high living.*

Lao Tzu seems tireless in harping upon the theme of noninterference or Wu Wei, so much so that the saying *"Wu Wei shih Tao"* (Noninterference is Tao) has gained currency in Chinese literature. In this chapter he attacks and denounces interference especially on the part of the government officials. He rebukes and warns those officials who resort to interference. He actually charges them with taxing the people to the point of starvation, thereby making them difficult to rule. Like Confucius, he considers high taxation as symbolic of bad government.

As the title of the chapter indicates, greed is harmful and is the underlying cause of interference. But Lao Tzu knows that the people are also greedy and interfere with their own lives and would even risk their lives for the sake of high living. The worst elements would commit crimes, while the better ones would work so hard and so long every day as to virtually become money-making machines. Unwittingly and unintentionally, they commit gradual suicide by overworking and overtaxing their energy in the hectic struggle for fame or power or wealth or pleasure. In Lao Tzu's view, people who live simply and preserve their life force and original nature are worthier than those who are eager to enjoy high living and luxury.

# 76
## ABSTAIN FROM HARDNESS
## Chieh Ch'iang

*Man is soft and weak at birth;*
*At death he is hard and rigid.*
*The ten thousand things, herbs and trees,*
*Are soft and delicate when growing up;*
*In dying, they wither and look haggard.*
*Thus hardness and rigidity are companions of*
*death;*
*Softness and weakness are companions of life.*
*Therefore armies, having become rigid, will not*
*win;*[1]
*Trees, having become rigid, will break asunder.*
*The big and rigid will be laid low;*
*The soft and weak will be lifted up.*[2]

In order to make out the sense of this chapter, it is helpful to remember what Lao Tzu has said in Chapter 40: "Weakness is Tao's function." What appears to common sense as weakness is a basic virtue from the standpoint of Lao Tzu's philosophy, conducive to the growth and development of other virtues such as humility, noncontention, and Wu Wei or noninterference. In this chapter, Lao Tzu considers it to be a necessary condition of life and points to the young plants as well as the infant, his pet object of contemplation, as evidence of this truth. The first line is reminiscent of Chapter 55 where he says of the infant: "Weak in bone and soft in sinews, he yet has a firm grip."

On the other hand, Lao Tzu denounces what is ordinarily considered to be strength. To him, strength tends to be rigidity and is a sign or condition of death. Life and death are, of course, the two extreme poles. In between the two poles, there is a wide variety of conditions. In general, it may be said that softness and weakness tend toward growth and good health, while hardness and rigidity tend toward poor health and decay. Softness and weakness are conducive to poise and relaxation, while hardness and rigidity lead to tension and stress.

Weakness and rigidity do not refer to physical conditions alone, but also to states of mind. Weakness is akin to humility and rigidity to pride or arrogance. As Lao Tzu sees it, humility is a favorable condition for success and victory, while pride or arrogance is a sure portent of failure and defeat. Just as a stiff plant which refuses to yield and bend will be broken by a strong wind, so an army which has become rigid will not win in war. A strong army is apt to grow rigid for more than one reason. First, a strong army tends to be arrogant and to underestimate the enemy. In Chapter 69, Lao Tzu says: "No disaster is greater than belittling the enemy." Secondly, a strong army often goes to extremes and fails to practice moderation, which violates another important Taoist teaching. (Cf. Chapter 31.) Thirdly, a strong army is prone to resort to unnecessary violence and is reluctant to show compassion and give quarters to prisoners. In both cases, it acts contrary to Taoist teaching. (Cf. Chapters 30 and 67.) An army liable to the above-mentioned faults will inevitably become rigid in its strategic thinking and tactical maneuvers. Very naturally, it will be impetuous to advance forward and seldom, if ever, think of retreat. Such an army may win some battles but will eventually lose the war.

The last two lines of the chapter sum up the wisdom of the preceding lines. Incidentally, it is worthwhile to note that Christ sees eye to eye with Lao Tzu when he says: "Every one that exalteth himself shall be abased; and he that humbleth himself shall be exalted." (Luke, 18:14.)

---

1. Cf also Chapters 30, 31, 69.
2. Cf also Chapters 77, 78

# 77
## THE WAY OF HEAVEN
## T'ien Tao

*The Way of Heaven,*
*Is it not like stretching the bow?*
*What is high is brought low;*
*What is low is pulled up;*[1]
*What is superfluous is taken off;*
*What is deficient is strengthened.*
*The Way of Heaven takes from what has a surplus*
*To supply what has a deficit.*
*The way of men acts differently.*
*It takes from what has a deficit*
*To serve what has a surplus.*
*Who will use his surplus to serve the world?*
*Only the man who is possessed of Tao.*[2]
*Thus the Sage acts but does not presume on the*
    *result;*
*He achieves success but does not claim any credit.*[3]
*Doesn't this show that he dislikes showing off his*
    *worth?*

The first eight lines of this chapter illustrate the Way of Heaven, which is another name for Tao. Tao is Yin and Yang in harmony; so Tao always tends toward harmony and balance. Hence what is high is brought low, and what is low is pulled up, and so on.

The next two lines show the way of men as contrary to the Way of Heaven.

The last few lines point out that the Sage follows not the way of men but the Way of Heaven. Hence he uses his surplus of goods to serve mankind. In so doing, he simply follows Tao and wants to establish harmony and balance or equality. He has no selfish ulterior motives.

Some commentators maintain that Christ's way is contrary to the Way of Heaven as conceived by Lao Tzu, by citing the following statement by Christ: "Whosoever hath, to him shall be given, and he shall have abundance; but whosoever hath not, from him shall be taken away, even that which he hath." (Matt. 13:12.)

However, Lao Tzu is talking about something like the distribution of wealth, while Christ is talking about the production of wealth. Immediately before Christ made the above remark, he set forth a parable about the sowing of seeds. Some seeds failed to produce anything while some fell on good ground and brought forth fruit aplenty. (Matt., 13:4-8.) It is but natural to sow more seeds on the good ground. And this is what Christ favors. There is no reason to assume that Lao Tzu would show objection to it. Lao Tzu also attaches great importance to prudence and frugality.

That Christ would show no objection to Lao Tzu's way of distribution may be seen from the following statement by St. Paul:

> For I mean not that other men be eased, and ye be burdened: But by an equality, that now at this time your abundance may be a supply for their want, that their abundance also may be a supply for your want: that there may be equality. (II Corinthians 8:13-14.)

---

1. Cf. also Chapters 76, 78.
2. Cf. also Chapter 41.
3. Cf. also Chapters 2, 10, 34, 51.

# 78
## Trust in Faith
## Ren Hsin

*Nothing in the world*
*Surpasses water in softness and weakness;*
*Yet among things that attack the hard and strong,*
*None can do a better job than water.*
*Nothing can serve as its substitute.*
*Therefore the weak overcomes the strong;*[1]
*The soft overcomes the hard.*[2]
*Few in the world do not know this;*
*Yet nobody is able to put it into practice.*
*Therefore the Sage says:*
*He who bears the blame for the ignominy of his*
    *country*[3]
*Can be called lord of the state;*[4]
*He who bears the blame for the misfortune of his*
    *country*
*Can become king of the world.*
*Statements of the truth seem paradoxical.*

This chapter is similar in tenor to Chapter 76. In both chapters, Lao Tzu deals with his pet theme: the superiority of the soft and weak over the hard and strong. In Chapter 76, he considers softness as the companion of life, whereas here he considers softness and weakness as the conqueror of hardness and strength. Water is one of his symbols for Tao; so in a sense this chapter proves that "weakness is the function of Tao," as set forth in Chapter 40.

He laments, however, that while most people know that weakness would conquer strength, none puts the doctrine into practice. As the title of the chapter indicates, they have no trust in their faith.

The last few lines were apparently intended as proof for the above paradoxical doctrine. He who bears the blame for the ignominy of his country and thereby is placed in a weak position would eventually rise to the highest post.

---

1. Cf. also Chapters 36, 43.
2. Cf. also Chapters 76, 77.
3. Cf. also Chapter 8.
4. Cf. also Chapter 13.

# 79
## Observance of Obligations
## Ren Ch'i

*In allaying a great grievance,*
*There is bound to be some grievance remaining.*
*How can this be called good?*
*Therefore the Sage holds the left tally,*
*But does not urge the other party to keep his*
*    word.*
*Thus the virtuous seeks to preserve the contract;*
*The unvirtuous seeks to blame the other party.*
*The Way of Heaven has no preferences,*
*But always suits the good man.*

The issue raised in this chapter is highly important in international as well as interpersonal relations. The issue is how to restore complete harmony between the parties concerned after some unpleasant episode has occurred—a harmony untainted by any trace of remaining resentment.

Lao Tzu's answer is that such restoration can be effected through the goodness or kindness shown by the party who has the upper hand. By way of illustrating his answer, he refers to the contract between creditor and debtor. In ancient China, a contract was made by splitting a piece of bamboo into two slips. The right slip was held by the debtor; the left slip, with the obligation of the debtor stipulated on it, was kept by the creditor. Usually the party with the left slip would press the other party for payment or lay some blame on him. But the Sage or the good man will not do this sort of thing, and his magnanimity would make the other party feel grateful instead of resentful.

The last two lines show that the good man will always be rewarded, not because he is preferred by Heaven, but because he acts in harmony with the Way of Heaven. This reminds one of the following remark by St. Paul: "And we know that all things work together for good to them that love God, to them who are the called according to his purpose." (Romans, 8:28.)

226

## 80

INDEPENDENCE
## Tu Li

*A state should be small in size and population.*
*It should teach the people not to use arms,*
*Even though arms may be found in abundance.*
*It should teach the people*
*To view death as a serious matter,[1]*
*And not to move to a far-away place.*
*Though there are boats and carriages,[2]*
*There is no occasion to use them;*
*Though there are arms and soldiers,*
*There is no occasion to stage public reviews.[3]*
*The people are taught—*
*To resume the practice of tying knots;[4]*
*To enjoy their daily food;*
*To wear beautiful clothes;*
*To enhance the comfort of their homes;*
*And to take delight in their social customs.*
*Neighbor states may be within sight of one*
*    another,*
*And the barking of dogs and the crowing of cocks*
*In one of them may be heard in the others,*
*Yet the people to the end of their days,*
*Do not maintain intercourse with their neighbors.*

This chapter outlines the features of the ideal state as envisioned by Lao Tzu. How simple and peaceful it is! Far, far more so than Sir Thomas Moore's Utopia.

People who know the social conditions of China may recognize that the description in this chapter fits almost completely the conditions of Chinese village life even in modern times. People in one village seldom have intercourse with people in another village. Their life is simple but not crude or devoid of refinements. There is social life but little luxury or vanity. Peace normally reigns, but there is no monotony. There are quite a number of festivals to celebrate during the year, and they are always occasions for joy and good will. Besides, there are weddings and funerals and childbirths and ancestor worship to stimulate activity and provide excitement. There is no use for boats or carriages, for villagers are strong and healthy and seldom travel far. There is no use for arms, for the people are usually friendly. In general, the conditions and the atmosphere are ideal for the development of virtue and spiritual cultivation. This is what Lao Tzu considers essential to life.

---

1. Ssuma Ch'ien, Grand Historian of China, has said: "Death may be as weighty as the mountain T'ai Shan or as light as a swan's feather."
2. Cf. Chapter 12.
3. Cf. Chapter 31.
4. To aid the memory, as in prehistoric times.

# 81
## EXPRESSING THE ESSENTIAL
### Hsien Chih

*Truthful words do not sound sweet;*
*Sweet words are not truthful.*[1]
*Good men do not argue;*
*Those who argue are lacking in goodness.*
*The seers of truth are not vast in learning;*
*People with vast learning are not seers.*[2]
*The Sage does not hoard.*
*The more he serves the people,*
*The more he gains.*
*The more he gives to the people,*
*The more he possesses.*
*The Way of Heaven is to benefit, not to harm;*
*The way of the Sage is to act, not to contend.*[3]

The last chapter reads like a general summary of the preceding eighty chapters. This is perhaps why it bears the title: "Expressing the Essential."

The first two lines remind us that Tao cannot be expressed in words (Chapter 1), and that even if expressed or suggested by symbols and similes, it does not sound sweet but rather insipid (Chapter 35).

The next two lines afford strong hints of such significant virtues as noncontention, humility, noninterference, contentment, nonviolence, and so on, which are featured in many of the preceding chapters.

The fifth and sixth lines are reminiscent of the contents of Chapter 48, wherein Lao Tzu says: "To learn, one increases day by day; to cultivate Tao, one reduces day by day."

The next five lines concerning the Sage illustrate the mystery of Tao and the contradiction between Tao and common sense. These two subjects also are frequently dealt with in the preceding chapters. For instance, "The Sage does not hoard" is only another way of saying that the man possessed of Tao "will use his surplus to serve the world." (Chapter 77.)

The last two lines again suggest the close relation between Tao and the Sage, who may rightly be regarded as Tao incarnate or the embodiment of Tao. From his actions may be known the Way of Heaven.

The last line may be an apt tribute to Christ for he says: "Take my yoke upon you, and learn of me; for I am meek and lowly in heart." (Matt., 11:29.)

The last line has another significance. It sets forth Lao Tzu's pet subject, Wu Wei, as conclusion of the Taoist canon. "To act, but not to contend" is a pat description of Wu Wei or nonaction in the sense of noninterference. It clearly shows that nonaction does not mean doing nothing, that it simply means action without contention and without interference with the rhythm of Tao.

---

1. Cf. also Chapter 1.
2. Cf. also Chapters 1, 48.
3. Cf. also Chapters 8, 22, 66, 68.

# Index

Nei Tan, 80
Neo-Confucianism, 10
Neo-Platonism, 101
Nirvana, 44
Non-Being, 25, 37, 130, 131, 142, 146, 147, 160, 179, 180, 183, 184
Non-contention, 94, 138, 156, 211, 213, 214, 218
Non-interference. *See* Wu Wei.
Old Testament, 74, 157, 209
One, the, 47-50, 53, 99-100, 146, 156, 177, 178, 182
Pao P'u Tzu, 79
Patanjali, 28
Paul, St., 50, 121, 193, 224
Peace, 138, 168, 227
Plato, 73, 120, 190
Plotinus, 28, 49, 57, 121
Po Chu-i, 197
Prajna, 38, 61-62
Psalms, ix, 46, 96
P'u. *See* Simplicity.
Quiescence, 66-71, 118, 134, 148, 158, 162, 174, 185, 199, 203
Reality, 103, 110, 156, 181
Reversion, cyclic, 13, 146, 149, 167, 179, 183, 197
Ruler, 6, 14, 54, 150, 199
Sadducees, 74
Sage, 13, 54, 109, 118, 130, 131, 132, 134, 137, 138, 139, 143, 162, 163, 166, 171, 172, 187, 189, 199, 200, 201, 202, 205, 207, 208, 211, 215, 216, 217, 218, 223, 225, 226, 228
Sai Yung, 115
Samadhi, 28, 52
*San T'ung Ch'i*, 76-78, 80, 86
*Secret of the Golden Flower*, 80

Senses, 40, 108, 109, 110, 113, 114, 118, 119, 123, 143, 192
Shen T'ai, 80
*Shu Ching*, 9, 48, 116, 120, 189
Shun, Emperor, 48, 55, 120
Simplicity, 12-13, 152, 169, 175, 178
Spiritual cultivation, 12, 15, 39, 53, 55, 62, 72, 77, 95, 97, 111, 112, 148, 158, 162, 193, 198, 210, 228
Ssuma Ch'ien, 2, 3, 9, 24, 75, 228
Sunyata, 35, 38
Su Tung-po, 91, 161
Tagore, R., 29, 59, 111
*Tah Hsueh*, 43
T'ai Chi, 22-23, 35, 38-39, 84, 130
T'ai Chi T'u, 84, 85
Tan T'ien, 82
Tantrism, 60
Tao, 3, 8, 10-13, 19-23, 24, 25-26, 27, 28-31, 37, 42, 44, 47, 49-50, 70, 72, 78, 92-93, 98, 100, 117, 130, 134, 151, 155, 157, 160, 166, 167, 171, 172, 174, 180, 181, 182, 186, 188, 191, 193, 194, 195, 204, 223
Tao Chia (Philosophic Taoism), 5
Tao Chiao (Religious Taoism), 5
Taoism, ix, 9-10, 15, 39, 44
Taoists, 29, 51-52, 75, 80, 95, 99, 112
*Tao Teh Ching*, x, 4-6, 8-12, 14, 15, 19, 22, 28, 30, 33, 44, 92, 114, 118, 176
Tathata, 38
Teh. *See* Virtue.

QUEST BOOKS

are published by
The Theosophical Society in America,
a branch of a world organization
dedicated to the promotion of brotherhood and
the encouragement of the study of religion,
philosophy, and science, to the end that man may
better understand himself and his place in
the universe. The Society stands for complete
freedom of individual search and belief.
In the Theosophical Classics Series
well-known occult works are made
available in popular editions.